A Way Was Opened

A Way Was Opened

A Memoir

By Ruth Brunk Stoltzfus
with Eve MacMaster, editor

Foreword by Nancy R. Heisey

Herald
Press

Scottdale, Pennsylvania
Waterloo, Ontario

Library of Congress Cataloging-in-Publication Data
Stoltzfus, Ruth Brunk, 1915-
  A way was opened : a memoir / by Ruth Brunk Stoltzfus
with Eve MacMaster.
    p. cm.
  Includes index.
  ISBN 0-8361-9203-6 (pbk. : alk. paper)
  1. Stoltzfus, Ruth Brunk, 1915- 2. Mennonites—United
States—Clergy—Biography. I. MacMaster, Eve, 1935- II. Title.
BX8143.S76 A3 2003
289.7'092—dc21   2002013705

The paper used in this publication is recycled and meets the minimum
requirements of American National Standard for Information Sciences—
Permanence of Paper for Printed Library Materials, ANSI Z39.48-1984.

All Scripture quotations are from *The King James Version*, or *The Holy Bible,
New International Version*. Copyright © 1973, 1978, 1984 International
Bible Society. Used by permission of Zondervan Bible Publishers.

All photos are courtesy of the Stoltzfus family except for those noted in captions.

A WAY WAS OPENED
Copyright © 2003 by Herald Press, Scottdale, Pa. 15683
    Published simultaneously in Canada by Herald Press,
    Waterloo, Ont. N2L 6H7. All rights reserved
Library of Congress Control Number: 2002013705
International Standard Book Number: 0-8361-9203-6
Printed in the United States of America
Cover design by Gwen Stamm
Book design by Merrill R. Miller and Gwen Stamm

10 09 08 07 06 05 04 03 10 9 8 7 6 5 4 3 2 1

To order or request information, please call
1-800-759-4447 (individuals); 1-800-245-7894 (trade).
Website: www.mph.org

To the memory of Grant Moses Stoltzfus, my husband, who inspired, advised, and supported me in every aspect of my life.

Contents

Foreword

Mary Malone, a retired history professor from St. Jerome's University, a sister university to Conrad Grebel University College in Waterloo, Ontario, is writing a three-volume history of women and Christianity. In the introduction to her first volume, Malone describes the steps of the process by which women have come to be noticed in historical research.

The first step is to notice the absence of women in much traditional writing. *The Story of Christianity*, a two-volume history by Justo Gonzalez, published in 1984, is still considered to be one of the best surveys of Christian history and is widely used in colleges and seminaries. In the entire table of contents of Gonzalez's first volume, from the early church to the Protestant Reformation of the sixteenth century, only one woman is named in a chapter heading— Macrina, a theologian and sister of two great fourth-century male theologians. This observation should raise a question: how can it be that in 1,600 years of Christian history only one woman is important enough to make it into the summary of the story? When we ask that question, we are beginning the process of bringing women into their rightful place as part of the Christian story.

A second step, says Malone, is to notice that when women are included in the history, it is often in an accidental or even hostile way. For example, repeated prohibitions by church authorities in the early centuries against the preaching of women tell scholars that women were indeed preaching. Otherwise, there would be no reason for rules forbidding them to do so.

In the third stage, historians begin to compensate for the long absence or downplaying of women in the historical record. Biblical scholars have done a great deal of research into the women who are included in the Bible—and so many recent studies discuss Miriam, Deborah, Ruth, Mary Magdalene, Priscilla, and Lydia. Mary Malone's work lifts out names from Christian history such as Perpetua and Felicitas, two women martyrs in the year 203; Paula, a monastic woman who was a friend of the Bible scholar and translator Jerome in the fourth century, and who may have done some Bible translation herself; and Hilda, the abbess of a seventh-century monastery in England where both women and men lived and served.

The fourth stage is to notice that the few records we have of women are usually available because these women were "outstanding." We need to dig deeper to understand the lives of ordinary women (this is also true about the historical search to understand the lives and the importance of ordinary men). In the process, we become much more interested in context: What was the world like in which these women lived? How do we learn about their daily joys and struggles? Women's letters and diaries have become important historical data in this deepening exploration of the women whose energies have shaped the church for 2,000 years.

This memoir by Ruth Brunk Stoltzfus ably participates in all the steps that Mary Malone describes. If a curious reader tries to locate this remarkable Mennonite woman and leader in the *Mennonite Encyclopedia*, it takes some serious sleuthing to track her down. Her father, "George R. Brunk," merits an article, as does the "Brunk Brothers Revival Campaign," the well-known effort of two of her brothers. Her husband, "Grant Moses Stoltzfus," is also present as an important Mennonite sociologist; his article includes the statement, "He married Ruth Brunk . . . Together they raised a family of three daughters and two sons." If the reader knows enough about Ruth, she might check the article on "Radio," which reveals that the Virginia Conference in 1924, when Ruth was nine, declared: "We deem it wrong to have the radio in our homes." But the curious historian needs to turn further to an article on "Broadcasting, Radio and Television," to learn in one sentence about the weekly women's radio program, Heart to Heart, that was established by Ruth in 1950. Amazingly, for as remarkable a woman as Ruth Brunk Stoltzfus is, only someone who is already informed could trace her in the historical resource that most Mennonites would turn to first.

A Way Was Opened provides readers with the outline of the life of this outstanding woman leader, throughout her ministry in the latter half of the twentieth century. It also opens to us her personal journey, through memories, fragments of letters, and personal journal entries. We meet the child whose parents turned aside her questions about how puppies were born, yet demonstrated the open book of their affection for each other in front of her. We read of the little girl whose commitment to peace and justice was born while listening to stories of the bravery of her grandmother, Susanna Heatwole Brunk, whose husband fled Virginia during the Civil War in order to avoid forced conscription. We meet the twelve-year-old girl who preached her first sermon to a group of friends and then proceeded to conduct a wedding service between two of them.

We learn of the women models who influenced her life—Sunday school teacher Bertha Berkey, English teacher Sadie Hartzler, and the well-known woman preacher Hannah Whitall Smith. We follow her journey into adulthood, marriage, and grieving the early death of her husband. And we learn of her growing call to ministry, early on in the work of Heart to Heart, and later as a pastoral leader in a series of congregations. Finally, we agonize with her through the long and frustrating process of becoming the first woman ordained to ministry in the Virginia Conference, including the opposition from members of her own family.

This story matters because Ruth Brunk Stoltzfus has been a mentor and an encourager to many younger women and men in Mennonite circles. It matters because she has provided a broader, less traditional model of what church leadership looks like. It matters because she has been part of the historic train of women and men who seek to live together in a way that witnesses to God's love in the world and builds up God's community, the church.

As one who, through WEMC radio, still has the opportunity to hear the voice of "Your Friend Ruth" every morning while preparing for work, I give thanks for her life, and for this story, which will help many more of us to join in the faithful witness and joyful encouragement she has so long given to us.

—*Nancy R. Heisey, President*
Mennonite World Conference

*The providential hand of "the God who has
been my shepherd all my life to this day."*
—Genesis 48:15

Prologue

One summer my children, grandchildren, and I decided to go swimming. If we took the shortest way to the water, we would have a problem: how to get Grandma (me) and the babies down a dangerous, 100-foot high cliff. Family consensus was that some of us should take the long, winding, more level way around the cliff.

With little Nathaniel in his arms, my son-in-law John led a small crew of us for what seemed to be a mile. Along the way we feasted our eyes on ferns, wild flowers, and trees, and we were delighted to find some blueberries. As we stopped to eat the ready-made refreshments we enjoyed conversation across the three generations.

But our path was not always easy. Farther on we encountered briers and thickets with branches snapping back at everyone coming in line. We helped each other get through.

Finally we reached the swimming place. Some of us headed for the water and some sat on bumpy rocks, bathing our feet while holding little ones.

When it was time to go, I said to my son Eugene, "I don't want to go the long way back. I want to go by way of the cliff."

"Mother!" he said, "The cliff is so steep that I have a long rope hanging all the way down so we younger ones can make it."

"I'll try it," I said. "You can climb behind me to help if I slip, and I'll hold onto the rope ahead of you."

We started up the cliff. It was hard to get a toehold anywhere with my leather shoes. (It had been a sudden decision to go to the water.) Sometimes Eugene held the heel of my shoe in his hand so I could take one more step. As I crawled upward, my body flat against the steep cliff, I was sorry I had never put to use the jeans my children had given me. Before I knew it, the rope I was pulling on took me over a yellow jacket's nest and I was badly stung.

When we finally reached the top, I was panting and hurting, but at the same time experiencing a feeling of satisfaction. The climb meant struggle and pain, but it also meant challenge and success. It felt good to have done it with the help of a son.

As I thought of this hard climb and the berry-strewn stroll earlier in the day, it struck me as an allegory of my life of pleasure and pains, satisfaction and stings. I thought of my parents and the love and sturdiness they built into my life from the very beginning. I thought of my deceased husband, Grant, and how our son symbolized the way Grant had often helped me to take "one more step" in my struggle to do the work I was called to do.

On June 16, 1950, I began the Heart to Heart broadcast for mothers and homemakers and continued as speaker for eight years. Support by Christian businesses, church groups, and individuals eventually put the broadcast on thirty-two stations. This brought invitations to speak in hundreds of pulpits in the United States and Canada, led to my weekly, illustrated Family Life Series for newspapers and to Minute Messages for radio. Later came the requests to serve as interim pastor in Ohio and as co-pastor in Virginia, and in 1989, when I was 74, to my becoming the first woman ordained by Virginia Mennonite Conference.

It did not just happen. God made a way when there wasn't any way for a woman to use the gifts the Spirit had given for public ministry.

This book would not have been possible without the work of my dear friend Eve MacMaster, who took seventy years of my writings, journals, letters, articles, and messages—totaling thousands of pages—and skillfully shaped it into the story presented here.

PART ONE

CHILDHOOD AND YOUTH
1915–1937

Chapter 1

Nurtured in Love

Denbigh, Virginia
March 1915–1920

Papa, a young Mennonite bishop from Kansas, came on a preaching mission to a country church in the Valley of Virginia near Harrisonburg. As he sat on the platform at Lindale Mennonite Church, he noticed a certain tall young woman walking in the assembly. He leaned over to the minister beside him, asked who she was, then said in his heart, "She's the one!"

She was. In six weeks George R. Brunk and Katie Wenger were married.

In later years, when people raised their eyebrows about such a short courtship, Papa would say, "I've been courting her ever since."

In the course of time, when we children began dating, our parents urged caution. "Take plenty of time," they would say. "There is no hurry about getting serious."

"But what about your getting married in six weeks?" we asked.

"Well," Mama would say, "Papa was twenty-eight and a bishop in the church and I was twenty-five."

We couldn't argue with that. We weren't twenty-eight, a bishop in the church, or twenty-five.

My birth
I was born March 15, 1915, at our home in rural Denbigh, now Newport News, Virginia. Mama was almost forty; Papa, forty-three. My parents named me Ruth Wenger Brunk, the only one of the nine children given the maiden name of my mother as a middle name.

I was the eighth of nine children, and the fifth daughter. The first five children were born before the family moved to Virginia from

Kansas in 1910. My brothers and sisters and their ages when I was born were: Esther, 13; Truman, 12; Stella, 10; Edna, 8; Menno, 5; George Jr., 3; Katie, almost 2.

I grew up in a ten-room frame house built by my father and helpers, in a Mennonite community called the Denbigh Colony. When my parents came to Virginia in 1910, Papa bought a tract of land, which he considered the best land in the Colony. They settled on a ten and one-half acre plot, which came to be known as Big Oak Farm.

Housekeeping

Mama was well-taught in the ways of thrifty homemaking when she and Papa were married. She made all of Papa's shirts and those of their four boys, as well as all the dresses and most of the other clothing for herself and their five sometimes hard-to-please girls.

In the early part of her marriage Mama first washed clothes on a board, then had the luxury of a washing machine turned by hand,

George and Katie Wenger Brunk at Big Oak Farm in Denbigh, Virginia.

then one run by a gasoline engine. When I was in my teens, we had the utmost in convenience for that day—an electric washer with a wringer. But we continued to boil all the white clothes to near-perfect whiteness. I can still see that big kettle stove full of clothes and feel the extreme heat as I stood there in the washhouse, poking and stirring the clothes with a sawed-off broom handle.

Letters from Papa

When I was twenty-three months old, my youngest brother Lawrence was born—the ninth child in the family. Of the effect on me Papa wrote:

> Little Ruthie feels pretty bad now, for yesterday a little brother came and pushed her out of Mama's bed. She goes about the house like a poor little lost lamb. She is not so broken up, only looks so confused and put out of being rocked a good deal since the new brother came.

At one point when he needed to be away from home for months because of a heart condition, Papa wrote letters not only to Mama, but also to each of us children. I cherish the letter he wrote to me when I was two years old:

> Ruthie, my dear little snowbird baby [referring to my white dress made by Mama], I get your letters and they are sweet and precious to me. I can read them as good as the rest. I get very lonesome for you to be here and put your head on my breast and suck your little thumb. I think of you every day and in my mind I see you when you play. I get very tired in my heart to be away so long and get no kisses on your face and not hear you talk so many things. Papa loves you all the time every day. Be a good baby for Mama. Bye, bye, Papa.

The letter was read to me, and I was allowed to hold it as my very own. I have it in my possession, yellowed by the passing years.

Times were hard for Mama and the older children, digging and marketing potatoes to survive while Papa was away. Mama wrote to Papa's Kansas relatives:

> We are so homesick and lonesome for our dear Papa I just think sometimes I can't stand it. I felt a little more hopeful last week. I even began to imagine how it would be to have a home again with George around. The things I looked at even seemed different, but last night his

letter was more discouraging. It made me feel sick. I thought I couldn't go to bed. The wind howled and roared just like it often did when we were together and spoke of how it would seem if one was gone.

If I don't hear more favorable [word] tomorrow, maybe I will go up to see him. I will surely take Ruthie if I do. I can hardly get over it, either, that I didn't take her the other time, but you know their clothes were so run down that I thought I couldn't get her fit to go on such short notice.

We couldn't get very much help digging potatoes so we're not quite through yet. Could have finished yesterday if it had not rained again. Five of us worked at it steady when weather was fit. Esther or Stella or I stayed at the house all the time (with the little ones).

Near this time my adult cousin Amos Brenneman, who was almost like a member of our family, took me along with him by train to see Papa, a trip I vividly remember. After our trip Papa wrote to the Kansas relatives:

I was so glad the next time when Amos brought her. I was afraid she would feel strange at first, but just as Katie opened a crack of the door, she saw me in bed, gave a spring on her mother's arm and said, "Hello, Papa!" exultingly. And the way she snuggled up to me and refused to be moved or allow her wraps to be taken off, would have done the heart good of any king or beggar if he had a heart.

I was too nervous, though, to keep her. She was like a little snowbird sure enough, out and in, up and down, hopping around and flitting about, but it seemed very dark when the time came for her to go. Mama went along to the train and she left us both that way and went home with Amos, saying, "Mama stay, Papa see get well?" She is always so good to stay or go just as we say.

When I was four, Papa wrote:

Ruthie and Bud [Lawrence] had a good time playing in the sand while Truman and I made a cement wall. They say a lot of cute things. I called Ruthie skinny and she said, "Papa, what YOU say that for?" I said, "Well, Truman says that." She said, "Well, Truman is a boy." She seemed to think I ought to know better."

School

In the fall of 1921, at age six, I began first grade at Denbigh Elementary School, two miles from home. School was scary the first few days but generally a good-enough experience. During the first

First grade, 1921.

part of that year, the Warwick County school system took us by horse-drawn wagon, then by school bus.

At home I was uneasy about learning to read, so Papa took me and my reading book into the parlor to help me. On page one of the first grade edition of *The Howe Readers,* he patiently pointed to the picture of young Fred with a spade, then to the words "Fred" and "spade," helping me to get the connection. In my mind's eye I can still see Fred and his spade.

I soon learned at school that the southern speech of the teachers and other pupils was different from the way we spoke at home and in our close-knit Mennonite community. The letter "r" was missing when they said "mothah" for mother and was added when they said "winder" for window.

I learned to use two sets of speech manners. At home and at church, I was expected to simply say a respectful "Yes" or "No" when answering my parents and other elders. At school it was "Yes, Ma'am" and "No, Sir" or I was considered impolite.

Mrs. Ercel B. Ingram was my seventh grade teacher. She combined good teaching methods and personal interest in her students. In later years when I taught the fifth grade for five years in that same Denbigh Elementary Public School, she was the principal.

Our community

My best friends were from our church community rather than those from the public school. We went to each other's homes for Sunday dinner and an afternoon of play. Sometimes we had special Sunday school class activities.

The teachings and practices of our church separated us from people outside our community. We didn't participate in worldly amusements like going to the movies or theater, own radios, take opponents to court, swear oaths, or go to war. In those days members of the Mennonite Church could be distinguished from outsiders by our plain dress: black jackets without lapels or neckties for men, devotional head coverings and long-sleeved cape dresses for women. Women didn't wear jewelry or cut their hair. These were the rules of our church, and I accepted them.

When I was fifteen I wrote to a friend from the Mennonite mission in Newport News, urging her to accept the church's teachings. "Even if we don't see the sense of some restrictions," I told her, "we should obey because Christ commands us to obey the church. We are disobeying God when we disobey the church, even if some of the rules aren't in the Bible."

My first sermon

In April 1986, after I spoke at an evening meeting in a series at Tiskilwa, Illinois, Mary Yoder Nice, who grew up with me at Denbigh and was in the same classes with me in school and Sunday school, came up to talk. Mary spoke as if she knew the answer, but asked, "When would you say you gave your first sermon?"

I tried to think whether to say 1950, when my Heart to Heart Broadcast brought a string of invitations into church pulpits all over the United States, or 1982, when I went to the first of two Ohio churches to serve as interim pastor.

Mary said, "Do you remember that day when a bunch of us girls, age twelve or so, were invited to Cora Miller's home for Sunday dinner—Malinda Shenk, you and I, Eva Hostetter, Ruth Hertzler, Ruth Shelley?"

"Oh, yes!" I told her.

"Do you remember that we played church in the afternoon?"

"Yes, and I recall the church service was held outdoors near the garage."

"You had the sermon," Mary said. "It was a wedding sermon, and when you finished you married Cora Miller and Malinda Shank."

First cars

I was four when Papa bought our first car, a 1917 Model T Ford. My first driving lesson began with operating the steering wheel of the Model T while seated on the lap of my cousin Amos. A dairyman who lived a mile away, Amos would often stop by to see if we children wanted to ride along on his errands to a hardware store some miles away or to see a farmer nearby. It didn't matter which, we wanted to go. I remember what it was like to sit on Amos' lap and get the feel of the wheel—learning to turn it not too much or too little in order to keep the car on the road—knowing that Amos could rescue the situation if need be.

One morning in 1922—I was seven years old—Papa announced that there would be a family surprise at a certain time that morning. We children were consumed with curiosity and time seemed to stop as we kept our eyes on the clock. Our older sister Edna tried to speed things along by turning up the clock. Papa talked like that might delay everything, but he went to the phone on the wall, cranked the required number of longs and shorts, and said, "You can bring it now." The surprise was a spanking new, beautiful black 1922 Model T Ford! I can still smell the odor of the car as my sister Katie and I sat in it almost by the hour.

In 1927, when I was twelve, it was in that Model T that I had my first experience driving alone. A driver's license must not have been required, since my parents let me drive one mile alone on a country road to Aunt Annie Brenneman's house. It made me feel wonderful.

Parental discipline

The first problem with peace in our family that I remember was when, as little girls, my sister Katie—twenty-two months my senior—and I had human relations problems, and one of us bit the other. Papa took us into the parlor, that large, carpeted room with potted plants and a musty smell. We didn't use the room except for guests and those special occasions when you needed a private conversation or you needed to be disciplined. Papa talked with us and then had us kiss each other. I don't remember that I felt like kissing Katie at the time.

As a child I did not know of any words that carried more weight than the two words, "Papa said." On those rare occasions when he had to punish he used only his hand, not a switch or anything else, because, as he said, "then I can tell better how much it hurts." I can testify that his hand was enough for the one spanking I remember.

Mama spanked even less. She was so gentle that it was hard for her to keep from looking pleasant even when she had to discipline us. One time, when Lawrence, the youngest, misbehaved, Mama hurried him into another room to deal with him alone. The older siblings peeped through the keyhole to see him get the punishment they felt he deserved. What they saw was Mama putting her arms around her little boy and saying, "Mama's baby!"

Playfulness

Mama was a gentle person, but she was no pushover. When I was seven, Papa wrote my sister Esther, away in nurses training in La Junta, Colorado:

> The other day Mama wanted me to tear out a closet in the dining room but I was not in favor. She kept on and got a hammer and chisel and began to knock off the boards and took off the door. After she got stuck and had the boards broken up, of course I had to finish it. "Whatever Papa says" [a frequent statement of Mama's].
>
> Mama wanted me to move the new chicken house and take the whole lot for garden. I talked her out of it seven times but it was like a ground squirrel in the ground. In a minute it pops up again. So the other day Ray [a neighbor] and Alfred [a nephew] put their big teams on it and pulled it south. Yes, "Whatever Papa says."

Later that year Papa wrote about tearing out a partition to make a larger "cook room," as he called it, and how this gave Mama more ideas:

> Then the little room, BEHOLD, was discovered to be too small for dining room so I tore out wall and double doors and set partition

THREE FEET BACK. I guess I will have to tear all the upstairs down and pitch it out the windows.

Teasing and playfulness were ingrained in us and encouraged from an early age. I was eight when Papa wrote in a family letter about spraying the chicken house for mites (chicken lice). "But they manage to get onto everybody that goes in there," he wrote. "Ruth was hanging on me at the supper table. I asked her if she wanted to divide the mites with me. 'I want to give you half of them,' she said. 'I don't want to be stingy.'"

When he was fifty-four, Papa wrote to his sister Min:

> Katie and I are all in all to each other and it would surprise you how young and silly we act—of course mostly Katie, I reckon. I claimed she cracked my rib one day but she says "it ain't so."

Mama, fifty, wrote:

> I've read the letter George wrote you and he is a great one. He won't even hardly let me touch him till he says, "Now don't break another rib." I tell you he's the bestest ole Pappy and can make faces just as funny as he used to, and gets a new one in occasionally.

Mama and her "bestest ole Pappy" in 1932.

Sex education

When it came to sex education, I learned more from a book my parents had on hand than by conversation with them. It was not the custom in those days for parents to encourage and answer questions about the facts of life and birth as we now think is best.

I remember asking about the matter, as a small child, when our dog gave birth to puppies. "That isn't a question for you to ask," Papa said. This puzzled me, because he had always answered my other questions.

Even so, I remember seeing him come in from the lawn and place a rose in Mama's hair or return from the orchards and put in her hands the largest peach or apple he had picked. Often her response was to say affectionately, "You big old Pappy!" (He stood six feet and four inches tall.)

The virtuous woman

Mama was always loyal to Papa. We children never heard her utter a word of criticism about him, nor he about her. She was aware that as a prominent Mennonite Church bishop, he had critics. Occasionally I heard her say of a person, "He doesn't like Papa." Mama's husband was "known in the gates," but few people ever knew how accomplished the woman was who held things together at home.

I remember how Mama looked as she kneaded dough for the twelve loaves of bread and rolled out dough for the six pies she baked at one time. But what I remember most about my mother was her kindness. She was devoted to her husband and children. From her I learned to love babies, to work inside and outside the house, to express southern hospitality, to invite guests, and to give gifts to neighbors and friends.

She was a living example of the virtuous woman in Proverbs 31. She reached out to those in need, she was honest in all her dealings, and "she opened her mouth with wisdom and in her tongue was the law of kindness."

During one of Mama's last illnesses, we children began to reflect upon her life as we had never done before. As we compared experiences, no one could remember a time when she had ever lost her temper or let her voice get loud or snappy. You can be sure it was not that any of her nine children were above trying her patience.

Outside the Colony

Our family enjoyed wholesome recreation. I remember when Papa took us to a health movie at our public high school—unusual for a Mennonite bishop in the 1920s. When the circus came to town, entertainment at the tent was off limits for us, but Papa took us the ten-mile trip to see the circus animals parade down the street on their way to the tents. On another occasion at the Newport News shipyard, we saw Mrs. Coolidge, the president's wife, christen a ship as it slipped into the James River on its way to the sea.

At Yorktown we witnessed mock revolutionary battles and other sesquicentennial celebrations. At Williamsburg we heard an Indian chief speak. Afterwards, when we went up front to meet him, Papa said, "The Mennonites never fought the Indians." A man who overheard him yelled, "You didn't fight the Germans either!" At age ten, that was my first experience with hostility because of our church's peace position.

Chapter 2

Papa's Story About His Parents

Hagerstown, Maryland
1860–1864

A family story about Mennonite non-resistance was familiar to me, for often in the evening after supper Papa entertained us with stories of his parents, Henry G. Brunk and Susanna Heatwole Brunk, their early life in Virginia, and his own childhood among the Kansas pioneers. I loved to hear about Grandmother Brunk's bravery during the Civil War. Years later our daughter Helen set the story to music and presented it on the stage. My grandmother Susanna's bravery inspired me when I left home to drive north for my first interim pastorate.

This is the story as I first heard it, in Papa's own words:

My father, Henry G. Brunk, was a strong man of about six feet two and powerfully built. He was of a cheerful, jovial nature, ready wit, sound judgment, and industry. He was apprenticed to a plasterer and became an expert at that trade. Later he learned harness-making and shoe-making.

My mother, Susanna Heatwole Brunk, was above average in size and a strong woman when they were married about the time the Civil War clouds were ready to break in tempest upon the nation. While they were poor, they had a wealth of love and health.

When the war broke out, Father refused to enter military service and was imprisoned in Harrisonburg for some time, finally agreeing to drive a feed wagon as a compromise. Taking sick with typhoid fever, he was sent home and never reported back for service. He was listed as a deserter and was compelled to keep hidden when the southern soldiers were about.

He was caught on the road one time by a Rebel scout, John Aery, who did not know him. When Aery asked if he knew the whereabouts of Henry G. Brunk, Father pointed him to a house and said those people might be able to tell him something. Being a deserter, he would have been shot if captured.

He worked in secret at whatever he could to earn bread for his wife and two babies. Making willow baskets was one kind of work he did. The payment he received for one basket being as much wheat as would fill it.

The hiding grew more and more perilous. When my baby brother Johnnie took sick and died, Father could not even be with Mother at the burial. He had to peep over the shoulders, at a distance, as he concealed his identity in the crowd, undetected by the searching scouts. He hastened away out of sight while the hymn was being sung and the grave was being filled.

The pressure got too strong and dangers too great. Father and Uncle Reuben Heatwole, with a dozen or so others, decided to strike out through the mountains for the north and safety. Father told mother to go to Maryland if she could, and if alive, they would try to find each other.

She could not bear the suspense and uncertainty. She took baby Sarah and started with a horse and spring wagon. They followed the Union army as it fell back north and consequently were between the two armies as the Rebels followed up as close as they dared.

One time she was captured by Rebels, who unhitched her horse and were taking it from her, but she refused to let go of the bridle. Just then a scout galloped by and cried, "Yanks! Yanks!" and the rebels began to throw their things together to get away and ordered her to hitch up her horse and follow them back. But she said, "I'll do no such thing," and hitched up and kept going north.

At Harper's Ferry the bridge was burning and she was too late to cross it. A miller told her when and how some people drove across the river. Nothing could daunt her—she held her baby tight and plunged in.

At last she drove into Hagerstown, having no word of whether her husband was living or dead. She stopped in the street and did not know what to do or where to go.

When she was at her wit's end, she looked at the faces of all that passed by but could not hope to see him. She looked through the windows of a storefront—and there she saw him at a shoemaker's bench, making shoes!

What followed was a storm of conflicting emotions—love, laughter, tears, and thanksgiving for their marvelous adventure and kind Providence's glorious intervention.

Chapter 3

Everything But Money

Denbigh, Virginia
1920–1925

I have memories of waking up in the mornings and from my upstairs window hearing Papa singing and the accompaniment of the clip, clip, clip of his shears as he pruned the shrubbery. The grounds of our farm were like a park, with flowers and evergreens and a fish pool on our front lawn that Papa made.

It was my lot to work out-of-doors much of the time, especially when Papa gave up other kinds of farming and planted peach and apple trees on most of our thirty acres at the home place, and forty acres at our second farm, a mile away. Many an hour of many a day my younger brother Lawrence and I "hoed trees," which meant making a wall of soil around the young, newly planted trees to hold tank loads of water hauled by our older brothers. Papa had first taken a hoe and carefully showed us exactly how it was to be done. Those trees thrived, grew, and produced until they became the main source of family income. They also provided excellent illustrations for Papa's sermons about spiritual growth and enemies of growth.

Fighting enemies of the trees meant spraying them seven times each season. I can still feel the windblown spray hitting my old straw hat and my back as I sat on the sprayer, driving a team of horses—later driving the tractor—while my older brothers Menno and George did the spraying. I was teased about the straw hat when someone spied me wearing it while I was working in the kitchen, frying potatoes.

Picking peaches in the summer was a family project. Early in the morning, promising that we could catch up on sleep later in the day, Papa would call up the stairs with an original sing-song rhyme to get up ". . . as soon as you can see the peaches on the tree." The tree-

Sisters at play. I am pouting because Katie got to hold the best doll.

ripened peaches were trucked to the city of Newport News, ten miles away, in time for women to buy them in the stores that morning.

Money management

From an early age and mixed in with family work, we children had experience with money management. Unusual for those times, Papa gave us a weekly allowance of five cents.

In a letter to Esther, away in nurse's training, Papa reported that Edna had bought from George three pairs of pigeons for a dollar. He wrote:

> George has been selling a good many squabs [baby pigeons]. They are all trying to get money ON THE BOOK [deposit on each child's account]. Edna is SICK for a wristwatch but hates to take it off the book. Whenever they want what they don't need I say, "Well, take it off the book." They don't like to hear that.

Papa then stated the balance in each of the nine children's accounts. At age eight my balance was $2.48. I remember yet that important day of the week, Friday, when we younger children would each get our allowance of five cents to spend as we saw fit. We were trusted to pull down the little gray wooden bucket of change from a kitchen shelf and get our own nickel.

As a young girl I took an interest in Papa's business transactions and records, a type of interest that has stayed with me. I remember when I asked the amount of our family debt and he told me the figure.

I often stood by as Papa dealt with customers who drove as many as ten miles to our Big Oak Farm—as Papa advertised it. That was a part of my business education and more, as I witnessed many transactions turn into discussions between Papa and the customers about the Bible, politics, and anything else you can imagine. My first business idea was to set up a soft drink stand for customers, even though we had no such drinks in our home. I had checked with cousin Amos, who did business in town for us, as well as for himself, that he could get cases of drinks for me at wholesale prices. All that my plan lacked was Papa's consent, which he wisely withheld.

Although money was scarce, all our needs were met and we children were free from worry. We had nourishing food, adequate but not extravagant clothing—mostly made by Mama—and a big ten-room house. Our rich and happy home had everything but money.

Different gifts

I made some efforts to be a good cook like my mother. In addition, I took home economics in my sophomore year of high school. In that class we were to cook a dish from time to time at home, have someone eat it, then write a report on the results of the recipe and the comments of the eater. I put off cooking several dishes until the night before reports were due. The poorly timed project took place after supper, when no one was hungry, and lasted long after bedtime. But my patient sister Katie stayed up until the food was ready to eat so I could report her comments.

Even as an adult, wife, and mother of five, I never experienced cooking as a field for creativity as my sisters did. Our son Allen and his wife, Anne, once told me how different their mothers were when it came to cooking: "Anne's mother cooks with a real flair. Allen's mother cooks because it is necessary to eat."

I said, "Well, what you mean is that Anne's mother cooks for fulfillment and I cook for 'fillment!'"

Hospitality

We lived with generosity and hospitality. In my memory I stand as a little girl holding to Mama's skirts and see her giving and giving—a jar of fruit, a piece of her needlework, a bouquet, or something else to a departing guest.

We often had company. I remember the Sunday morning when Mama said to Papa, "I have things on hand and ready enough that we could invite company for dinner today." They agreed to invite two families but failed to decide who would do the inviting. After church it developed that each had invited two good-sized families!

The mother of ten (with most of her children along) said, "Katie, let our family go home and come some other time," but Mama insisted that they all stay. She peeled more potatoes, added things here and there, and somehow had enough for thirty-five people, including those of our family still at home.

Each time we told this family story Mama would add, "And I said, 'If they all had as good a time as I did, they had a good time.'"

I remember at age twelve sitting across the table from some unusual guests—the black preacher, Elder L. Michaux, and his co-worker. They had come to witness a Mennonite communion and foot washing service at our church and had been invited home for Sunday dinner by my parents, a thing unheard of in racially segregated southeast Virginia in those days.

Other contacts with people outside our community came through my father's travels as bishop to churches in our district, and through meetings and other contacts he had with the wider church. More than once people who knew him would stop at our home on the way to Florida or some point farther south. And with plenty of fresh garden products or canned and cured food on hand, my mother was equal to cooking for unexpected guests.

Neighbors, including non-Mennonites, came to get help at Papa's shop with its many tools. The blacksmith forge, where tools were heated and shaped over hot coals, was a popular part of the shop. Though Papa studied, preached, and wrote articles, he was also good at doing things with his hands. I grew up thinking that all men could build and fix anything.

Papa's spiritual guidance

Although a heart condition disrupted his work at times, Papa had multiple responsibilities as a farmer, an unsalaried bishop with oversight of a number of churches, a writer, a counselor, and a traveling evangelist. I can still smell the smoke on his clothes and feel the kisses he gave when he returned from train trips. I can hear him giving to Mama an account of the church work and conversations—some controversial—with church people.

Busy as he was, Papa took time to give his children spiritual nurture, sometimes one to one. At age eleven I was hospitalized with pneumonia. When I returned home, Papa had to be away in church work, but he left a note:

> Dear Ruthie,
> Bye Bye. Pappy hates to go just when you come home. Take awful good care not to catch cold. Be fat and rosy till I get back. I want to see you about ready to romp and play by the time I come home.
> Papa [A hand-drawn turtle with "KISS" on its shell.]

I remember the day he taught me my first prayer. Rather than the alarming "if I should die before I wake," he taught me to say:

> *Jesus, tender Shepherd, hear me,*
> *Guard Thy little lamb tonight.*
> *In the darkness be Thou near me.*
> *Keep me safe 'til morning light.*

"Then," he said, "you can add words of your own, maybe something like this: 'Bless Papa and Mama and all the little children in the world.'"

I also remember the first Bible verse he taught me to memorize: "How shall we escape, if we neglect so great a salvation?" (Hebrews 2:3)

I see Papa yet as he read to the family from the Bible. I particularly remember the times he read, in installments, the story of Joseph and his brothers. It must have given me an early and lasting concept of God's providential hand in a person's life.

Another scene is imprinted upon my mind forever. We had gathered at the table for a meal. After reading from the Bible and speaking about evil influences and his fear that some of the children might go wrong, he laid his head down on his arm and wept aloud. I can still hear his sobs and see his big shoulders shake as he yearned for the salvation of his children.

Papa's influence was broader than our family or even the Mennonite Church. When the flag salute was required in the Newport News schools, he addressed the State Board of Education on behalf of a youth who refused to salute. As a result, the majority of the board members voted to excuse the boy from giving the salute.

At the hearing, Papa and the other Mennonite leaders explained that the Mennonite Church held to "the absolute separation of church and state, and the freedom of conscience. . . . Our practice of peace and non-resistance is not due to unfriendliness or disloyalty to our country, but to the firm conviction that it is a positive requirement of the Gospel of Christ."

When Papa prayed we were in touch with heaven. His prayer at mealtime often included, "Bless this food to its intended use and our souls in thy service."

"Our souls in thy service. Our souls in thy service!" The words riveted themselves into my mind, heart, soul, and into the marrow of my bones. He meant it. I meant it. The church preached it. I grew up with no other idea than that my life would be lived in service to Christ and the church.

Chapter 4

Spiritual Struggles

Denbigh, Virginia
1925–1930

An utterly happy and secure childhood did not mean that there were no spiritual struggles. When a black woman came to buy grain, I stood by in the barn as a young child, and when she paid Papa, I saw a nickel drop from her purse into the straw. I did not pick it up for her or tell her she dropped it. I wanted that nickel and took it for myself when she left. Oh, the grief! I suffered vastly more than a nickel's worth of pain before I got relief from that guilt. I put a nickel in the church offering many times before I felt forgiven.

One time I was a bit careless with the truth, even though my motives were good. Esther, my oldest sibling, recently returned from nurses training in Colorado, was asked to speak at our Sunday night Young People's Meeting. During her talk on "The History of China Missions," she said by mistake, "the history of nursing."

When we got home, Esther was feeling bad about her slip of the tongue. The way I tried to comfort her was to say, "Esther, I was sitting in the service where I could see just about everyone, and nobody was listening anyway."

I experience forgiveness

When I was ten, my sister Stella told me the big secret that she was going to be married. "Now, Ruth," she said. "Don't tell anyone."

At school, when I was with my best friend, Eva, it was too hard to keep the secret. Back home after school, Stella asked, "Did you tell my secret?"

I answered, "No."

That night was miserable. I tossed and turned and worried because I knew I had not told the truth.

In the morning when Mama called the older girls to get up, I decided that when Stella came down the hall, I would run out to her and make things right. But when she came by my bedroom door, I was frozen in my bed.

Just before she reached the bottom of the stairs, I jumped out of bed, ran down the steps, and said, "Stella, wait! I said I didn't tell your secret, but I did. Will you forgive me?"

She put her arm around me and said, "Yes, Ruth, I forgive you."

Suddenly my heart felt free and clean—like it was washed, starched, and ironed!

My baptism

That same year, my tenth, I sensed the call of the Lord on my life during a series of revival meetings conducted by evangelist B. B. King at our Warwick River Mennonite Church.

At home I talked to Papa about it and said, "I want to stand during the invitation at the next service."

As a bishop in the church and a father who faithfully taught his children, he would surely be glad for his daughter to respond. But he wanted the experience to be real, so he gave me words of caution. "Don't come because others are coming," he said. "Come because you hear Jesus calling you."

Soon afterwards, on April 12, 1925, I was baptized into the church by Papa, who was assisted by deacons S. E. Hostetter and A. P. Shenk. Others were baptized in that service, including my sister Katie, twelve, and our brother Lawrence, eight.

The baptism was by pouring. As Papa said the words, "Upon confession of your faith," he cupped water in his hands from a basin held by a deacon. As he said, "I baptize you in the name of the Father, and of the Son, and of the Holy Ghost," water fell from his hands upon the head of the kneeling person being baptized. As he said, "Amen," he laid his hands on the person's head for a meaningful moment.

Warwick River Mennonite Church

Whether Papa was officiating at a baptism, wedding, funeral, or other service, he did so with dignity, faith-building words, and well-timed pauses. As bishop he had extra responsibilities in other congregations as well as ours. He and two other ministers usually took

turns preaching our Sunday morning sermons. I was always glad
when it was Papa's turn.

Our church was a simple, white, rectangular, wood-frame building large enough to accommodate an attendance of some 200 people. Inside, the women sat on the benches to the left and the men to
the right. This arrangement and the custom of kneeling for prayer
changed in later years.

Our singing was always in four-part harmony without the aid of
any instrument. I still feel the moving of God's Spirit—as I felt it
many times during the singing, preaching, and observance of the
ordinances in that place of worship.

Evangelists John Grove and J. D. Mininger were among those
who came to our church for revival meetings and influenced me
profoundly. I remember the call of God on my life as I felt it in their
meetings. There was no question about it. My life would be lived in
service to the Lord and the church.

Influences

As I built on the sturdy foundation of my secure childhood and
needed to become a person separate from my parents, three women
had a profound influence on me, some without their knowledge. I
remember as though it were yesterday:

• • •

I am twelve, in a Sunday school class of girls. Bertha Berkey, a
pleasant, caring teacher speaks of the Scriptures with such clarity
and conviction that I continue thinking about them outside of class.
She helps us plan for additional class meetings in our homes. I love
and admire her and want to be with her all I can.

I am fifteen, snuggled under the covers on cold winter nights,
reading *The Christian's Secret of a Happy Life* by Hannah Whitall
Smith. Years later I learned that the author was a woman preacher.

I am eighteen, a senior and a dormitory student at Eastern
Mennonite High School. Miss Sadie Hartzler teaches my English literature class during the week and my Sunday school class on
Sunday. You don't skim lightly over any lesson in either class under
her. You study and you think. In the Sunday school class she makes

insightful points, asks relevant questions, and writes on the black-board brief concluding statements that stick. She is a teacher worth imitating. Her sincerity and dedication are worth following.

• • •

Among the books that impressed me was the handsome 620-page, gilt-edged *Portraits and Principles of the World's Great Men and Women* (1899) from Papa's library. Six women, among "over fifty leading thinkers," were described in such terms as "proprietor and manager of a publishing house," "having keen literary tastes," "rare business ability," "devoted to the great needs of the common people," "prominent in hospital work," "leader in temperance work," "able writer," "popular lecturer," "president of the World's Woman's Christian Temperance Union," "graduated from seminary in 1855," "began teaching," "became principal of her alma mater," "high liter-ary ability," and "a personal force in her home and public life."

But along with the influence of good books, the powerful effect of my parents' lives, the way they taught and dealt with me, the impact of church life, and the reality of God's presence brought me to the sure understanding that faithfulness and usefulness were what mattered, more than personal fulfillment or success.

Papa, the church statesman, and Mama, the generous and gracious hostess, were powerful influences in my life.

Chapter 5

Grooming for Ministry

Denbigh, Virginia
1930–1937

Papa did not seem to buy the belief that women, including his daughters, should strive for incompetence because they were female. I grew up without believing that line. His niece, Florence (Friesen) Cooprider, the first woman medical doctor among Mennonites, was spoken of in our home with affection and admiration.

At thirteen, I was sitting in the Sunday morning worship service when Papa saw missionary Sarah Lapp in the audience and invited her to the pulpit to speak. She stood a little to the side of the podium as she told of the work in India. I had never seen a woman speak from a pulpit before. When we got home, Papa was pleased that she had stood a little to the side. But it was unusual that a woman stood there at all in the late 1920s, and it left an impression on me.

Women's role

While Papa did not believe in the ordination of women, he had much to do with grooming me for a speaking ministry. A minister once wrote to him, "What are we going to do with those verses about the silence of women in the church?" He answered, "Men can't latch on to one or two verses in the Bible about silence just to please our own egos."

When I was twenty-two, I began a special study of those other Bible verses about women as leaders: prophets as well as wives and mothers, a judge, buyer of real estate, seller of clothing, messengers commissioned by Jesus, workers with Paul, a woman who held office in the church, a woman apostle (according to Bible scholars), instructions for women speakers in the public assembly, and more.

My first experiences of public speaking

My first taste of public speaking was as a child in my home church. Children recited Bible verses at the Sunday evening Young People's Meeting. Boys and girls read topics, no doubt written by a parent. Women as well as men gave talks, though the final speaker was always a man.

Beginning at age fifteen I was active in church as a Sunday school song leader, Sunday school teacher, and summer Bible school teacher. While a teenager myself, I taught the teenage girls' class at the mission station on 34th Street in the city of Newport News. One of the girls, Frances Dean, became a lifelong friend. In one letter to Frances I expressed my concern to her about listening to preachers on the radio!

When, at age sixteen, I was elected president of the Literary Society of our church youth group, Papa helped me with my inaugural address: "I thank you for your confidence in electing me president. . . ."

That society, with its opportunities for leading singing, reciting readings, giving talks, leading discussions, and debating, was a piece of the puzzle that made up my preparation for radio broadcasting. When I was asked to memorize readings for programs, Papa helped me to select readings up to twenty minutes long and had me rehearse them before him for pointers on gestures and voice variations. On a public program where I held a goblet of sparkling "wine" (grape juice) to impersonate a young woman speaking against drinking, he had me let the goblet crash to the floor at a crucial point.

Papa helped me with speeches and debates while I was at home, but also when I was away at Eastern Mennonite High School and College. I wrote to him for help on an Easter message. I treasure the letter in which Papa wrote five points for me, calling them, "Some things that could enter into an Easter address."

On the other side of the paper he had typed a moving poem, "The Star of Love," by an unknown author, for me to give along with my address. He wrote suggestions for voice variations and body language at certain places in the margins: "Lofty subdued tone," "Shrinking as from some great calamity," "Soft, tender confidence," "Put feeling into the Bible quotation," "The balance more rapid with firm, joyful confidence." At the bottom of the page he wrote, "Ruth, here is a grand climax for your piece. It will be effective if you enter into the spirit of it."

Encouraging words

Although we were often given words of love and encouragement, compliments were not frequent, no doubt for fear that they might foster pride in us. But I remember Papa's brief but strong words of praise after hearing the song, "Precious Peace" (sung in four parts, unaccompanied), which my college friend Mildred and I had written—she the words and I the music. "I claim that is a good song," he said.

It meant a lot to receive a letter from my parents, which I still have, for my nineteenth birthday when I was a senior at Eastern Mennonite High School in Harrisonburg, Virginia, 200 miles from home.

This is your birthday and we remember it with pleasure to us and good wishes to you. Your childhood has only pleasant memories for us

*As a young woman
at Eastern
Mennonite College.*

and we appreciate the LOYALTY and HELPFULNESS of your life. We trust you may have many useful and happy years in the service of the Lord, and even if evil times come, that you will stand true until the end.

Do not fail or be discouraged, for life in the highest sense only begins when the last of the passing years are struck out by the clock of time and the light of Eternity dawns upon us.

Yours affectionately, Papa & Mama

More than once Papa's letters said, "Ruth . . . service in the church . . . service in the church." The time came when I wondered, could my service in the church be a speaking ministry?

With college friend Mildred Kauffman.

PART TWO

COURTSHIP, MARRIAGE, AND FAMILY 1937–1949

Chapter 6

Two Hearts Are Joined

Harrisonburg and Denbigh, Virginia
1937–1941

I had my first date at age fifteen but was not allowed to go out with everyone who asked me. "He's not your stripe," Mama would say. Later on I understood better what she meant.

One winter night, years later, I was sitting alone, thinking the long, long thoughts of youth. I wondered if marriage might be in my future, and my thoughts turned into a prayer: "Lord," I prayed, "if there is someone you have in mind for me, guide him to me and me to him. And whoever he is and wherever he is, please bless his life now."

I did marry, and years after our marriage Grant said, "You know, one night before I ever met you I prayed that God would guide me to the woman for me and then I asked him to bless her, even though I did not know who she was."

Eastern Mennonite School

When he heard that my high school classmates called me "Bean Pole Brunk," Papa gave me fifty dollars "for being the tallest of the girls." (I was five feet, ten and a half inches tall.)

In September 1932 I transferred to Eastern Mennonite School (EMS) for my last two years of high school. I felt more at home in Harrisonburg, Virginia, 200 miles away, than at the local high school.

"Try to keep first things first and remember that CHURCH and HOME come ahead of school," Papa advised me.

I lived in the dormitory at first, then boarded with my sister Stella and her husband, Ward Shank. I found the literary societies a place where I could practice writing and public speaking skills, and I enjoyed most of my classes. "It is wonderful to be here at EMS,"

47

I wrote to my friend Frances Dean: "There is always a Christian atmosphere and I enjoy the Christian fellowship of the other girls."

After high school graduation I worked in Denbigh picking chickens for market (scraping off pinfeathers, etc.) to earn money to go to college. Each day, after ten hours of work, I walked home with chicken blood on my apron and one dollar in my pocket.

The next year I returned to EMS for the two-year teacher-training course. In addition to class work and practice teaching, I participated in the student work at a small mission in Harrisonburg. I wrote to Frances about one Sunday's experience: "I consented to have the children's meeting, whites in the morning and colored in the afternoon. Dealing with the little black children was a new experience for me, but how I enjoyed it! They listened better than the white children and did so more intelligently. They were cleaner and dressed nicer. Sang better, too."

My father and brothers were frequent visitors at EMS. Papa was one of the founders of the school and a leader of the committee that gave oversight. I wrote in my diary when I saw my brother George in the halls, "He has an admirable dignified air about him. I am proud of my family. . . . My heart began to thump when Truman walked in."

I skipped classes to go along with Papa, my sisters Stella and Katie, and Stella's daughter, Audrey, to see the place where the Rebel soldier met Grandfather Henry Brunk. We visited Bank Church cemetery, where Papa's little brother Johnnie was buried.

On my birthday I wrote: "Can hardly realize that I'm twenty-two years old. Seems only a short time since I was rolling tires, shooting marbles, playing baseball, and climbing trees."

Love is born
My diary recorded my first date with Grant, February 27, 1937:

> Mary Emma [Showalter] has invited a group of college students to her house Saturday night. Grant Stoltzfus asked for the "pleasure" of my company. He seemed a bit excited. I consented. . . . Pleasant time at M. Emma's. Pulled taffy. Grant made possible a very happy time for me. Said it was a "memorable evening" for him.

Grant wrote home that he went to a party, but "not Ruthlessly." His brother answered that " 'ruthless' has no capital R."

Grant and I continued to date through the end of the school year, attending musical events, picnics, and outings. On May 1 we went to Natural Bridge just south of Harrisonburg with Hubert Pellman, Grant's good friend, and Mildred Kauffman, my good friend, on their first date.

On April 28 I wrote in my diary:

> *Love has been born in me.*
> *I know not how it came*
> *Except that his soul touched mine*
> *And gave it birth.*
>
> *Oh, this love!*
> *May it grow and deepen*
> *Into a thing of sacredness*
> *That can never be shaken—bonded in God.*

"Wrote that little poem in history class," I told my diary. "Hope no one sees it till a long time hence and maybe not even then. Grant has dreams of being a high school teacher."

Papa's death

After graduation I returned home to Denbigh and sought a teaching position. When I didn't hear the decision of the board, I went to find out for myself. I was so thrilled to discover that they were glad to approve me that I came home blowing my horn at a great rate. But I confided to my diary, "I have my fears about teaching. May God give strength."

In the spring of my first year of school teaching, on April 30, 1938, Papa died suddenly of a heart attack. I wrote to the Kansas relatives:

> No words can express the sorrow and distress we are feeling since Papa left us. We need him so much. I cannot see how we will ever get along without him. His seat is empty. We miss his counsel and advice, his love and kisses, his singing, smiling, and his prayers. It's painful to go to the table and not hear him pray.

Our family Christmas that year was sad. I wrote in my diary:

> Papa left us all of a sudden. We can't get over it. We had no last words and no good-byes! I have many, many regrets. Oh, if only I had

tried to make Papa happier while he was here. I look back and see times when I should have been more loving. He always appreciated my show of love. Mama spends much time with Papa's clothes in their closet. She buries her face in them and cries until we hardly know what to do.

Deepening friendship

Soon after Papa's going I began to think of the advice he had given me about Grant. He said I should be careful not to fool him in any way; I should drop him if I felt I didn't care for him. We had kept in contact, but I was uncertain about him, despite, as I wrote to Frances Dean (now Mrs. Arthur Strickland), the fact that Grant was "distinguished and popular at school."

I wrote a letter to Grant saying that I felt our friendship should end. He answered that no one could ever mean to him what I had meant, but if I did not feel what he felt then he must be willing to do as I wished. I suggested that we dissolve our friendship for a few months to see how we felt about each other. Then I went to Harrisonburg, staying with my sister Katie and attending summer school at Madison College. By the end of that summer I was terribly lonesome for Grant and eager for him to write.

In August his letter came. Sure enough, he wrote, "I still love you." He came to see me in September, and the last night before he left we had our first heart to heart talk. I felt afterward that we were beginning to understand each other, but then he left for Indiana, to complete his degree at Goshen College.

The day after Christmas Grant arrived for a visit. I was proud of him everywhere we went. Our friendship and our love deepened. In February he wrote that he remembered well the blue dress I wore the night of our first date, two years earlier. I didn't remember that. Then he wrote that he was discouraged and afraid he could never make me happy, and I thought that was a smooth way of getting rid of me. Later I realized how wrong I was and how honest dear Grant was to tell me how he felt. It was a bitter time for both of us.

He finished his year at Goshen but did not return to Virginia the next September. When my school started I wrote a matter-of-fact letter, asking him to send me my letters. To my surprise, he wrote saying that he still loved me and always would, even if I did not love him. Of course that awakened my love, and I accepted his love again, and his friendship.

During his visit to Denbigh that fall I came to understand him better. As our friendship deepened, we were convinced that God had led us to each other.

That Christmas I visited his home. Grant had a fine family, and I found their home to be lovely and hospitable. The snow-covered hills and valleys of eastern Pennsylvania were beautiful to my eyes. The heater in the car made us feel cozy and secure as we drove through the snow. I came home from that trip a happy girl.

We exchanged gifts. I gave him a picture of myself for his birthday on February 12, and for my birthday he gave me a large candy Easter egg in a little cedar box.

In May he wrote, suggesting that we go fishing with a group the next time he visited. When he came, he didn't want to go fishing, but to a place where we could talk alone. We found a spot in Mariner's Museum Park, near Newport News, and there, on May 25, 1940, I promised to be his wife. Later he said, "A man can't ask his sweetheart to be his wife while with a group on a fishing trip."

Our wedding

While Grant finished his degree at Goshen College, I taught another year at Denbigh. Then on June 17, 1941, we were married. On the day of our wedding Grant wrote in his diary, "It came off just as we wanted it to come off. Now we belong to each other."

Our simple wedding was in line with family tradition—the quiet church or home weddings of my parents and most of my eight siblings. I can still see the lawn of our home that evening:

• • •

The wedding decorations are the flowers, shrubs, and trees that my parents have loved to care for over the years. Mama sits with two other honored guests—Grant's parents, Sylvanus and Lydia Hartz Stoltzfus. Most members of both families are present.

Enter my brother, Truman H. Brunk, officiating minister, who stands, waiting. Edith Shenk, Lois Shenk, and Ruth Smith sing "I Love You, Truly," a popular love song we approved. Next come my small nephews, David Brunk and Bobby Hertzler, who take the marriage license to Truman. Grant, the bridegroom, and his attendant, Hubert Pellman, all up front. Then my attendant, Mildred Kauffman Pellman, and I join Grant and Hubert in front of the minister.

Our wedding day:
June 17, 1941.

Truman gives a brief message, the ceremony is performed, and our promises are made to each other. The women's trio sings, "Two Hearts Are Joined," the wedding song Mildred and I had composed—she the words, I the music—for both of our two weddings, six days apart. Enter four couples to manage arrangements and serve refreshments on the lawn: my brother Lawrence Brunk and sister-in-law Dorothy (who had made my white wedding dress), friends Esther and James Burkholder, my sister Edna and brother-in-law Arthur Hertzler, and my sister Katie and brother-in-law John Shank.

• • •

Leaving home

As we drove off on our wedding trip to Elizabeth City, North Carolina, Grant said, "Sweetheart, I'll try to make you as happy as I can."

At the end of June, Grant left for summer school at Hershey, Pennsylvania, and I stayed at Denbigh and helped pick the peach crop. Two weeks later he came to get me and my things.

When the moment came for me to leave, the fact that I was leaving home, mother, church, and friends flooded in on me all at once. I felt my heart being torn. I could not speak when I said good-bye. I just walked around and kissed each one. Mama was out in the kitchen, saying she didn't know how she could stand this loss, so soon after Papa's death. Only love could make me leave everything to go to Pennsylvania.

On July 6, in a car loaded with my belongings acquired since babyhood, as well as our wedding gifts, we made our way to our new home—two rooms in the stone house near the mill in Morgantown, Pennsylvania, which Grant's folks had bought and moved into shortly before. Grant took some college classes and worked at a market. I taught Bible school and canned peaches, apples, and tomato juice.

One Sunday at Grant's home church, Conestoga Mennonite, we participated in an ordination service. At that time ministers and deacons in some Mennonite churches were chosen by lot from among the (male) membership of the congregation. This Sunday Grant was in the deacon's lot. On a table in front of the church were several identical black books, one for each candidate, and in one was a slip of paper. It was an intense moment when Bishop John Mast looked in Grant's book for the slip of paper. The slip was found in Ira Kurtz's book, and we were all pleased that he was the new deacon.

During the service the men in the lot sat on the front benches and their wives sat with them. It was almost as if the woman was being ordained with the man.

Chapter 7

My World Becomes Larger

Akron, Pennsylvania
October 1941–September 1943

In October 1941, four months after our wedding, Grant and I moved to Akron, a small town in Lancaster County, Pennsylvania, where we worked at the office of Mennonite Central Committee (MCC), the united relief and service organization of the Mennonite and Brethren in Christ churches. Both of us worked full time for a combined salary of seventy dollars a month, plus room and board, at MCC headquarters.

Under the direction of office manager Ernest Bennett, I kept track of expenses for the Civilian Public Service (CPS) camps run by MCC. These camps were being set up under the Selective Service Act of 1940, to provide alternative service so that religious conscientious objectors, if drafted, could do "work of national importance under civilian direction"—and under civilian financing.

The church paid all the expenses for the boys in the camps. The first year we had 525 campers, and later there were several thousand. I also monitored progress of a debt liquidation drive for Mennonite Board of Education under the supervision of Orie O. Miller, executive secretary of MCC.

The work gave me a view of the wider Mennonite Church and enlarged my view of the other peace churches (Church of the Brethren and Quakers). Information came across my desk about young men from non-peace church denominations headed for CPS camps as conscientious objectors. Most of those were Methodists.

It was valuable continuing education. As publicity director, Grant was close to the news. He reported on MCC programs for our church papers and prepared news releases about the MCC workers overseas.

We were in close association with Orie O. Miller. I don't know of a person in the Mennonite Church who put his positive stamp on more people, or did more to motivate good projects. He kept regular hours at the MCC office to maximize his time away from his family-run shoe manufacturing business and other responsibilities in his home and church.

Orie and other leaders of the historic peace churches made many trips to government offices in Washington, D.C., on behalf of alternative service for conscientious objectors. We heard some news from those trips, and along with the other MCC staff, we held nonstop discussions about national and world events. Quaker visitors sometimes joined the MCC family dining table. This enlarged our view of our church, other churches, and the world of politics.

Preparing for war

On Sunday afternoon, December 7, 1941, we heard the news of the Japanese attack on Pearl Harbor. I remember the sinking feeling I had in my heart as Grant and I drove back to Akron from a visit with his parents in Morgantown. I can feel now the apprehension I felt as we talked about what the war might mean for us and multitudes of others.

For the next year and a half Grant worked with Mennonite Church leaders as they prepared to set up CPS camps for conscientious objectors (COs). They visited farms in the Hagerstown, Maryland, area and met with officers of the Soil Conservation Service. MCC purchased land and prepared for the arrival of COs from Ohio and Pennsylvania.

While Grant was gone I had fun teaching myself to type and even began to enjoy "romping with numbers," especially when the books came out right. But Grant was exhausted from his work and from traveling back and forth between Akron and Hagerstown. When he was home, I felt abandoned because he had so much business downstairs in the MCC office. We had one common project we both enjoyed—editing a little paper called "Office Memo."

I wrote to my friend Frances Dean Strickland, "I never suspected that I would ever be so happily married, even though I was sure that I was very much in love. It is ever so much sweeter than I even imagined or hoped . . . I think my heart will burst . . . I marvel that God gave me a husband so wonderful. I never deserved it."

In August 1942 we moved from our room above the MCC office to a four-room apartment three houses down the street. It was wonderful to be in our own nest, but I was never a conventional housewife. One Sunday we were at friends' for dinner, and when one of the older women stepped aside to let the men go to the table first, I stubbornly said, "Oh, no."

"Well, that's the way we were always taught," she answered.

Waiting for induction and baby

When we visited Virginia, I delighted in playing with my brother Lawrence's little Janet, a special pet of mine. (After she was grown she signed a letter to me, "Your first baby.") Our hopes for a little one of our own were realized with the confirmation that a baby was on the way, due to arrive July 3, 1943.

Because of the war, Orie turned much of the bookkeeping over to me, and in February I moved my office from the MCC building to our apartment three doors down. I arranged a little office, with a sewing machine table for the secretary, Helen Lehman, and her typewriter. I had my own desk and a steel file. I worked seven hours a day at forty-two and a half cents an hour and considered a good part of my pay to be the enjoyment and satisfaction of doing church work. While I worked at bookkeeping and waited for the baby, Grant visited CPS campsites and waited for his induction notice.

I wrote to Frances Strickland, "The more serious the war becomes, the more we nonresistant people are hated and misunderstood. I love my country as much as those who fight for it, but I believe the New Testament teaching on loving enemies. I cannot conscientiously take part in any killing."

My reflections came after an incident a few days earlier. I had met a woman on the street who evidently knew my position on war. I spoke to her as everyone in our small town usually spoke, but she gave no response to my friendliness except a hateful look. My natural inclination, as I walked on, was to feel bitter toward her, but I realized that if I allowed myself that feeling, I would be contradicting the very doctrine of love that made me oppose participation in war. I walked on, praying for her and thinking, "Maybe she had a son or husband killed in battle. Maybe some other sorrow crushed her mother heart."

Grant and I at the MCC House in Akron, Pennsylvania.

On the day before my birthday, Grant was drafted and classified as a conscientious objector. Two days later he was transferred to full-time work at Akron. While we waited for his induction notice, he took on the correspondence work for the new MCC Peace Section Office in addition to the publicity work he had done formerly.

My mind was in a whirl. As a CO in a CPS camp, Grant would not receive a cent of salary, only his room and board. The support of our family would rest solely on me. I loved the work at MCC, but felt I had to consider jobs that paid more.

Should I accept the teaching job offered by the Mennonite Parochial School Board? But if I left our little baby to someone else's care, someone else would make the first impressions on baby, receive the first smile, and see the first tooth while I was slaving at a money-making job and Grant was away with CPS.

Should I accept a bookkeeping job that the owner of a large hardware store was begging me to take? Office work would demand less of my time than school teaching.

Should Grant try for a farm deferment? If he did, we could keep our family together. But his folks did not favor it, and Grant felt he should stay with MCC. Grant's parents were thoughtful of me.

They said I should not plan to work; this situation was a call for them to sacrifice, too.

Ernest Bennett, the MCC office manager (later head of the Mennonite Church Board of Missions), and his wife, Earla, were also expecting. Should we follow up Ernest's suggestion that our two families live together, split expenses, and hire someone to care for the babies while Earla and I worked?

Should the baby and I go to live with Grant's family or mine? Life felt like a jigsaw puzzle with missing pieces.

Our second wedding anniversary, June 17, 1943, was supposed to be Grant's day of induction into CPS, but his local draft board was growling. They were not satisfied with the authorization Grant had to stay in Akron on detached service. They would not consider him inducted until they got official notice from Washington.

The arrival of our little one also continued to be postponed. I was ready and eager, with clothes and supplies and suitcase packed. The baby's due date, July third, came and went.

Birth of Allen Grant

Our dear little Allen Grant was born at 1:00 a.m., July 9, 1943. Grant was with me all of the time except for my stay in the delivery room. "He has a round face, large nose and feet," I wrote in my journal. "His Mommie thinks he'll make a fine looking little boy." I knew then that I couldn't leave our baby for a job.

Grant wrote in his diary, "The doctor came into the hallway where I was and told me, 'Your son is in the delivery room.' That gave me a strange sensation. He weighs 7 lbs. 8 oz. and is a heavy-set little lad. It surely is a moment to see a little bundle of humanity, the earthly (and heavenly) part of your own immortality. I hope God will ever give us the wisdom to be to this boy what we should be . . . I sent telegrams to Ruth's mother and sister Esther and mailed the formal announcements. Everyone is rejoicing with us." Grant said to me, "You have your MA degree now."

We named the baby Grant for his Daddy and Allen because we thought it went well with the name. People said he looked like his father.

The next day Grant brought disappointing news from his local draft board. The plan for us to stay in Akron was canceled.

On the fifth day after the baby's birth I was allowed to sit up, and on the eighth day I sat on the edge of the bed and dangled my feet. That same day Orie Miller met with Grant's draft board, but the interview was fruitless. Grant was ordered to go to Hagerstown. I felt another disappointment when Dr. Reynolds said I should give up nursing because the baby was not getting enough nourishment.

On July 20, Grant's twin sisters, Ada and Ida, brought Allen and me home, and Ida stayed to help until I regained my strength. Five days later, Grant packed his bag and left sixteen-day-old Baby and me for the CPS camp at Hagerstown, Maryland. I thought of the couples who were separated more than we would be. "How can they stand it?" I wondered.

Allen and I agree to be inducted

When Orie Miller asked me about our future plans, I said we would rent our apartment to MCC people if he would arrange for Grant and me to live together near Hagerstown. He laughed, then said we would get about ten dollars rent per month for our furniture. I saw that Grant and I could be together and make ends meet with the fifty dollars we would receive if we were both in the camp program.

On September 1, Grant became director of all four units of CPS in the Hagerstown area. I stayed in Akron until the auditors examined the books, and then I went to live with Grant's folks at Morgantown while Allen and I waited to be inducted. On September 28 we joined Grant at Clear Spring, Maryland.

Chapter 8

Our Little World

Clear Spring, Maryland
September 1943–May 1944

I served for eight months as camp matron at the Civilian Public Service (CPS) camp near Clear Spring, in the hills of western Maryland. The campers were good-natured and intelligent, a mixture of college graduates and farmers. They did soil conservation work under government supervision, with some equipment supplied by the government, but the churches paid the campers' allowances.

As matron, I planned meals for about thirty-five campers, supervised cooking, cleaning, and laundry, and periodically inspected the barracks to see if cots were made neatly, shelves and closets kept in order, and floor swept clean. "Don't tell anybody how my closets used to look!" I wrote to Mama.

I found the meal planning the most demanding job, even though I had three cooks under me who did the actual work in the kitchen. On Sunday mornings I let them sleep while I got breakfast. Sunday was our hardest, busiest day, because of visitors. As the only woman, I was also expected to meet and act as hostess for all visitors.

Grant lost weight in the camp. He was on the run, looking after three other CPS camps, teaching a Bible class at the Amish camp, arranging for inter-camp activities, and going into Hagerstown twice a week to buy supplies for the farm and food for us all.

I liked to tell my family and Grant's family and a few friends about interesting things and characters in my little world at camp, but I soon got tired of writing about the same incidents over and over. So I began to mimeograph a two-page news sheet, "My Little World," promising publication "as the author receives inspiration," with personal notes added by hand. In the first issue I took note of "Conchie," who "got his name from Conscientious Objector even if he is just a dog, but he does have a conscience about keeping the chickens chased off of the yard and garden."

In January, I took on Grant as a columnist, and "My Little World" became "Our Little World," with the banner headline: SENSATIONAL NEWS RELEASE: BABY CUTS A TOOTH.

Camp routines

Our days began at 6:00 a.m. with a rising bell. At 6:30 we had breakfast and devotions. Twenty-five men left at 8:00 for project work outlined by Soil Conservation (SC) officials, and two went to the SC office in town. At 12:00 noon we served dinner at camp for the laundry man, the farmer, three cooks, the office clerk, Grant, and me. Those leaving for work had taken lunch with them. At 4:45 p.m. the project fellows and two office men returned. We had sup-

Baby Allen's first home was at the Civilian Public Service camp in Clear Spring, Maryland.

per at 5:30. Once a week we held a prayer meeting at 7:30. Bedtime was 10:00.

Grant noted that "The CPS man's delight is a rainy day when he can spend the day reading, writing, wood working, developing pictures, etc.," but "Rain on Sunday is a GI [Government Issue] rain to them!" Our real government issue included army cots, blankets, a big army stove, and cooking utensils.

A typical day's menu began with a breakfast of tomato juice, cooked Ralston cereal, scrambled eggs, and hot Postum to drink. The noon meal consisted of leftovers at camp or a lunch on the project of celery and potato soup and sandwiches: chicken, egg and mayonnaise, or jam. A typical evening meal included chili con carne, candied sweet potatoes, pickled beets, string beans, peaches, and homemade doughnuts.

I was pleased with the camp cooks. I planned the menu, but they deserved the credit. "Our Little World" reported:

> "This can't be CPS!" Those words came from a new camper whose eyes fell on the big pieces of peach pie on the Sunday evening supper table. Another fellow said he had planned to sell some clothes that were too large for him, but now he thinks he'll just keep them. I deserve no credit, but somehow I take those remarks as a bouquet given in style.

Under the story I drew a stick figure of a camper presenting flowers to the matron.

Visitors and helpers

Our families supported Grant and me with gifts and visits. His sisters Ida and Ada were busy schoolteachers, but they took time to make a dress for me, complete with snaps, buttons, and collar. My brother George and my sister Stella's husband, Ward Shank, came as guest preachers for our Sunday services.

Mama, my sister Katie, and Katie's husband, John Shank, came in late November, bringing six big turkeys. That treat fed thirty-four campers for two big meals. At the Sunday meal the boys were so quiet that I wondered what was wrong. One of the big talkers spoke up and said, "Well Ruth, you know what you told us—that Mama was coming and that we should be good."

Alice Beiler from Grant's home church in Morgantown wrote

that their sewing circle would gladly furnish curtains for seven of our closets in the boys' quarters. We considered that a great favor and a sample of the way sewing circles across the country responded to camp needs. We received twenty-four sturdy white aprons from a sewing circle in Kansas.

Local Mennonite people also helped. Women from the community came every two weeks to do mending for the boys. Eleven of them breezed in one day and housecleaned the whole place, even washing and ironing the curtains.

Widening our world

Once in a while we took a Sunday away from camp to attend a local church. We learned to know the community and enjoyed fine hospitality in local homes. One conservative congregation amazed us with its requirement that all the women wear aprons, every man wear a frock-tailed coat, and no one wear wristwatches.

Grant and I (4th and 5th from the left) with other Civilian Public Service personnel in Clear Spring, Maryland, 1944.

At the Amish CPS unit twenty-two miles away I attended my first Amish service. There was no Sunday school, but the preaching, in German, lasted from 9:30 a.m. until nearly noon.

One weekend Grant was in Lancaster for a special Sunday school meeting, so the visiting minister and spiritual advisor had no one to introduce him at the Sunday worship service. I knew that the Quaker women were active in their churches, and I had a notion to turn Quaker long enough to take charge of the meeting and introduce him!

I tried in various ways to make a contribution to the welfare of the campers, most of whom were away from home for the first time. I put up quotations on the blackboard in the dining room, such as: "He that ruleth his spirit is better than he that taketh a city" (Prov. 16:32).

At the camp Christmas program I tacked up profiles of the campers that I had made by rigging up a strong light and letting them pose while I traced their shadows on the wall. The cutouts looked so lifelike, I made one of Allen and sent it to friends with the newsletter.

Civilian Public Service camp barracks at Clear Spring, Maryland.

For Christmas, Grant and I gave each other a twenty-five dollar life subscription to *Readers Digest.* I wrote home, "We'll sit in our little upstairs room with its crude furnishings and uneven floor while the *Digest* widens our world."

In February, boys from every Mennonite camp in the country and from about every Mennonite community came to attend a four-month Rural Life School at our camp. From this new group we learned about Mennonite communities in Kansas, Indiana, Oklahoma, Ohio, and Pennsylvania. Considerable disagreement existed about which one was the "garden spot."

The school brought speakers and visitors on rural living and the Mennonite rural community. The county agent, local veterinarians, and extension men came to the camp to lecture on topics related to farming: poultry, orchards, animals and their diseases, soil and fertilizers, and farm woodlands. When they stayed for supper, Grant enjoyed "the splendid opportunity" to answer their questions about the CPS program and our faith. Even though many of them had sons or brothers in the armed forces, Grant found them "congenial and understanding of us."

Discouragement and frustration

One Sunday we had a visit from Paul Hume, secretary to Paul French, the executive director of the National Service Board for Religious Objectors. NSBRO was the link between the camp programs of the historic peace churches and the Selective Service bureaucracy.

Another Sunday, the Sidling Hill Unit directors and their wives visited us. We poured out to each other the troubles and headaches of CPS life. Consequently, we started the week feeling better in spirits than we had for many a week!

One of the headaches was the persistent problem of running over our food budget, despite my attempts to cut down on our consumption of meat and eggs. Mary Emma Showalter from Virginia, the traveling dietitian for the MCC camps, spent a weekend with us to help us reduce our food expenses. MCC set policies for all CPS camps, but the cost per man per meal was higher for a small camp like ours. It was hard not to use all the meat and eggs we wanted when we produced them on the farm. I felt frustrated about being charged market prices for food we produced.

By May, Allen was a heavy ten-month-old baby and camp duties were heavy, too. For some time, I had thought that my place should be filled by a woman who did not also have responsibility for a small child. I wrote a letter of resignation to Orie Miller on May 28, and after an eight-month stay, Allen and I left camp.

Chapter 9

Lonesome at Home

Denbigh, Virginia
June 1944–June 1947

Although I missed Grant, and even missed the campers and the cooks and the small talk in the kitchen, I was glad to be away from camp. Grant's folks invited me to stay in Morgantown and teach while Grant's mother kept the baby. I ground away at a bookkeeping correspondence course, prodding myself by making a list of the 192 pages of workbook material I had to do and striking them off as they were finished. I also worked for sixty-five cents an hour at a pea viner in a contract that Grant's folks had with the Campbell Soup Company. The pea vinery, or huller, was across from the Conestoga Mennonite Church. Farmers mowed the peas at night for high moisture and got them to the vinery as soon as the sun was up.

Even though I felt at home with Grant's family, I was eager to get back to my home church and my family. After a month in Morgantown, Allen and I moved to Denbigh to live with my sister Edna and her husband, Arthur Hertzler.

My brother Truman had a rush with the peach crop and needed me to help, so after a few weeks with Edna, Allen and I moved into a downstairs room at Truman's. I picked fruit, drove truckloads to Yorktown, kept house, painted signs to advertise the peaches, and sold peaches at the house.

In August, Allen and I settled into a three-room cottage belonging to my sister Esther and her husband, Henry Shenk, across the lawn from their big house. Henry paid me twenty dollars a week for selling fruit and gave me all the milk I needed and other food, besides free rent. Through the rest of the summer I sold peaches, as much as 100 dollars' worth in one day, at the house and at the Colony Market (a Mennonite farmers' cooperative) in Newport News.

Back to school

I always said no one but me would love and train Allen, but war and economics made me eat my words. A number of women from the Parent-Teacher Association (PTA) begged me to teach school at Denbigh Elementary, where I had taught for four years before Grant and I were married. My brother George said I should teach, since there was such a shortage of teachers, and Esther would be nearby in an emergency. What made me finally consent was the dire need for a teacher. The PTA mothers said it was my patriotic duty.

I engaged the help of Betty Brenneman from across the road. She was dependable, she loved children, and she knew how to do household tasks. Since Allen slept a long nap, I was away from him only four hours of his waking time each day.

The busy days passed quickly. I got up at 6:00 a.m. to write to Grant. At seven I woke Allen and dressed and fed him. Each day I rushed home to Allen, sat down with him clinging tightly, and read Grant's letters. When I asked, "Where is Daddy?" Allen looked right at the picture of Grant on the dresser in the living room.

Grant's Exchange

In addition to teaching, I was involved in a small auction business. I was so pleased with the $86.87 I made from the first sale that two weeks later I held another one, charging ten percent to sell

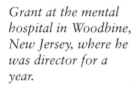

Grant at the mental hospital in Woodbine, New Jersey, where he was director for a year.

other people's items. "Tell me now," I wrote to Grant, "are you ashamed or proud of me? I sold things that you will not even miss when you come again—little gadgets and duplications in dishes, etc."

I called the business, Grant's Exchange. I got a merchant's license and ordered a sign for the end of the lane and wore myself out running around buying things. It was fun, but the sale did not yield as much as I expected. I came out with a profit of 15 dollars on 128 dollars worth of goods.

I soon found another source of income. Truman said I could have half the rent of a vacant six-room house that he owned if I took care of the headaches: advertising, dealing with the people, and furnishing the house, which I could do at a small cost with the furniture left over from the sale.

The way of the transgressor

At my request Grant bought me a radio, but because of church rules I had to keep it in a hiding place. "Thanks for locating a good radio at a good figure," I wrote to him. "The next problem is for me to use it peaceably without a lot of criticism."

Later I wrote to Grant:

> The radio has been out from its hiding place a few times and works very well. Last Wednesday while still in Harrisonburg, I took it to Miles Music Store for repairs and just as I was about ready to hand it over, my nephew Rowland was standing by and I did not want him to see the forbidden radio. I told him to go and find where my brother-in-law John had parked and to meet me at Penneys. What a hard way the transgressor has! I get a lot of stations now and have a good aerial on the radio.

I enjoyed Firestone's Fine Music Hour and the Bell Telephone Company program that followed. I heard President Roosevelt and listened often to Fulton J. Sheen. But there was so much opposition, I kept the radio in my bedroom upstairs and used it only when I was resting or at bedtime, when there was no likelihood of any visitors.

Mental health work

In January 1945, Grant was asked to take leadership of a new CPS unit at a hospital for feeble-minded boys in Woodbine, New

Jersey. He wrote in his diary, "A note from the Mental Hygiene fellows says that if the CPS fellows produce the goods, there is a possibility that a permanent Mental Hygiene program will be possible through a grant of the Rockefeller Foundation. I want to do what I can in this, for it is a great contribution that we as COs can make in World War II to a great social problem."

Mennonites vs. the world

In the spring, a few of the teachers decided we'd have a game of baseball and invite people in the community to play with us. When we Mennonite women arrived, we found that the Denbigh people were pitting themselves against the "Dutchmans" (Mennonites) and had planned that kind of competition for a week without saying anything to us.

We didn't want to act scared, so without any practice or organization we played as a team. It was the nearest I ever came to praying that my side would win a baseball game. Many people from the Denbigh community came, all cheering for the other side, but by the time the ninth inning was over, the "Dutchmans" had beaten the world, ten to eight!

The end of the war

One morning in May 1945, the whole Denbigh school went into the auditorium to hear President Truman and Prime Minister Churchill's speeches on the ending of the war in Europe. When school was out that year, I thought I had never felt so relieved and carefree in my life. I decided not to go back to teaching, but to stay with Allen while we waited for Grant to be discharged. In order to make ends meet, I drove the Warwick River Christian School bus, with Allen standing up beside me or sitting on the front seat behind me for the thirty-four mile round trip.

"I'm ready any time for our breadwinner to get home," I told Grant. I kept him up-to-date, writing about everything Allen did:

> Yesterday in church when everyone knelt for prayer, I remained seated while holding Allen. The little fellow must have thought all the church was playing peek-a-boo and hiding their eyes because he said, "Boo!" during the prayer. When the people still hid their eyes, he said, "Boo!" a little louder.

Allen began to develop frequent whining spells when he wanted something, but I nipped it in the bud by refusing to listen to his request unless he "asks Ma-ma nice." I reported to Grant how well Allen responded to my teaching methods, and how glad I was that I had decided to stay with him instead of teaching another year. "A whining habit is one of a dozen things that requires a mother's close watch," I wrote.

While I was keeping my eyes on Allen, I had some things to learn too. One day I was trying to show home movies of Allen when the sweet child himself was at my side, interrupting the show with his talk. I wanted him to be quiet so we could see pictures of him!

I hoped each day for news of Grant's discharge. In my September 30, 1945, letter to Grant, I said, "Your letters do me so much good. Each time I get one I think maybe it contains special news of your discharge. That is what I ache and dream for each moment of each day. The days and nights are so long without you, and it's no fun going places always without you."

Grant met with A. J. Metzler, manager of the Mennonite Publishing House, to discuss a job after demobilization, but demobilization seemed to take forever. Meanwhile, we anticipated our discharge pay. A Virginia Mennonite Conference committee was planning on giving the Virginia boys about 200 dollars if they had been in camp over two years. Grant's twin sisters, Ada and Ida, sent two checks of ten dollars each, and we received 110 dollars from my family.

In November Grant was transferred to the mental hygiene program of the National Mental Health Foundation in Philadelphia. There he could do the type of work he enjoyed most. His assignment was to prepare public education pamphlets about mental health and to research church-run mental institutions.

As soon as I realized that Grant would be receiving enough for both of us to live on, Allen and I joined him. On January 5, 1946, we moved to a third-floor apartment in the home of Grant's great-uncle, Moses Hartz, near Grant's work and the University of Pennsylvania.

Grant was discharged from CPS on May 24, but he continued to work at the Mental Health Foundation for another month. Because I thought Allen needed good country air and sunshine, he and I moved back to Denbigh in early June. Also, I was expecting our second baby in October.

Waiting for baby

That summer Grant commuted between Denbigh and Scottdale to work at his new job with Mennonite Publishing House, and I waited for the birth of our second child. Grant was editing a new magazine, *Mennonite Community*, which featured news and photographs about life in Mennonite communities across the United States.

While Grant was managing writers and photographers for the new magazine, I was managing workers for the moving of our cottage to a better lot on a half-acre near my brother Lawrence's house. I savored the feeling of living on land that someone else did not own, and I was thrilled with my plans to partition off part of the living room to make a little study for Grant. My brother Truman was a great help, advising me on everything from the price I should pay for land to the kind of cinder blocks to buy.

After everything was completed, on October 11, 1946, Eugene Harold, our second child, was born. Grant wrote in his diary, "Today the miracle happened again. The little fellow seems like a pretty good lad with a round face and a nice body. He weighs 7 lbs. 1 oz. He was yawning when I saw him."

Chapter 10

Under His Wings

Scottdale, Pennsylvania
June 1947–December 1949

In June 1947, we moved from Denbigh to a second-story apartment next door to the Mennonite Publishing House in Scottdale, Pennsylvania. The people at the publishing house completely cleaned it before we came, and when we arrived, they offered us multiple invitations to Sunday dinner. The profit on the sale of our house and lot in Denbigh cleared our debts. Grant said we were as we had been at birth—breaking even.

The burning of soft coal made everything in Scottdale sooty. Even when there was not much smoke, the wind blew black stuff from the rooftops onto and into our house. I ached for a house where we could get Allen and Eugene down onto the good earth and out into clean air.

Business enterprises

While I was still in Denbigh, I had taken a correspondence course from Ellis Business Service, Cedar Grove, North Carolina, at a cost of sixty dollars. Now under my business name, Reliable Bookkeeping and Tax Service, I had thirteen small businesses paying two dollars a week for my services by mail. After Grant pointed out that I was keeping books for a dozen businesses and could do the same for us, I set up a budget arrangement. Why should the shoemaker's children go barefoot?

In April we bought and moved to a two-story house. In July, nine months pregnant, I invested my bookkeeping earnings in a mail order business called the Mail Order Shop. I told my sister Katie, "I will never be satisfied until I get into some kind of buying and selling, so I plan to start here at home on a small scale for the present." I mapped out an advertising campaign for the next year. I even thought up schemes for my mother, at seventy-three, to make some money knitting booties and kimonos, but she declined.

Under his wings

On July 17, 1948, our third child, Kathryn Esther, was born. Grant's comment, "A nice little baby girl who will bring a lot of joy into our home" turned out to be true, but not until after we had experienced a serious crisis.

I spent four days in the hospital and then hurried home to look after Allen and Eugene. Then I became very sick with an undiagnosed illlness. The doctors at Mt. Pleasant hospital near Scottdale decided against surgery and sent me home again. I think I would have died except for the arrival of my brother Truman from Virginia. From the start, my recovery from that illness was due to God's orchestration of human instruments.

My sister Edna, a nurse, came and took baby Kathryn home with her to Denbigh, where she kept her for two months. People from my home congregation donated blood. Many prayers were said on my behalf.

Truman got clearance from the doctors for me to go by Pullman train to Washington, D.C., where he met me and took me to Denbigh. The pain on the train trip was so great that at one point my sister Esther, also a nurse, asked if she should try to have the

Our house in Scottdale, Pennsylvania.

train stopped. When we arrived at our destination, I was readmitted to the hospital. Meanwhile, I continued to experience excruciating abdominal pain that was only partially alleviated by regular injections of morphine. I became aware that my life could end soon, but God gave me such assurance that a prayer formed in my mind. I asked the nurse for paper and pencil and wrote:

> *Lord, I care not whether now*
> *Or in later years*
> *You call me Home.*
> *Must I retrace those steps*
> *I lately took toward You?*
> *To go on would mean perfect joy.*
> *To stay—joy mixed with pain and tears.*
>
> *But, Lord, here are our boys*
> *And baby girl*
> *Who need me so!*
> *If I may stay to help and teach*
> *And love them,*
> *I will take the joy mixed with pain*
> *Instead of perfect joy.*
>
> *O God, You know the end*
> *From the beginning.*
> *Your way is best.*
> *I care not whether now*
> *Or in later years*
> *You call me Home.*

When the time came for me to go for surgery, Grant was by my bedside. My mother, Esther, and Truman were in the room too. But their presence was no more real than the presence of God. Truman read from Psalm 91:

> I will say of the Lord, He is my refuge and my fortress: my God; in him will I trust. . . . He shall cover thee with his feathers, and under his wings shalt thou trust. . . . Thou shalt not be afraid for the terror by night; nor for the arrow that flieth by day. . . . For he shall give his angels charge over thee, to keep thee in all thy ways.

It is impossible for a greater peace to come into a person's soul than that which flooded my soul that day. I knew that I was in

Grant as editor of Mennonite Community.

God's hands, and that he knew what he was doing with my life, whether it meant death or not.

The surgeon successfully removed a large gangrenous cyst. Esther, who was with me after surgery, told me afterwards that I was saying "under his wings" when I began to regain consciousness.

When Grant returned to Scottdale friends supported him with meals, while in Virginia my family watched Allen, Eugene, and baby Kathryn. Friends were generous with money to help.

After I was out of the hospital my family meant more and I felt closer to God than ever before. I realized that every breath I took was because of a miracle. Grant, too, felt that something had changed. He wrote to me from Scottdale, "You are living by nothing short of a miracle. This is a new beginning in my life. God has been good to us beyond words. You and I are going to be closer together than ever before."

I returned to Scottdale in late October, but it was months before

I was completely well. It was a lesson in patience, having to go on week after week unable to take care of my little baby, or even to rock Eugene comfortably.

Within seven months of my surgery I was pregnant again.

At home in Scottdale

In September 1949, Allen went off to school, eager and unafraid. Grant and I both went along the first day and met his teacher. It gave us a funny feeling to leave him at school in a large grade with about forty others. But I was beginning to feel at home in Scottdale. I wrote my family back in Virginia:

> We have lived here long enough now that we are getting pride in the place. I do like the people (most of them) and dealing with the outside people who appreciate the Mennonites is a treat. Wherever I go I am usually treated with respect. So far the schools seem fine and understand when there are activities that our children cannot engage in.

We were on a tight budget, so I started several moneymaking schemes. I bought a list of 100 hosiery mills and wrote them for the permission to sell their goods. I ran an ad in *The Mennonite Community* and also mailed out direct sales letters to a list of parochial school teachers, offering items they could buy from the Mail Order Shop to give their children as Christmas gifts. I also sold baby caps that my mother knit and pecans she sent me from Denbigh.

I enjoyed working on our household budget to see if we were keeping our expenses within limits. In November I calculated that we owned a little over one square rod of our acre. I made a chart, marked the debt off in fifty-dollar blocks, and when we paid that amount, filled in a block. It seemed childish at first, but it affected a decision when Allen wanted a bike and I wanted an automatic toaster and Grant wanted a new briefcase. Allen filled in the first block and kept a good interest in the game. Grant said I was making a business fellow out of him.

I devised several projects to improve our house. I rented a sander and sanded the living room floor around the edge of the rug to get a lighter finish. I stretched a curtain across one end of our upstairs hall and measured and schemed until I got a vanity dresser in and reserved enough space for a rollaway, fold-up bed that I ordered from Sears. I reminded myself of Mama, fully armed with a yard-stick, hammer, and nails.

Our growing family

On December 21, 1949, Ruth Carol, our fourth child was born. We named her Ruth, after her mother, and Carol, for Christmastime.

I was serenely happy. When Grant prepared to go downtown on Christmas Eve he asked if I wanted anything. "No," I said, "I have everything: two boys, two girls, and a good husband!" In February I described our family life in letters to Mama and my sisters:

Our growing family in January 1950: (l. to r.) Allen, Ruth Carol, me, Grant, Kathie, Eugene. In just six months I would begin a weekly radio broadcast that would grow into a full-time ministry.

I have tax work I want to get aside this afternoon while the babies are sleeping and before 3:30 when the big question box and cyclone combination [Allen, six years, seven months] comes home from school. . . .

We have just come in from a nice time together outdoors. Grant was a bucking bronco for the boys a while and then Allen had a lot of questions about the distance of the stars. We listened to an owl hooting in the trees in the hollow. Later we had worship out beneath the stars. Somehow, after thinking about God's greatness as Creator, and that He has us in His great plan for life here and heaven later, worries are soothed and smoothed away.

We did four different hitches of canning this past week. We never canned so much before, but we want to can more yet and try to lick the high food cost instead of eating out of the store. Grant's late corn crop is doing well.

Maybe my scheme will not work, but I have decided to buy time-saving equipment and make monthly payments on it instead of paying a hired girl. We have already bought a GE automatic washing machine—placed in the kitchen, and it's a honey! Next will be a few modern cupboards around the corner of the kitchen near the sink, and I even consider an electric dishwasher. Am I crazy in my idea?

I can't give up the bookkeeping because it requires only about one day a week to earn the $24 that comes in. I can be at home and earn that but I feel like saying, "No," to everything that requires me to be away from home.

PART THREE

HEART TO HEART
1950–1958

Chapter 11

Heart to Heart Begins

Scottdale, Pennsylvania
June 1950–July 1952

On a Monday morning in May 1950, only God knew that the six-mile trip to radio station WCVI, Connellsville, Pennsylvania, would determine my Christian service for the rest of my years. Ever since my sickness two years earlier, I had felt strong inner urgings to start a weekly broadcast for mothers in the home. Grant listened seriously when I told him about it, and we began to discuss ideas for such a venture.

As I studied the content of radio programs for women, it was not what was said, but what was not said, that spoke the loudest to me. There were many suggestions about accumulating things, little about building relationships or living for what will matter in 100 years and more. This, when mothers had the lives of little children in their hands? Women needed and deserved a program of more substance.

One Sunday evening we attended a United Church of Christ service in downtown Scottdale. After the service Grant said, "Let's go up and talk to the pastor about your idea of a women's broadcast."

Pastor Sparks warmed up to the idea right away. "I know the folks at WCVI," he said. "I can go along with you tomorrow morning to talk to them."

On the way in our old 1941 Ford, I told Grant and the pastor, "I felt led to pursue this idea, but if the interview is not favorable, I will take it as God's will that I do not start a broadcast." I prayed silently, "Lord, I don't care if the door is open or closed. Please, just make it plain."

It seemed very plain. The station manager was not in, and the assistant manager said there was no available time.

Just as we were leaving, the manager came in and invited us back to his desk. After listening to our ideas and looking over my written plans he said, "Yes, there is available time, and I will give you religious rates—twelve dollars for each fifteen-minute broadcast. Could you put the program on five days a week?"

"No, we have four children," I told him. "I could do the broadcast only once a week." We settled on Friday of each week.

Out on the street as we headed for the car, Pastor Sparks said, "You were wondering about Providence. You have Providence walking right with you!"

Preparing to go on the air

Soon I made final plans with S. C. Cunningham at Scottdale, one of my bookkeeping clients, who had expected to be my sponsor. He would pay fifteen dollars for each broadcast to allow me three dollars for gas and other expenses. At the first and last, the announcer would do a commercial about the sponsor's two nut shops and bakery. After organ strains of "O God, Our Help in Ages Past," I would have twelve and a half minutes to say what was on my heart. I would go on the air June 16 and each Friday at 11:00 a.m. under a six-month contract.

As June 16 approached the newborn broadcast had to have a name. Grant and I discussed this one evening after we had the chil-

Recording one of the first Heart to Heart broadcasts in 1950.

dren settled in bed. "Well, what do you want to do on the broadcast?" Grant asked.

"I want to share ideas about Christian family living, tell stories," I told him. "I just want to talk heart to heart."

"That's your name," he said.

The first broadcasts

That first broadcast, being near Father's Day, centered on the theme of the father's importance in the family. It foreshadowed an emphasis, by myself and others, that fathers are parents too. It is for the children's best spiritual and emotional welfare—their serenity, self-identity, purpose in life—to have the closeness of their father as well as their mother.

Each day I offered a special thought like "Mothers who stay at home with their work can go around the world with their prayers" or "The greatest teacher in the world is the mother of a little child." I signed off with "Good-bye, and God be with you right there where you are."

On the air I identified myself only as "Your friend Ruth," since the name Stoltzfus would not be easily understood. I found later that the name Ruth has the Hebrew meaning of "friend"—another cause for rejoicing in God's leading ahead of time.

I wrote to Mama and my sisters about my goals for the program:

> I'm scared to tell you about a plan I have, for fear you will not approve. But you have learned to never be surprised at anything I do.... Maybe you never prayed for a radio broadcast, but I want you to pray for this one. . . . I will have to do as I feel God is directing me no matter what [some] people think. . . . I feel the sin would be if I turned down the opportunity that has been thrown right in my lap.
>
> I want to reach mothers in these scattered mining towns, encourage them to go to church, to teach and read to and pray with their children, to give thought to life's important things—most of all, a right relationship with God.

In June I wrote to them:

> Two broadcasts are over and I do enjoy the experience. The first was on "Fathers." I gave some of my memories: the white bag of candy that showed up among the packages when Papa came home from town, the circus parade he took us to, the trip to hear and meet

the big Indian chief at Williamsburg, the thrill at Newport News of seeing Mrs. Coolidge, the president's wife, christen a big ship as it slipped out into the water of the James River on its way to the sea. Papa understood the heart of a child, but he also understood the soul of a child, and he taught us about God. I tried to develop the Christian theme from that point.

Yesterday the broadcast was on love and patience, with fifteen points for listeners to test themselves: "I am patient," "I do not boast," etc., and then I read 1 Corinthians 13, which deals with all those questions: "Love thinks no evil," etc. I have a lot to learn, but it is a good experience.

The broadcast continues

Near the end of six months of broadcasting, I hesitated asking S. C. Cunningham for further sponsorship, and I thought I should end the broadcast. I wrote at the bottom of my bill to him, "Thank you again for sponsoring my Heart to Heart broadcast. It was very generous of you. I have reason to believe the broadcast was helpful to many people. Sometime when our children are older, I hope to do something of this type again. December 8 is the last broadcast."

When the news got around that I expected to discontinue the broadcast, a small group of women from the Scottdale Mennonite Church called a meeting and a number signed up to donate several dollars a week. Other listeners also began to respond with small donations.

Three days before the last scheduled broadcast, the mail brought a letter from a listener saying how much the broadcast meant to her:

> I want to thank you for your wonderful program. I think it is one of the best on the air. May I ask you to pray for my son, as he is not a Christian. I heard you speak on the importance of good books. I would like information on a good book that will do something for a fourteen-year-old girl and a sixteen-year-old boy. I would also like to have a small Bible suitable for a soldier to carry, as my son will be going into the army in the near future.

I could not wait to share this letter with Grant, who was down the street talking over the fence with a neighbor. He read the letter and said, "You can't stop a broadcast that means that much to a listener."

Later, after a broadcast on which I read a listener's letter, the engineer said as I walked out of the studio, "I didn't know you were getting mail like that. We consider that one letter represents 1,000 listeners who plan to write but never get it done."

A check of seventy-five dollars from Grant's oldest brother, Ivan, encouraged me to take advantage of recording and duplicating services and thus go on more stations. One of these stations was WLAN, Lancaster, Pennsylvania, and going on there was crucial to the extension of the broadcast. I found that Lancaster County women wrote checks, and that they would underwrite some to my broadcast for expansion.

In time, Christian businesspeople and church groups sponsored the broadcast so that by March 1956, it was on twenty-four stations in Virginia, Mississippi, Pennsylvania, Vermont, Ohio, Indiana, Iowa, Kansas, and Oregon.

Encouragement from listeners

Listeners to the broadcast began writing words of appreciation and requests for the literature I offered. Letters from listeners and comments in person told me of people who became Christians, mothers who began going to church with their children, family relationships that were changed, confessions made, and husbands and wives reunited.

Christmas in Scottdale, Pennsylvania, 1951.

An eighteen-year-old girl wrote that she came from an irreligious home. She said she wanted her own home to be different. "I do not quite understand how or why God has become so important and inspiring to me," she said. "Perhaps your program has had a lot to do with it, and I am grateful from the bottom of my heart."

As a result of the broadcasts, hundreds of churches over the states and Canada opened up their pulpits for me to speak on

The children in 1952: Kathie, Ruthie, Allen, Eugene.

Christian family life relationships. An early word of confirmation came from people in Scottdale, a word that was significant in my calling to service in the church. Mary and David Alderfer sent me this note:

> Your worship service last evening was most edifying! We had planned to take our "brood" home after young people's meeting but felt so well prepared for what might follow that we did not want to miss the sermon, so we stayed and received further blessing. Thank you and more power to you and God bless you!

My regular study of books on Christian family living began when Alta Mae Erb, author and speaker, asked me to review some books for the Mennonite Publishing House.

I offered listeners a three-page Heart to Heart Lending Library that listed seventeen books—"just the books that will inspire you month after month when they're in your home . . . these books are the finest on the market. Read them and be inspired by them as I have been." The plan was to lend one book a month for six months for two dollars to cover mailing and handling costs.

Encouragement from home

Like my father, Grant had walls of books. Often he would pull down a volume and say, "Here you can find some help on that topic you're working on." After hearing him talk or pray, I would quickly jot down notes lest I forget his quotable words. Though busy with his own work, he would take time to look up information for the broadcast.

Everything on the home and devotional life that came to his desk he passed on to me. "Grant is such a help," I wrote to Mama and my sisters. "Right now he's typing up letters, sending for materials for program ideas."

Despite the help Grant gave me, I had more ideas of things to do than strength to do them. The Heart to Heart mail was so heavy I could hardly answer it. I hired part-time help with housework, reasoning that if I were a missionary on foreign soil, I would be expected to use hired help. I was a missionary on home soil. My office was in our home where the children were always near me.

Chapter 12

Expanding Ministry

Denbigh, Virginia
September 1952–June 1955

After selling our Scottdale house, we moved back to Denbigh, where we lived while Grant attended seminary at Richmond, sixty miles away. (He had finished a master's degree at the University of Pittsburgh while we were living in Scottdale.) Our plan was to finance seminary with loans and the profit from the sale of the house.

"Today several of our dreams are being realized," I wrote in my journal September 11, 1952. "Grant has begun work at Union Theological Seminary, as he has been longing to do for a number of years. Eugene, almost six, has started in the first grade at the Christian Day School here in the Colony."

The bottom of the money barrel

A brochure about Heart to Heart included a quote from John Wesley that described our situation: "Money never stays with me. I throw it out of my hands lest it should find a way into my heart."

I considered plugging along with bookkeeping and taking on more clients, working for my brother Lawrence in his retail poultry store, or opening a store of my own. My brothers did all they could to help me with housing and finances. Truman urged me to teach in the Mennonite school, but I told him I couldn't leave my babies. George and Lawrence, who operated the Brunk brothers tent revival campaigns, proposed having me operate an office for them in Denbigh. I said maybe I would if I could have a rocker in the office so I could stop and rock my babies.

George wrote:

> Ruth, I wish you could give full time to radio work. Maybe we [Brunk revival tent campaigns] can subsidize you. I'll talk to Lawrence.

. . . Go ahead with the Lancaster broadcast on your own. We'll pay for it. Your lending library is a good one. Enjoyed your fan mail. Think you can do a real service.

In February I sent five dollars to Grant at the seminary. "That leaves me with $1.00," I wrote, "but I think we'll be better off for this experience of being at the bottom of the money barrel. Chins up! The $1.00 will see me through today! I won't worry about tomorrow."

I avoided saying much on the air about our financial needs because I felt it cheapened the program. In August 1953, I sent out the first monthly *Heart to Heart Letter* to "the inner circle of Heart to Heart friends." In the letter I asked for suggestions to improve the program as well as financial support, and I shared feelings about the broadcast that I could not say on the air:

> At times I feel so alone in this work. The other day I was consulting a lawyer on the legal aspects of the program and he said, "Well, I don't know of anything else like this program, do you?" I said, "No, sir, I don't, but feel called to it as definitely as a minister feels called. I know God is with me."

Expansion of the broadcast

The broadcast continued to expand, adding new stations and new listeners. In 1954 mail was as high as fifty-four letters on one day. The mail was heavy with requests for the Mother's Pledge I read on several programs. I ordered a thousand for the first printing. Later we printed the pledge on heavy cardboard suitable for hanging on the wall, as well as in tract form for easy distribution. At least one hundred thousand of these were distributed and it was printed in four languages.

We also printed 10,000 copies of a Family Worship Decision Card in tract form and made it available in large quantities to those wanting to distribute them. We sent out thousands of other tracts, a thirty-eight-page booklet on "How to Conduct Family Worship," and a booklet for new mothers called "My Baby."

Sharing joys and sorrows

The mail reflected the joys and sorrows, victories and defeats of many hearts and homes. Listeners requested prayer and wrote of prayers that had been answered and help received.

A Mother's Pledge

I will do my part to make our home a happy place of work, play, love, and worship. I will give Christ His place in my life and help each family member to be loyal to Him and to the church.

I will be a loving companion to my husband, mentally, physically, and spiritually. When misunderstandings come, I will be quick to forgive and to ask forgiveness. I will encourage a happy relationship between my husband and our children.

I will take time to enjoy our children and to appreciate each one individually. I will discipline out of love and not to relieve my inner feelings. I will help our children to befriend people of all races and to live above petty grievances. I will answer all their questions about life and teach them about eternal life in Christ.

I will maintain an interest in people and their lives wherever I meet them in the course of my day. I will PRAY, GIVE, and GO as God leads me to help those in physical or spiritual need.

I will look upon this life as only a part of God's great plan for me. I will keep busy and happy, with an enthusiasm for life, but with my face set toward my Father's house of many mansions.

God helping me, this is the kind of person I will be that my life might be a blessing to my husband, to our children and the generations to come, to the church and to the world.

**No. 84RS © Concord Associates For a free copy, ask for No. 84 and send a long, self-addressed, stamped envelope to:
Concord Associates, 1111 Mt. Clinton Pike, Harrisonburg, VA 22802**

One woman wrote:

> The program has helped me so much—words cannot express it, but God knows my grateful heart. I had a conviction that my life was not a victorious one. Your program has had a big part in reviving my soul.

I was so touched by the cross section of human heartaches represented in the prayer request column of the *Heart to Heart Letter*; I invited readers to join me in prayer for each one. A woman wrote:

> Some days I used to become disgusted and impatient and the world seemed upside down. But, praise God, I have asked Him to give me victory over this and He has. Just a whispered prayer in a trying circumstance can take away feelings of remorse and impatience.

A young woman wrote:

> I am twenty-one but fearful about establishing a Christian home because I feel that I understand so little. My mother never gave much information because she said such things were too dirty to talk about. Do you advise going to a close friend if you don't feel free to talk to your mother?

I answered, "Yes, and read a good book on sex. Sex is not bad except when misused. If you ever have children, answer their questions."

People told of the help they received from reading the Bible daily, especially after I promoted the Heart to Heart Bible Reading Fellowship. "I like the word fellowship," I wrote in the *Letter*. "We have common problems and concerns and a common need of the Savior in our hearts and homes. Now we can have Christian fellowship together by means of reading the same Scripture selection daily, even though we are scattered far."

Extending the idea of fellowship, I put people with common concerns in touch with each other. When I took on speaking engagements, I listed meetings "where we can talk not only heart to heart, but face to face!"

One listener reported:

> I was touched to find that today the prayer helpers will be remembering my sister-in-law who had polio. Her situation has been miracu-

lous thus far—being able to leave the hospital exactly two months after she was stricken so severely. Even the doctors could not explain that. She has a long way to go but if prayer has done so much thus far, who needs to fear that continued intercession won't accomplish the rest?

In one *Heart to Heart Letter* I gave a step-by-step suggestion for a daily quiet time of prayer and Bible reading:

> As we read these Scriptures, may God's spirit expose, rebuke, and remove every ounce of race prejudice in our hearts. Modern scientists tell us that blood from one race is no different from that of another race. But they have nothing on Doctor Luke. He reported that truth long ago in Acts 17:26, "And [God] hath made of one blood all nations of men." Let's be wise and humble enough to make present-day applications. Souls don't have color.

Along with personal devotions, Heart to Heart promoted family worship. A woman in Sugar Creek, Ohio, wrote, "We began family worship again last night after hearing your talks. We want the family worship booklet. . . . I am glad for the little decision card and calendar."

Listeners felt the same personal connection I did. One woman wrote, "Seems you are right here in my home talking to us."

Some responses were light-hearted. "I would rather listen to the Heart to Heart program than eat breakfast," one person said. A male listener in Kansas wrote, "Are you married? If not, would you be interested in marriage?" Grant told friends, "I took the letter home to Ruth and she decided to stay with me."

Financial struggles

We continued to struggle with finances, believing that God would see us through. When Grant left one morning for another week at seminary, he pulled out a long grocery store tape, our largest grocery bill ever: $17.87 for fifty-four different items. "Keep it as a souvenir," he said. That spring we built a house in the Denbigh area, acting as our own contractor and working directly with the electricians, plumbers, plasterers, lumber dealer, and builders.

I wrote to Frances Strickland:

Since March 15, 1954, I have been a freer girl because I have dropped all thirteen bookkeeping accounts, and yet the Heart to Heart Program work is expanding so rapidly that I am kept more than busy! But my days are too full for any relaxation.

While my brother George and his family were in Canada that summer with his tent campaign, we helped with their fruit crop. Truman had charge of the peaches and we took care of the apples. Grant trucked peaches for brother-in-law Henry Shenk to Norfolk almost day and night, putting in as many as eighty-five hours a week. Allen directed people to George's orchard, where they could pick up apples at a dollar a bushel.

Allen and Eugene helped out with household tasks. I gave them each a list of jobs to do daily, and once a week they exchanged job lists. As soon as each job was completed, it was checked off so I could tell at a glance how things were going. Each boy received a quarter a week as a minimum allowance, but if they completed all of their jobs for one week without being told and without too many careless touches, then they each received two dollars a week. As well as keeping the boys occupied, that system relieved me of some of the household tasks and enabled me to devote time to my radio work.

The faith of children

One evening during family worship Grant prayed for the children and that each one would grow up to be a Christian. Eugene, who was then five years old, latched onto the "grow up" idea. After Daddy's, "Amen," he said, "Now, Mommy, am I bigger?"

We were still living in Scottdale when Allen made a start in the Christian life during the Brunk evangelistic campaign in nearby Johnstown. I will never forget how he looked up into my face during an invitation hymn and said that he would like to go up front with those confessing Christ. I immediately sat down and talked with him to make sure he understood what that step would mean. Then together we went to the front of the tent and later Uncle Lawrence dealt with him. During the testimony period he said a few words and I expressed thankfulness that we lived in a day when the Spirit called boys and girls and men and women to Christ.

On the way home that night, while Allen slept on the back seat of the car, Grant and I talked of ways in which we could help him to have a real Christian experience. Grant said he hoped that Allen would escape some of the doubts and unsatisfactory experiences that he had had in his own youth.

"Turning on the faucet"

As the number of speaking engagements kept increasing, I worked at balancing radio work with family life, taking the children with me whenever possible. I was not able to be at all the meetings that were requested, and I turned down some invitations because of family responsibilities.

Sometimes I took the children. Sometimes the whole family went together. Often we stayed with friends or made new friends in the homes that offered hospitality. I spoke in churches, in the Brunk evangelistic tent, and sometimes in school buildings when the crowd was too large for a church.

Our family in 1953. From the left: Eugene, me, Ruthie, Grant, Kathie, Allen.

One evening I was invited to speak at our home church about the radio work. It was just a matter of "turning on the faucet," because I was full of the subject. I told them, "When I have the opportunity to stand before a microphone once a week for fifteen minutes and talk to thousands of mothers in four states, I can't turn it down. Maybe you think I should, but I can't."

The women's side

The Heart to Heart program schedule cards that I passed out in those days listed the schedule of broadcasts on one side, and on the other side was printed:

> Listen to the Heart to Heart program conducted by Mrs. Grant M. Stoltzfus, mother of four (Your Friend Ruth). A new and different women's program, emphasizing not the right look, but the right Book—the Bible; not household hints, but happy home hints; not only temporal needs, but the deep spiritual needs of hearts and homes.

The motto at the bottom of the card read "Man does not live by bread alone, and woman does not live by baking the bread alone."

When I distributed the cards in conservative areas like Lancaster County, Pennsylvania, I wondered whether radio work was approved. Practices in those areas were different from those we were used to in Denbigh. One time I arrived early at a church in Lancaster, needing to spend some time in study and meditation and prayer before the meeting started. However, I did not want to be found sitting on the men's side when the audience began coming in. On which side should I sit? Did this church even have separate seating for men and women?

I knew that if the committee deciding on the location of the clock was made up of men only, they would likely place the clock where it could best be seen by the men. So I sat on the side of the church where I could not easily see the clock. Sure enough, when the audience arrived, they found me sitting on the women's side!

Strength to the weary

After suffering with a persistent backache for weeks, in April 1955, I called the doctor and went to bed. He checked me thoroughly and then announced that my trouble was arthritis of the spine. The drug he prescribed made my pain better but my pocket-

*At a speaking
engagement in
Kansas, October
1954.*

book sick. All the while I kept wondering if I would be able to leave by plane on May 6 to keep seven speaking appointments in western Pennsylvania and eastern Ohio.

By May 3, after being in bed for a week, I began to doubt whether I could go. I thought of the hardships of traveling commercially, going about with little physical strength from house to house to visit and from church to church to speak. I thought of the uneasiness I always felt when I was away from the children. I worded a telegram to send to those who had scheduled the Heart to Heart meetings: "Health reasons force cancellation of meetings. Letter will follow."

But I didn't send the telegram. I began to think of the relative ease of travel by plane and of the radio program's need for freewill offerings to pay a debt for airtime. Although I did not have the strength to travel, I believed that God would make a way for me if it was his will for me to go. But his will was not clear.

On May 5, one day before I was scheduled to leave, I felt impressed to discontinue the drug my doctor had prescribed. It kept me weak and I decided that I would prefer to have some pain if I could gain strength. That night I rolled and tossed, half awake and half asleep, half convinced that I should go and half convinced that I should not.

Finally, at 3:00 a.m. on the morning I was to leave, I turned on the bed lamp and looked to God in prayer. "Lord," I said, "help me to know what to do. You seem far away, and I can't tell if you want me to go or not. I am willing to go or stay. It doesn't matter which, but please make your will plain to me. I know you are able to make me strong enough to go, but I cannot claim your strength unless I am sure it is your will for me to go."

God seemed to speak a message as plain as these written words: "Go to my Word for your answer." I reached for my Bible, intending to browse through it until I came to a message that I felt was the answer. But before I could browse, my Bible opened, without any fluttering of the pages, to Isaiah, chapter 40. As I read, the verses seemed to have been written especially for my problem.

When I came to the last verses of the chapter, I heard God's answer, clear and plain:

> *He giveth power to the faint;*
> *and to them that have no might*
> *he increases strength.*
>
> *Even the youths shall faint and be weary,*
> *and the young men shall utterly fall;*
> *But they that wait upon the Lord*
> *shall renew their strength;*
> *they shall mount up with wings as eagles;*
> *they shall run, and not be weary;*
> *and they shall walk, and not faint.*

There was my answer! I would not force my interpretation upon anyone else, but I believed that "they shall mount up with wings as eagles" meant that I was to take my plane that morning. After this answer, and meditation on the Word, all tension was gone and I was sleepy. I had my answer, so why worry? I soon lost consciousness and slept soundly until 7:00 a.m., when I awoke refreshed and happy.

I packed my suitcase, including the bottle of drug tablets in case of sharp pain in my back, and vitamins, which I determined to take to build up my body.

The air travel and the meetings went well. At the annual meeting of the women's sewing circles of Allegheny Mennonite Conference I felt impressed to speak of Christ as a real person and to refer to my experience the previous morning.

In an evening service in Johnstown the minister introduced me by saying, "She is the daughter of George R. Brunk I, sister of George R. Brunk II, and the wife of Grant M. Stoltzfus." When I went on to speak in a church in Ohio and the leader asked for information to introduce me, I said, "Just say she's a daughter of the King."

In Ohio I visited a home where a family was bereaved because the father, in a period of deep depression, had taken his own life. While in this home I asked God to help me know whether to mention the tragedy. I felt that the wife wanted to talk, and we did, at some length. I expressed the belief that her husband had not been himself when he died, and that he was saved. That, with the assurance that God provides strength for each day, seemed to be the comfort God would have me give.

Before I returned home, I asked the Lord to continue to strengthen me. I prayed, "If you take me back looking worse than when I left, I will get some attention. But if you take me back looking better, you will get a lot of praise."

At the Newport News airport my sister Esther greeted me by saying, "You look better now than when you left!"

Chapter 13

Rich in Happiness

Harrisonburg, Virginia
July 1955–July 1957

On May 24, 1955, Grant graduated from seminary, marking the end of three years of financial struggle. He felt it was God's will for us, and that all would work out, even though we had built up a tremendous debt. He took a position as Secretary of Literature with the Mennonite Hour, the radio ministry of the Mennonite Church, which had its offices in Harrisonburg, Virginia. I was happy to think of living in Harrisonburg, and we moved there in July 1955.

Allen, Eugene, and Kathie went off to school in September, but Ruthie was two and a half months too young for first grade. Since we felt she was ready for some systematized work, and she was tall for her age, we said, "Why hold her back another year and make her unnecessarily larger than her classmates, perhaps all the way through the grades?"

So we sent her to a nearby Christian day school with the intention of sending her to second grade at Park School the next year. When we received a printed statement of the purpose and ideals of the school, we agreed with the requirement that girls were either to wear full-length stockings or go barefooted. However, not admitting Negro children seemed a classic example of "straining at a gnat and swallowing a camel." Grant wrote to the school:

> We have a question about how these high ideals are to be reconciled with closing the school to Negro children who need and deserve Christian nurture as much as our own. According to Matthew 25, we will be judged more by the way we act toward 'the least of these' than some other things which are often stressed. Both the Virginia [Mennonite] Conference and General Conference [of the Mennonite Church] have passed resolutions on the race question that are true to the Bible teaching. By God's grace we should try to live up to them.

In May 1956, Heart to Heart Broadcast became the official women's radio broadcast of Mennonite Broadcasts. Watching me sign the contract are my sister Katie Shank, president of the Heart to Heart Broadcast board, and Lewis Strite, president of Mennonite Broadcasts.

Family devotions

I tried to practice what I taught on Heart to Heart. Since I was encouraging Bible reading, especially in the family, along with devotions, our family started private devotions in conjunction with family worship. We chose after breakfast as the time least likely to be interrupted by phone calls and demands of all kinds. We gave direction to the small children for their private time and at the end of five or ten minutes, we rang a little bell and gathered together in the living room for family worship.

I oversaw the private worship and Grant conducted the family worship. Then Grant went to work, and the children were off to school. It seemed better than devotions in the evening, when everyone was tired and we were likely to be interrupted.

Experiences with prayer

When I couldn't go to a Heart to Heart meeting in Denbigh in October 1955 as scheduled, I told my recording engineer, Richard Weaver, about it. He said, "Why don't you send Katie Shank (my sister and a board member), Mrs. Lehman (Myra Lehman, also a board member), and Mrs. Landis (Eva Landis, my secretary)—all three—down there to give a program?"

They went and gave an excellent program. While they were in Denbigh, I was home in bed with a threatened miscarriage. The next morning I got up, dressed, and thanked God that I was better, not knowing of their prayers for me the previous night.

As my pregnancy progressed, Kathie and Ruthie began to ask questions about my appearance, so I took them into a room and told them our secret. I said that Allen had been told, but not Eugene, so we called Eugene in to hear the good news. Then Ruthie asked, "Does Daddy know?"

Becoming official

The Heart to Heart broadcast kept growing as new stations picked it up and more and more mail came in and went out. We had as many as 206 pieces come in one day, with the average climbing toward 200 pieces of mail a week. Our greatest problem was assembling our monthly mailings. Church groups and friends generously donated their time to help.

One evening in April 1956, a group of friends invited me to Frances Harman's house to assemble 9,000 pieces of Heart to Heart printed material for mailing. Before the evening was over I found that a baby shower had been planned in my honor.

Despite such help, I saw the need for some kind of organizational backing and asked God to show us the right plans. Soon after that, Henry Weaver Jr., radio secretary of the General Mission Board, and Lewis Strite, president of the Mennonite Hour, asked about Heart to Heart becoming affiliated with the Mennonite Hour.

Grant and I met with representatives from the General Mission Board (Mennonite Hour's parent organization) to talk about a possible merger. We suggested that the parent organization over all the church's radio work be called Mennonite Broadcasts, rather than the Mennonite Hour, which was the specific name of one program. On May 22, 1956, a ceremony was held at the Radio Building in Harrisonburg to sign a contract placing Heart to Heart under the supervision of Mennonite Broadcasts. By that action, Heart to Heart became the official women's radio broadcast of the Mennonite Church.

The Heart to Heart office

The Heart to Heart broadcast continued to be self-supporting, with our own board of directors: my sister Katie F. Shank, Myra Lehman, my secretary Eva Landis, our secretary of literature Miriam Weaver, and me. The others were responsible for financing and directing the program, so I could be free for writing and speaking. Eva and Miriam worked in the offices in the Mennonite Broadcast building. I kept a small office there, but I did most of my work at home. I wanted to practice what I preached about mothers staying at home with their young children.

Each week I dictated my script on a recorder for Eva to type and then went to the Weaver Studio to record the messages. Eva transcribed the message, corrected it for punctuation, and inserted titles I had written to make the message easier to read. Then she retyped, mimeographed, and mailed the messages in monthly sets. Our outgoing daily mail also included books, schedule cards, and tracts.

My sister Katie contributed guides to the monthly Bible study, my niece Audrey Shank compiled a list of suggested recordings for home listening, and my friend Mildred Pellman helped out with proofreading.

The *Heart to Heart Letter* expanded from a single mimeographed sheet to a four-page printed newsletter with a regular column, "From Your Friend Ruth," and feature articles, as well as excerpts from letters, the broadcast schedule, the Bible study guide, and a daily prayer list.

By October 1956, with 100 to 150 listener letters a week, the task of counseling by mail had become too large for one person, so I enlisted Katie and Myra to read and answer letters from people who needed help. Eva Landis described it well: "We feel women send the broken pieces of their hearts to us and ask us to help put them together again."

A channel of blessing

An exciting testimony came to me at our local radio station, WSVA. While Virginia Lindamood (Lindy) of the staff was interviewing me on the air, the announcer sent word that he would like to see me at the close of our discussion.

"One time when I was airing a tape of your Heart to Heart broadcast," he began, "you said something that made a difference in my marriage. The statement was, 'We do not *find* happiness in marriage. We *create* it.' I was separated from my wife at the time but I got to work. Every weekend I drove a thousand miles round trip to visit her until I won her back. Now we have a baby son. I am the happiest man in the world and I just want to thank you!"

There were also some grave and seemingly unsolvable situations confided to me. I tried as best I could to give counsel by mail or refer the correspondents to Christian professional helpers in their local area. A few times in my travels, I looked up people who seemed in need of a personal visit.

Ora H. Troyer, president of the Indiana-Michigan Mennonite Conference women's association, wrote to me in 1956, "I don't believe any of our meetings ever go by without some reference to the Heart to Heart program. It seems to fill a need for many busy mothers and we feel they would be interested in meeting their friend Ruth."

Later she wrote:

> One day a local minister's wife came to the office where I work, with a burden on her heart that she said she was unable to shake off. She has long listened to your program and feels the women of our area do not take advantage of your program as they could, perhaps because they do not know about it. I asked her whether she had heard that we are expecting you as our speaker in May. To my surprise, she began to weep tears of joy, for that is the real reason she had come—to see if we would ask you to come.

Once while driving from a speaking engagement in a Franconia Mennonite Conference congregation, I had the strong impression that I should stop to see Harry Brackbill, a Christian businessman. Owner of seven farmer's markets in the Philadelphia area, he had inquired about putting my weekly Heart to Heart broadcast on a station in the area.

I argued, "Lord, I wrote to him about it twice but he never replied, and I am embarrassed to go."

The answer was, "I said you are to go."

I went. His wife met me at the door and said her husband was out in the field getting corn for their markets. As I walked toward my car, puzzled, he drove in.

I said, "Brother Brackbill, I'm embarrassed to appear to ask you to sponsor my broadcast, but the Lord made me come."

He said, "Sister Ruth, the Lord was talking to me in the cornfield just now about your broadcast, and I told him I would sponsor it."

Rich in happiness

I was struck many times by our family's happiness. I wrote in my journal, "We have some fusses, but our family does enjoy being together."

Once while I was burning trash, Grant and the boys were working nearby in the garden, and the girls were picking up stray pieces of trash and sticks from the lawn, Kathie said, "This is more fun when we all work!"

About that time I wrote a poem called "Rich in Happiness" for the *Heart to Heart Letter:*

> *Not rich in wealth am I*
> *But rich in happiness.*
> *Rich in memories*
> *Of Father, Mother,*
> *And childhood home.*
>
> *Rich in love of husband*
> *And precious children.*
> *Rich in friends*
> *Who stood by me*
> *In my darkest hours.*
>
> *Rich in thoughts*
> *Of God and heaven—*
> *In hope for things to come.*
> *Rich in work to do*
> *And hearts to help*
> *O God, how rich am I!*

Birth of Helen Joy

In the first six years and five months of marriage we had four children. Six years and six months later we were due to have our fifth child. As the time came for the birth of the baby, we discussed names with the children. I made out a slip for each family member with two names for a boy and three for a girl: John Ray, John Dale, Norma Joy, Helen Joy, and Deborah Joy. The vote was tied, so we talked it over and agreed on John Dale for a boy and Helen Joy for a girl.

On June 3, 1956, Helen Joy was born. When the plump little baby lay in my arms, the months of inconvenience and hours of pain were forgotten. I wrote in my journal, "Our cup of joy is full and running over!"

The house on the hill

On July 27 work began on our house on a two-acre hillside lot two miles outside of town. We wanted a house in the country so we could have privacy and the children could have room to play. We felt we couldn't afford to build from the standpoint of our finances and we couldn't afford not to build from the standpoint of our children, who would soon be grown and leaving home.

Life in the house on the hill was joyful during those years. I wrote in my journal:

> Little six-year-old Ruthie is asking more questions than I can answer. Her imagination works overtime. One evening while I was making the baby's formula, she asked, "Did God create germs or did they just come popping out?" I hope we will be smart enough to answer her questions when the door of her mind is open, instead of hurrying her off to bed, as we almost did last night. I pray that she will use her

Our new home on the hill in Harrisonburg, Virginia.

mind and her talents for the work of the kingdom of God. I thank God she will live at a time when our church is more willing to use a woman's abilities.

A heritage of the Lord

We often gave programs as a family. One time when we were invited to give a program for the Church of the Brethren in Mount Solon, Virginia, I spent some time arranging topics, verses, and assignments for each of the children. I drilled them on new verses from the Proverbs to give "with good expression and even some gestures."

When I gave the children the list of lessons, messages, and verses for memory work, at first they said, "Do we have to learn all of that?"

I said, "No, you don't have to learn any of it unless you want to. Just go as far as you can and want to. I thought maybe for this program you could do just the first line." My strategy worked.

While some of my teaching methods were successful, I did sometimes question my own behavior. When I noticed that Grant and I were fussing about noise, I wondered whether the problem was the children's noise, our nerves, or just our need for quiet. I also noticed that when we had our minds on our work, we did not enter enough into what the children were saying, especially at the table.

But the children were appreciative. One evening I was scheduled to speak to the college women's prayer circle at Eastern Mennonite College. My topic was "The Two Shall Be One," with a discussion of engagement and marriage. At the supper table before I left, Grant wished me the Lord's blessing in the talk. Kathie spoke up and said, "Mother, just think. Your talk might keep a girl from getting a divorce some day!"

Grant was a constant support and encouragement. When he bathed the children, he called the process "the sheep dip." In the middle of one cold night when he came back from checking if the little girls were covered, he said, "I just stood by their bed and prayed for them."

Once when I was taking off by plane for speaking appointments, I said to the woman beside me, "See my husband and children by the fence? I am leaving them to go to Kansas to tell those mothers to stay home with their children."

Chapter 14

New Directions

Harrisonburg, Virginia
June 1957–May 1958

The Heart to Heart program went off the air during the summer months of 1957, the first time in its almost seven years. Expenses for radio time, recording, and administrative help remained the same during the summer, but income always ran low. In the May-June *Heart to Heart Letter* of that year I reported a debt of $3,200. We could not risk a summer that would put us deeper in debt.

Along with the financial pressure, I felt the need for a break from my schedule of preparing the weekly radio talks, answering problem letters, directing the overall program, and traveling out of town for speaking engagements. I went through a period of deep searching and testing. It was a time of transition for Grant, who was leaving Mennonite Broadcasts to join the faculty of Eastern Mennonite College to teach sociology and church history. Should I also leave so I could be free to answer the frequent invitations Grant and I received to speak in churches?

After weeks of frustrating indecision, but with the certainty of God's leading, I felt I should resign. When I announced to Mennonite Broadcasts Incorporated (MBI) my decision to turn the program over to them, I also submitted my resignation, to be effective June 1958. "It is abundantly clear to me," I wrote to a friend, "that I must be free from constant radio deadlines and be on a more flexible schedule. I will continue with the same interests but *with* my family instead of *apart* from them. It will be a satisfaction to have founded Heart to Heart and to have kept it going for eight years, and a joy to know that it can go on whether I go with it or not."

In a letter to Lewis Strite, chairman of the board of MBI, I wrote of a "growing conviction that I should give my time to my family and thereby be more of an example of the thing I have been telling mothers over the air."

By fall the Heart to Heart debt was wiped out, and by the beginning of October, I was back on the air.

Mama's death

On October 7, 1957, after a long illness, my mother died at the age of eighty-two. Just one day before being afflicted by a stroke, she had finished a project of knitting bandages for relief and neatly folded her work away, as though signifying that her life's work was ended. During the next two weeks, and up to the time of her passing, Mama was not able to talk to us. But at times we children were sure, by the expressions in her eyes and the way she reached for our hands and clasped them, that she knew us and could hear us speak.

In our childhood Mama had helped and comforted us. Now it was our turn to help and comfort her. Many times she had helped us to face life. Now it was our opportunity to help her face death. I remember the early morning scene as my brother Truman came to her bedside. Conscious that the end was drawing near, he bent over, stroked her head, and said in gentle, assuring tones, "Don't be afraid, Mommy. God will take care of you. Just trust in him. Everything is all right." Then he poured out his heart in prayer for her. Later that morning she slipped peacefully away.

On a snowy day in February 1958, I wrote in my journal:

Today when I was trudging up the hill in the deep snow, I thought, "I must write Mama about this unusual snow," and then suddenly I realized with an ache in my heart that she is gone. How it hurts to be without someone whose life has been intertwined with yours for so many years. And it does not ease the pain to think of the times when I should have written and visited Mama oftener and comforted and helped her in so many ways. But God knows my heart was in the right place and we had many exchanges of love.

Dear Mama—so gentle, so naturally sweet, so sincere, so loyal, so generous, so patient, so unassuming, so kind, so concerned about her children.

Last night as I lay awake during the wee hours, I felt impressed with the thought of carrying on Mama's prayer burdens for her now that she is no longer here. How much of this earth scene does she know about? Would she have us children plead with God for each other? Yes, I am sure she would have us befriend and help each other and share burdens together also.

How could I love her if I did not love her other children? Somehow in these family experiences, I have gotten an insight into the words in

1 John 4:20: "If a man say, I love God, and hateth his brother, he is a liar." We can't love God if we do not love his other children.

A further aspect to His truth has opened up to me in my own experience as a mother. I can easily see how difficult it would be to believe that any one of our children would have sufficient love for me if he or she did not truly love a sister or brother, my other children.

Brainstorming

I could not understand the future or why my decisions had taken the turn they had, but I felt that God was moving in my life and everything that happened was according to his purposes. I wrote in my journal, "I rejoice that I will have more freedom to do things! But oh, we are so lacking in necessary capital to get started."

When I made lists of possibilities for family life ministries, Grant encouraged my brainstorming. "You can afford to have many ideas if just one works," he said.

Ella May Miller became the speaker of Heart to Heart after I resigned. [Mennonite Media]

"I believe there are great possibilities," I lamented in my journal, "but how can I exercise my flair for ministry without feeling that I am neglecting my housework and family responsibilities? [My sister] Stella is making me several dresses. In my youth I made my own dresses and got along fine, but it seems sewing (and housework in general) is not my line."

Transition

When Heart to Heart was fully integrated into MBI on January 1, 1958, Richard Weaver was appointed interim director. He took care of business correspondence and management, and the offices and departments of MBI took over the responsibility for publicity, processing the mail, and handling the money.

In a little office in our home I answered a flow of problem letters and prepared the radio talks. We took an audience poll to measure interest and coverage. Many people said, "We enjoy your program and want it to continue." We sat up and took notice when one listener responded with: "Do we want the program to continue? Does a kitten like milk?"

When the Heart to Heart broadcast committee met to discuss the question of my successor, they asked Lewis Strite how much of a job this work would be. He promptly answered, "full time." "And," he continued, "being the speaker of the Heart to Heart program is a big enough and important enough job to justify having someone move here from a distance—a woman, her husband, and her family."

At my suggestion, Ella May Miller, who was serving on the Heart to Heart board, was invited to take the assignment as speaker on a trial basis. The committee was unanimous in recommending her to the MBI board, which officially appointed her.

I wanted to acquaint the Heart to Heart audience with Ella May before my termination, so they would feel that the broadcast was in good hands. In a letter to listeners I expressed my satisfaction with the new speaker, "My successor is a Christian wife and mother with deep understanding, a warm heart, and a consecrated spirit."

After Ella May's appointment I discovered a letter in my files that she had written four years earlier, expressing convictions similar to mine and giving me assurance of her deep concern and faithful prayers for the work.

My last Heart to Heart program

I conducted my last Heart to Heart program on May 22, 1958. On that program, which aired on June 7, I told listeners, "It was not easy to decide to discontinue as Heart to Heart speaker, but never in my life have I been more sure of God's leading. While God was leading me, he was leading in the life and in the selection of the new Heart to Heart speaker." Then I introduced Ella May and in a little ceremony I commissioned her. Turning to the listening audience I recalled the years we had spoken together "heart to heart," the times we had talked and prayed, laughed and cried about our joys, problems, and responsibilities:

> I leave you with a promise from the Bible that I am claiming personally. I know Mrs. Miller is claiming it, too. I trust that you will be able to claim, as your very own, this promise of God to his children, found in Psalm 32:8: "I will instruct thee and teach thee in the way which thou shalt go: I will guide thee with mine eye." Good-bye and God be with you right there where you are.

And just like that, it was over.

PART FOUR

"HOMES MAKE THE NATION"
1958–1974

Chapter 15

Babies, Books, and Baggage

Harrisonburg, Virginia
May 1958–December 1961

While I was preparing to leave Heart to Heart, Grant and I began a ministry called Christian Family Service. It included counseling, literature promotion, and speaking, all in the interest of building better family relationships.

"Since we can't have a family farm," I said, "we want to have a family firm, and we trust that it will be not only a firm, but a ministry also." Christian Family Service would be our way to fulfill the need we saw for sex education, spiritual training, Christian counseling services, and family conference work in the churches.

Our speaking engagements raised questions for our family. Which children to take where? Who would stay with those who stayed home? When we were invited to serve together in churches for weekend family life conferences, we often took the children along in the station wagon that Grant said was for "hauling babies, books, and baggage."

Doors open

I felt a conviction that someone should be reaching out with Christian, home-strengthening ideals. I believed that parents who were too busy to read a book on home building would read a short newspaper ad. Some current ads stressed the importance of going to church, but none went to the roots of family relationships. Grant encouraged my idea of launching an illustrated family life newspaper series.

The doors started opening. I happened to hear of Judy Preston, a professional artist who had recently moved to town. A talented woman, she agreed to do art and layout work for us immediately.

But who would make engraved metal plates and mats for the ad? We learned of an engraver who also had just moved to our area. He proved to be a Christian man, intensely interested in our plan and ready to assist us.

We would need high-quality photographs. How would they be supplied? The first professional photographer we talked to offered every assistance to help our project materialize.

More doors opened. As we traveled into communities over the states for speaking appointments and presented our plan to Christian businessmen, almost without exception we found them enthusiastic about our ideas.

When we showed a sample ad and explained that the newspaper space would be paid for by sponsoring businesses, who would then be listed below the ad, one man said, "This is the kind of advertising I have been wanting to do." He, like many others, wanted more from life than earning money. He wanted to give a Christian witness to the homes in his community.

God continued to prepare the way, next at the bank. On my first visit I requested a one thousand-dollar loan to pay beginning production costs. When I went back for an answer from the board of directors, the banker examined the sample illustrated, four-column family life ads I took along. Then he said, "Well, we figured that if this didn't succeed, you'd dream up something that would. So we'll lend you the money."

I walked out of the bank thanking God.

Concord Associates

When it became necessary to select a business name for the production of family life ads, we chose the name Concord Associates, which included all our Christian Family Service activities—radio, newspapers, conferences, and literature (which included posters, cards, leaflets, thousands of copies of the best-selling "Mother's Pledge," and a new "Pledge for Husband and Wife"). The word concord means "harmony." After we had already selected it and had letterheads printed, we found that the word also had the connotation of "happy family."

The family life ad was about one-fourth the size of a newspaper page, adaptable to varying column widths. In order to attract the attention of readers, each ad featured a large photograph on some

TO BE REMEMBERED

They are golden moments of warm companionship when mother and children pause from rush and routine for happy times together.

Sometimes they are spellbound moments that stretch the mind with insights and adventures. Other times they are quiet moments that nurture the spirit with thoughts of God. Every time they are vital moments that build lasting values into precious lives.

When the fleeting moments have blended into years, the children will not remember if the ironing was done in record time or if the house was always in perfect order. But they will remember if Mother took time to be with them, to laugh and read, talk and pray. They will be eternally grateful for priceless moments to be remembered.

Concord Poster 199
© Concord Associates
Harrisonburg, Va.
Request free copy from above address.

A Concord Associates ad featuring two daughters and me.

phase of family living, along with an appropriate Christian message of 100 to 150 words. Every ad included a small logo and the motto, "Homes Make the Nation," drawn by artist Judy Preston.

A number of local businesses agreed to sponsor the Concord Family Life ads for a period of six months at a time. By sharing the costs, each one paid only a small amount, and the united effort made possible an imposing ad that was noticed and read. The business sponsors were listed below each ad. Reprints of the weekly ads were distributed as Concord Family Life Features, which we mailed out in monthly installments at $2.50 for a year's subscription.

I began the newspaper series in late 1959, and in a few months the first issues were carried weekly by the *Daily News-Record,* our Harrisonburg, Virginia, paper, and the Archbold, Ohio, *Buckeye.* These were the first of seventeen papers that eventually carried them. God led so that bit by bit, by writing or planning four or five illustrated, four-column messages for one month at a time, we produced a total of 365, with most written by Grant and me and some by other writers: Robert Baker, Urie Bender, and James Fairfield.

Her Heart and Home

About this time I put together twenty-four messages from my Heart to Heart broadcast as a book called *Her Heart and Home,* published in 1959 by Moody Press. Grant gave me advice about promoting the book and gave hands-on help as well, especially with writing.

When I was doing the Heart to Heart broadcast, I had noticed that when he was asked to discuss the Sunday school lesson over Eastern Mennonite College's FM station each week, the writing of a script was easier for him than for me. Over time, I learned to take pen in hand and begin pushing it until ideas came. Of all the things I did, writing the family life ads for newspaper was the hardest.

A few times Grant and I did writing projects together. Grant's first draft was always more presentable than mine, and he did little rewriting. When I labored too hard rewriting an article or a talk, he would say, "There is such a thing as cooking it to death, you know."

"I don't write pieces," I would tell him. "I rewrite them."

Mediation in action

Some messages for the family life ads grew out of conversations after which I would say to Grant, "Will you write that up for the newspapers?" More than one resulted from our own satisfactions or struggles in family living. Our home life, with its mix of joys and frustrations, convinced me that the biggest job for parents is to teach children how to get along with other humans.

I adapted one family story from an incident that occurred when Allen and Ruthie were about fourteen and eight years of age. (For the newspaper, I changed the names.)

> One evening at our supper table there were human relations problems between Allen and Ruthie. They were fussing and snapping at each other, the worst ever. Grant and I looked at each other as if to say, "We have to do something about this." We had thought this was a problem of sibling rivalry that these two would outgrow, but not so.
>
> We said to Allen, "Now you keep quiet while Ruthie tells what she thinks is wrong. Then she will keep quiet while you say what you think is wrong."
>
> The family of seven listened and talked and cried and prayed. The experience was like a family council, revival meeting, and communion service all rolled into one. Allen and Ruthie patched up their differences—forgiving and asking for forgiveness.
>
> It was Ruthie's turn to do dishes, and although it was a major family problem whenever it was Allen's turn, he got up from the table and voluntarily helped her.

Kathie was a ten-year-old observer at the time. Years later, as an attorney conducting a workshop on mediation, she spoke of this incident as her first observation of mediation in action.

A visit from George

My brother George came to Harrisonburg in January 1960 to preach a series at Weavers Mennonite Church. After a week of preaching powerful revival sermons with no visible results, George preached on a text he had never preached on before: "We have toiled all the night, and have taken nothing" (Luke 5:5). He said he believed there was "sin in the camp" and a spiritual "heaviness" about the congregation.

I thought he had discerned a problem that I had experienced firsthand. I had felt a lack of freedom of the Spirit in the church, especially a failure to acknowledge that the Spirit is able to work in a woman's life. "Is that the reason many of my messages are given in other denominations?" I wondered. "I do not want recognition for myself, but a real revival in my own heart and in the whole church."

I gave George a copy of *Inspired Letters* by Frank C. Laubach, and the next morning he called and said I should read verse 22 in the letter to Philemon from that translation. I read the Apostle Paul's request to Philemon for a guest room in words that sounded like George: "Will you also please get a room ready for me?"

The meetings closed memorably. George invited the audience to commit to try to win one soul to Christ in 1960. So many people surged forward that not all could get up front. Many stood in the aisles while George led an impressive prayer of dedication. I was happy to see that twelve-year-old Allen was among those who stood.

When George was leaving to return to Denbigh, he said, "Well, we are proud of the work you are doing. Keep up the good work." It did me good that he mentioned it. My brother Truman was a big encouragement, too.

A troublesome question

Others were critical. A letter expressed concern: "Why is it that in your ad we never see a Mennonite woman who is obedient to the Scriptural requirement of the devotional covering? Is it not true that wearing the covering is a sign of woman's sanctification to the Lord?"

I knew that many people in the church interpreted Paul's instructions in the first letter to the Corinthians to mean that women should cover their heads to show their subordination to men. In my studies I had come to a different conclusion. I answered, "I do not know that it is. Jesus did not say anything about it, and Paul, in straightening a local situation, taught it as showing the leadership of man as far as human relations go."

The question was troublesome. Our ad was for all people, regardless of denomination, and sponsors from other denominations had joined us in our concern for Christian homes. I thought we had to use conventional attire or stay out of the paper. We were careful to avoid jewelry, which the Mennonite Church forbade at that time.

I told the writer of the letter that even in our Mennonite Church there was a difference of interpretation as to whether a woman should wear the covering all the time or just during public worship. I said I did not feel we could settle the question in our ad. I also said our main concern was not the "clothes line."

The question of nonconformity in dress came up again in a subscriber's letter and comments made to one of our salesmen. But neither George nor Truman said a word about the clothing pictured in our ads. When I discussed attire with George and told him about Allen's respecting and consulting us before he wore a tie instead of the traditional plain suit, George said, "Well, I would have liked to see us keep the plain coat, but it is gone now." I had noticed that some key men on his board no longer dressed "plain"—in a simple, unadorned black suit, the jacket without lapels, worn buttoned up to the neck, over a collarless shirt and no tie.

But the criticism continued. Someone wrote to one of our salesmen about the seriousness of the pictures in our ads being a transgression of the nonconformity principle (this was from the New Testament teaching that we should not be conformed to this world, which I agreed with but interpreted differently). Others objected that this was a case of a woman doing work a man should be doing.

Chapter 16

Opposition

Harrisonburg, Virginia
October 1959–July 1961

One weekend our plans to speak at a church suddenly changed. Our topics had been arranged ahead of time, but on Saturday night the pastor notified Grant that the topic "The Home and Discipline" would be the Sunday morning message and he, Grant, was to give it.

That was my topic but I, a woman, was not allowed to present it in a Sunday morning service. I loaned Grant my scribbled notes with all kinds of abbreviations. He stumbled through them as best he could while I sat on the front bench bursting with things I had prepared to say.

There were other put-downs. On a Sunday morning in a large Mennonite church in my hometown, I was in the audience when a bishop verbally spanked those who started projects and "then expect the church to take them over." Clearly, in the context, he was referring to the Heart to Heart broadcast I had started.

At another church a pastor engaging me for weekend messages thought it would be best not to "take the pulpit" for the Sunday morning message, since some members would be offended. Drawing myself up to my full five feet, ten and a half inches, I replied, "Fine, I do not need extra elevation." But at the service, when the worship and song leader, a male, spoke from the pulpit, while the one bringing the message could not, it struck me that somehow a special sacredness was attributed to maleness.

Return to radio

As a husband-wife team, Grant and I spoke in dialogue on the weekly, fifteen-minute Friend to Friend broadcast, which first aired on WGCB, Red Lion, Pennsylvania, on December 5, 1959. In response to our broadcast, a woman from Lancaster wrote:

I was thrilled to hear on today's program the Scriptural authority for the woman's role in the church. I have been active teaching children and women, and felt at peace with and in the will of God concerning this, but felt that there was no Scriptural basis for it. So you can see what a need your program filled, and may our Lord and Savior bless you for it.

We also produced Minute Messages by Your Friend Ruth, beginning February 11, 1960, on WSVA in Harrisonburg, Virginia. The messages were adapted from the family life newspaper series. Forty years later they are still aired by several radio stations as a public service.

First appearance on TV

When I told Virginia "Lindy" Lindamood, who was interviewing me on the local radio station, about my plan to do a series on success in marriage on WDAC in Lancaster, Pennsylvania, she said that WSVA, the local television station in Harrisonburg, ought to line me up for some work in that field. She introduced me to Bob

Grant and I began the weekly, fifteen-minute Friend to Friend radio program in 1959.

Lee, director of WSVA TV, who offered me thirteen free television programs from 6:00 to 6:25 each Tuesday evening.

I consulted three bishops. My brother Truman said yes, while favoring my publishing a note explaining that our family did not have TV and I did not wish to encourage anyone to buy one. D. W. Lehman said no, it would cause offense to many in the church, who considered watching TV a violation of the nonconformity principle. My brother-in-law Ward Shank said, "I will not say yes or no. You will have to decide."

When I told Bob Lee that I had decided no for the present, he said, "Any time you are ready, just give me one month's notice."

Meanwhile, Lindy persuaded me to continue coming out to WSVA radio each Tuesday morning to speak a few minutes. After the review of my book was finished, she wanted me to do condensed versions of my WDAC talks on marriage success.

Then Reverend Coffman of the Evangelical United Brethren Church in Mt. Clinton, Virginia called to see if I would serve on the Talk Back television panel. I said I would be interested. I saw it as a way to make a gentle break into TV work later on.

When we had a Brunk family gathering, with a potluck supper at George's, I told the family about Reverend Coffman's invitation. George seemed to lean toward my taking advantage of the opportunity to be on the TV panel. He thought it would be less offensive than conducting a program alone.

My first experience on TV was the evening of June 14, 1960, on the Talk Back panel discussing family worship. The chairman was Mr. Barnett of Bridgewater College. Other participants were from Cooks Creek Presbyterian Church and Harrisonburg Church of the Brethren. Grant and the children were watching at a neighbor's house. They said I looked best when I was speaking and the camera was close, but that I looked warped when the camera focused on the whole panel and caught me sidewise.

Struggling with finances and critics

Grant did not enjoy keeping records of family finances. Occasionally he would ask, "Where are we financially?" and I would show him a sheet that I periodically updated, with two columns headed, "What we owe," and "What we own," and the disheartening difference between the two totals.

In 1958 I began a fruitful association with Jim Burkholder, then a student at Eastern Mennonite College, who continues to procure business sponsors for the newspaper series to this day. Speaking engagements brought in some additional income, but if it had not been for Jim's successful salesmanship and his enthusiasm for working full time during the summer, we could not have continued. The newspaper ads also financed the production of my Friend to Friend broadcast and Minute Messages.

By the end of August 1960, our ads were appearing in eighteen newspapers, and the way seemed to be opening for me to sell insurance for Brotherhood Mutual Aid. At that time the Mennonite Church disapproved of such insurance as "worldly," believing the practice of mutual aid within the church was sufficient. When Virginia Mennonite Conference changed its ruling against insurance, I saw a chance to get our financial burden lifted, and I began to sell insurance to friends and acquaintances.

The next summer, Grant reported sentiment at Virginia Mennonite Conference against life insurance in worldly companies, another concern arising from the principle of nonconformity. But in the same meeting the ministerial aid committee reported how min-

Our family in 1959. From the left: Kathie, Grant, Allen, Eugene, Helen, me, Ruthie.

isters could apply for social security. "Isn't the social security 'company' a worldly company?" I wondered. And besides, it wasn't as good a policy as a regular life insurance company offered.

I encountered official church opposition in other matters. In September 1960, as Jim Burkholder and his fiancée, Marian Longnecker, made plans for their wedding, Jim asked a Lancaster County bishop if there would be any way he and Marian could have a woman give a message and then a bishop marry them.

"Jim and Marian said they wanted me to have part in the wedding," I told Grant. "You can imagine the answer!"

"Tell them we tried"

In those days I couldn't afford a secretary, but after hiring Lessie Hershberger to prepare meals, I was able to enjoy working in my office more. I wrote in my diary, "I cannot run my life after everyone else's pattern, and I am going to quit trying. I still love my family!"

Another area of frustration was family worship. Although we wanted to follow this spiritual discipline, it was hard for us to find the time in our busy lives. One Sunday evening as I was leaving to speak on the subject at a church in our community, Grant said, "Tell them we tried." Sometimes we had Bible reading in addition to the usual prayer at the table before the meal. Other times we left the dishes and went into the living room for worship after the meal.

One time Grant read 1 John 5:21, "Dear children, keep yourselves from idols." Then he turned to the family and said, "Now I'm going around the circle for each of us to say what comes the closest to taking the place of God in our life." The littlest one was too young to answer, but the other six of us named sports, high grades, fashions, too much work, and academic degrees. It was a searching time.

Chapter 17

Our Changing World

Harrisonburg, Virginia
August 1961–September 1964

I wrote in my diary in September 1961, "The children are growing and eating more. Kathie puts her hair up in 'swings' for school and church. Allen thinks he should be allowed to stay out at night later than 11:00." Kathie's braided pigtails, crossed and pinned at the back of her head, were a distinct step toward womanhood.

One day that summer the boys called from my brother-in-law Henry's in Denbigh, where they were working in the peach orchard. When Grant learned that Allen was wearing a beard, he urged him to shave it off. It was the beginning of the 1960s counterculture. I thought, "What will young people *not* do to assert their independence?"

Another change that year came when, for the first time in our marriage, our bills were paid up. Financially, the worst was over.

Changes
On October 16, 1962, I wrote in my diary:

> I have decided to drop the cape from my dresses. It has become a double standard, with many people wearing the cape only for dress-up occasions. At other places you see them dressed very differently, in short sleeves, etc. My decision is to wear a simple, modest dress everywhere I go, without the cape. [The cape dress not only concealed a woman's figure with an extra layer of fabric over the bodice, but also kept fashion at bay.]

I thought our church needed to make some changes in family life education. Don Augsburger, pastor and Eastern Mennonite College (EMC) professor, confirmed my conclusions that the church needed a parent-training program. I heard him speak on the influence of home and church on behavior and personality, citing a study he had done of several hundred students. His study revealed that not one participant had been led to Christ by a Sunday school teacher.

I told him we'd get better results from the money spent on a big Sunday school and Bible school program if we used it instead to study the nature of children and to set up a program to help parents be the teachers of little children.

Shocking news

We had had some concerns for Allen's spiritual welfare and were having long talks with him. His attitudes seemed good, and we assumed that he was behaving appropriately. Then on December 8, 1962, we were shocked to find that he and some friends had been found drinking beer on the EMC campus. Grant talked with Allen in our bedroom and called me up while I was preparing supper. Allen seemed penitent as we knelt to pray and weep, and later he went to confess to a college official.

For days I was in a state of shock, praying over and over, "Lord, have mercy and help us." I was shocked, but I was also baffled. Allen was a good boy and our relations with him were excellent. When I asked Allen if he would like to see us and the younger children drink beer, he said no.

I dreaded that the news would soon become known, not only in our local community, but all over the church. How could we go on with our family life work? My nephew Truman Brunk Jr., tried to comfort us. "This sort of thing happens in every Mennonite community," he said, "but most do not get the publicity of a case involving sons of the faculty."

Four days after we heard the news, an announcement was made in the college chapel about Allen and the other boys. Before chapel, I wept and prayed with the parents of one of the boys. Allen and the others were suspended from school for a week. When I heard some talk about Allen, I thought, "We must not be concerned about what people think, but with the spiritual welfare of our boy." But we felt sharply the pain of our situation when we went out to speak on family life. I prayed for courage.

Crossing barriers

Allen's announcement that he wanted to spend the 1963–1964 school year in Europe with a study abroad program created a disagreement between Grant and me. Grant said yes to the idea and I said no, because some of the boys involved in the drinking episode would be going on the same program. He went, and as he left to sail to Germany, I said, "Be a credit to the Lord and us."

"I'll try to," he answered.

At 11:30 a.m., August 23, 1963, when his ship was due to take off from New York, I was in a public prayer meeting. As I thought of Allen and tried to pray for him, I broke down in tears. "God, help me in these pains of parenthood," I prayed, "not only the letting go pains, but the pains of concern about his spiritual life and growth."

Five days later Grant and Eugene drove to Washington, D.C., with friends to participate in the Freedom March for civil rights. The girls and I rented a TV and saw some of the activities, including Dr. Martin Luther King Jr.'s "I Have a Dream" speech.

Later we learned that the chaplain of Hampton Institute (a historically black school) had written to thank the sponsors of our family life ad, "The Color of a Soul," which appeared in the Newport News *Daily Press*. That gave some sponsors new interest, but customers of one sponsor threatened to quit patronizing his business if he continued to underwrite such "controversial" messages.

About that time a missionary in Jamaica wrote about distributing our literature. She said our messages crossed the "barriers of culture." After we printed the "Mother's Pledge" in Spanish, we had requests from Mexico, Puerto Rico, and Argentina, as well as from Texas and other states.

In September 1963, our family moved our church membership to the Park View congregation, which was meeting at the college. One day Harold Lehman told me he had noticed that I was the only woman to speak up during a congregational business meeting. He felt that more women should have participated. I said, "I don't believe men realize how women have been intimidated."

Our family appreciated the Park View congregation, which was freer than the average Mennonite congregation. Only a few months earlier, while Grant and I were speaking at a church in Pennsylvania, we had been told not to sit together on the front bench because that might offend some people. Separation of men and women for worship was a tradition still observed in conservative churches. I felt we should sit together anyway, to teach them that it was all right for a husband and wife to sit side by side, but I was outvoted by the leader and Grant. The next morning, after we read the "Pledge for Husbands and Wives," I handed Grant a note: "Sit down with me as husband and wife should." He did.

During the afternoon discussion we were asked about families sitting together in church rather than following the tradition of men and women on separate sides. I resolved to speak on the matter. Although two bishops and some others in the audience were displeased, in the evening service about two dozen men sat with their wives.

Anointed

One time Grant and I went to Denbigh to attend a Saturday evening wedding. The next morning, while getting ready for church, I felt anointed of God for some task at church but had no idea what it would be. It was so real that I cried to the Lord for help, knowing that I had no notes along except those written in the margins of my Bible.

After Sunday school, when it was time for the sermon, my brother Truman, the bishop, announced: "Brother John Shenk was to give the message this morning, but he has been called away to take his wife to the doctor. I see that Grant and Ruth Stoltzfus are in the audience and I'm giving them one minute's notice to come to the pulpit to give the morning message."

Praying for one another

One evening we had a warm family worship time, remembering especially Eugene and his gospel octet as they got ready to leave on tour to New York state and Pennsylvania. While we were rejoicing over this, a phone call came that notified me in a kind, charitable way, that Ruthie, along with two friends, had skipped Sunday school class. Then my heart rejoiced again when Eugene returned and asked, "Mother are we going to have family prayer time again this summer?" I fixed a little card reminder for each family member to remember to pray for each other at 6:30 p.m. every day.

I was also strengthened by our neighborhood women's prayer

A Pledge
FOR HUSBAND AND WIFE

AS HUSBAND AND WIFE, we will take time for love and companionship. We will keep adding fuel to the fire of love by words and acts of appreciation for each other. When there is a misunderstanding, we will be quick to forgive and to ask forgiveness. We will allow no one to come between us.

WE WILL take a sane attitude toward money and decide financial matters together. We will take a mature attitude toward work, each carrying a proper share of family duties.

WE WILL take time for wholesome recreation and new experiences that are worth-while. We will keep a sense of humor and learn to laugh even at ourselves.

WE WILL avoid the home-wrecking habits of impatience, worry, nagging, jealousy, and all other forms of self-love. We will face all hardships with faith in God and each other.

IF GOD entrusts children to us, we will welcome them, love them, and give them good care and training.

WE WILL give Christ His place in our hearts and in our home, keeping in tune with Him by frequent periods of Bible reading and prayer. As a family we will be loyal members of the church, attending its services together regularly and sharing in its ministry to others.

BY GOD'S HELP our home will be an asset and not a liability to the church, to the community, and to the world.

Concord Poster 87-HF © 1963
Concord Associates, R. 2, Harrisonburg, Va.
Lithographed
in U.S.A.

circle. Our meetings were a bright spot in my week, and others felt the same about sharing their concerns for their families in prayer together.

Grant prayed this prayer one evening with our family of seven. I went to my desk and wrote it down before I would forget it, and used it in a newspaper message and years later passed it on to our children and grandchildren:

O God, we thank you for our godly parents and grandparents and all those persons of the past whose faithfulness made it possible for us to know you and to believe in your Son.

Help us to teach your Word diligently to our children, that they might teach it to their children—that the lamp of faith may burn brightly and be passed from generation to generation until the end of time. Amen.

On our 23rd anniversary, June 17, 1964, I wrote in my diary, "I think we are more in love than ever. Even when we have a misunderstanding or disagreement or are upset with each other, there is a sure knowledge that we belong to each other and love each other. These irritations are on the surface and do not touch the deep loyalty that calms the waters. If our children marry, I hope each one will marry as well as I have."

In the fall of 1964 Allen returned for his final year at EMC, and Grant returned to Union Theological Seminary in Richmond to complete his doctoral degree.

Chapter 18

A Time of Sorrow

Harrisonburg, Virginia
March 1965–December 1966

On my birthday, March 15, 1965, I said that I had had fifty wonderful years of life and I was happier than ever. Then began a period of grief and anguish. It was a time of sorrow, a sorrow deeper than anything I ever thought I would have to bear. Only by the mighty inner strengthening of the Holy Spirit was I able to eat, sleep, and take interest in my work or anything else.

In April Allen came to me and said, "Mother, I must talk to you. I must tell you that I am not a Christian." He claimed he was not an atheist but an agnostic. After breaking the news of his unbelief to me, he traveled to Richmond, where Grant was taking classes. I prayed that God would prepare Grant.

Grant's illness

Grant was at the end of a hard year of graduate study. He was facing examinations and the completion of his thesis, as well as writing a book on the history of Ohio Mennonite Conference. The shock of learning Allen's spiritual condition caused everything to crash in. He began to be depressed and to remain so day after day, week after week. I saw this dear man, who had lived with zest and purpose, lose heart and even his sense of humor.

In July Grant came home from Richmond, unable to complete his studies. He tried to write but could not concentrate. He turned to me one day and said, "Ruth, I'm confused. I think I need professional help."

After checking all possibilities for physical causes of the trouble and finding none, our family doctor arranged for Grant to see a psychiatrist. On the day of the appointment, we packed a suitcase, knowing Grant could be admitted to a hospital. The psychiatrist talked with him about half an hour and then called me in. "Your husband is significantly depressed," he said, "and should be admitted to the psychiatric wing of the hospital."

At the hospital I stayed with Grant as long as permitted. We had prayer together and I left. As I went down the elevator and out of the hospital, I could not keep the hot tears from streaming down my cheeks. "O God, help us," was all I could pray.

For days Grant was kept on heavy medication. I made frequent trips to see him and kept in touch with him by telephone. Each time I talked with him I got a sick feeling.

On Monday morning, eleven days after Grant entered the hospital, a visitor, Mrs. S., came to my door. She told me she felt led by God to come see me, but wanted this to be confirmed by two or three others. The previous night a third person had advised her to come. She was confident, and so was I, that God had sent her. "God revealed to me that your husband is going to get well, and that your son is going to be saved," she said. "While I was reading Isaiah 43 in my devotions, your name came to my mind. I am going to read the passage to you now and every time I read 'O Jacob' or 'O Israel' you substitute 'O Ruth' and take this message as a personal one for you today:

> *. . . thus saith the Lord that created thee, O Jacob (O Ruth),*
> *and he that formed thee, O Israel (Ruth),*
> *Fear not: for I have redeemed thee,*
> *I have called thee by thy name; thou art mine.*
> *When thou passest through the waters, I will be with thee;*
> *and through the rivers, they shall not overflow thee:*
> *when thou walkest through the fire, thou shalt not be burned;*
> *neither shall the flame kindle upon thee.*
> *For I am the Lord thy God, the Holy One of Israel, thy Savior. . . .*
> *Since thou wast precious in my sight, thou hast been honorable,*
> *and I have loved thee.*

"Yes," I thought, "this is wonderful. I have the confidence that God is with us and that I have a right relationship with him, *but what about my son?*"

Mrs. S. read on:

> *I will say to the north, Give up;*
> *and to the south, Keep not back:*
> *bring my sons from afar, and my daughters from the ends of the earth;*

Even every one that is called by my name:
for I have created him for my glory, I have formed him;
yea, I have made him.

"Bring my sons from afar. . . . Oh, God bring my son from afar,"
I begged silently.

Mrs. S. prayed fervently, with unusual power and authority. We
had real contact with God. She held her hand on my head as she
prayed God to lay his hand of healing on my husband "right there
in the hospital where he is right now." She was just as definite about
our son. "Speak to him right now where he is on the job," she
prayed, "and bring him back to you, somehow."

After more than two hours, Mrs. S. said good-bye. That afternoon the telephone rang. It was Grant. "I tried to wait until evening
to call, when the phone rates are lower," he said, "but I couldn't
wait. I had to call and tell you that something happened this morning. I can't explain it, but suddenly I was better!"

"I can tell you what happened," I said. "Mrs. S. placed her
hands on my head and prayed for you and for all of us."

Grant was released from the hospital with the expectation that
he would recover.

Heartache

Our women's prayer cell helped me by providing a bond of sweet
fellowship and strength in sharing testimonies, burdens, intercession, and praise. When I was called on to lead prayer meetings or to
speak, I felt that God was strengthening me for such service in spite
of my sorrow.

Grant was better, but not completely well. Because of our concerns for his health and Allen's spiritual crisis, we turned down invitations to lead family life conferences. I concentrated on other
aspects of our work. In 1965 we published the first of a series of
annual Concord Associates calendars, using photos and messages
from our family life newspaper ads. They proved popular with
Christian businesspeople as well as churches. We revised the format
in 1972 and published them as Family Life Memo Books through
1976. We also printed a soft cover book, *Two Hearts Unite*, for
newlyweds, which, like the calendars, we sold directly to bookstores
and individuals.

I continued producing the family life newspaper series, speaking on the radio, and selling insurance for Mutual Life Insurance of Fort Wayne, Indiana. During the 1966–1967 and 1968–1969 school years I also served as Acting Dean of Women at Eastern Mennonite College. Along with my administrative tasks at EMC, I often found myself counseling students who had received bad news or were suffering some special hardship: a mother with cancer, a friend killed in an auto accident, a sister who had died in childbirth. I tried to have a talk with each burdened person.

The arthritis of the spine that I had suffered in 1954 returned suddenly in January 1966. It was so painful that I needed a cane to walk and sometimes I could not go to work at EMC. But more than backache, I was experiencing heartache.

Helen's decision

One day, as she often did, Helen, age nine, came to me with a problem that she wanted to make right. She said that in first grade she had copied another child's work. I encouraged her to tell the boy about it and say she was sorry. Before leaving for school, she said she felt scared. I wondered, "What is the price of peace in such a case?" Since she had not done anything to hurt him, should she only ask God's forgiveness? Oh, for wisdom! Is our sense of Christ's forgiving love too limited when we think we must 'make everything right'?" We had prayer together, that God would make Helen strong and unafraid.

After school she reported that she told the boy but was not sure he understood. Should she go to him again? "No," I said, that was enough.

One evening we went to see a Billy Graham film at the college, and afterwards about nine people responded to the invitation to Christ. As I was tucking Helen into bed that night, she said, "Mother, I felt like responding but didn't know if I should."

I sat on her bed and we talked it over. Several times earlier I had prayed with her when she felt God was calling. This time she said she had mostly decided before that she wanted to be a Christian. Now she was deciding in a more final way. We went downstairs and had family prayers about her decision. "Now," I prayed, "all the children have made the Great Decision, though one is on a detour. O God, may it not be a permanent departure from you."

In touch with Allen

Allen graduated from EMC in 1965 and taught for a year at a local high school before going on to graduate study at Tufts University near Boston. In March 1966 he received notice that he had been awarded a Woodrow Wilson Fellowship, and he was honored at a dinner by the EMC history department. When the letter came from the foundation announcing Allen's award, I wrote to him:

> God has something in mind for you. I am praying that he will undertake, intervene, overrule, if necessary even baffle, confuse, hurt, in order to bring you to the place you need to be in your thinking, believing, living, and serving, so that you will fall in line with his plan and find a fulfillment that is beyond anything you can imagine, by his mighty power at work in you.

That year Allen became engaged to Elsieanne Hess of Lancaster, Pennsylvania, who had attended EMC and then transferred to the University of California at Berkeley.

Chapter 19

A Time of Joy

Harrisonburg, Virginia
December 1966–January 1967

Allen and Elsieanne (Anne) came for the Christmas holidays, bringing Ruthie along from Lancaster Mennonite High School, where she was a boarding student that year. We fell in love with Anne. I wrote in my journal, "Her personality is so likable. She is very intelligent, capable in housework, and so forth, yet she does not seem at all frothy and quick-spoken. She and Allen are very much in love."

While we were eating supper, Grant arrived from taking two weeks of doctoral exams at Union Seminary in Richmond, Virginia. We all got up and rushed to the door to meet him.

On Saturday evening at the close of the meal Eugene said, "I bet I know what Daddy and Mother are giving us for Christmas."

We decided to play the game of allowing ten questions to which we answered only yes or no.

"Is it a book?"

"No."

"Is it something that benefits a student?"

"Yes."

On it went, with each of the five children asking two questions, but no one getting the answer. Interest was at such a high pitch that some of them wanted the secret to be revealed at once, even before our devotions and gift exchange. But Grant said, "No! These dishes must be done first."

My nephew Truman and his wife Betty had come for dinner that evening, and they stayed to share the excitement. When Grant got the five envelopes and began to distribute them, Truman called out, "All open them together, to the count of three!"

Grant counted, "One, two, three!" and they ripped open the envelopes.

Eugene said, "A trip with the whole family!. . . ." and stopped short.

Everyone was breathlessly silent. Then the children began to exclaim and scream. Allen and Anne had a touching moment, kissing in the background. The other children jumped up and down and hugged and kissed Grant and me.

The typed statements said, "Your gift for many Christmases and birthdays to come is a trip with the whole family to the eighth Mennonite World Conference in Amsterdam, July 23–30, 1967, and with some travel beyond."

This just about pulled the house down. Immediately we began discussing whether we could buy a VW station wagon over there, travel eight to the load, ship the car home, sell it for what we paid, and thereby having the use of it at no cost.

We gave the rationale: Grant needed and deserved a vacation. We had traveled a lot, the children often with us, but almost always to meet appointments. Mennonite World Conference would give our children a view of the Mennonite Church around the world and where they needed to fit in. We had concluded that the trip was affordable, considering the benefits. We had never had a real vacation as a family.

After some discussion about schedules, Truman and Betty left to go home for their gift exchange. We quieted down, settled in the living room, and Grant read the Christmas story from the Gospel of Luke and had prayer. Then we opened the packages under the tree.

A little ceremony

Later that evening, I sat on the arm of the davenport next to Allen. He said, "Can we move over and make room for mother?" He found himself seated between two women, his sweetheart and his mother.

"Oh, this reminds me of a little ceremony I wanted to go through," I said.

"What is that?" Allen asked.

I told Kathie to get me a rope, but someone picked up Christmas ribbons and said, "Will this do?"

"Yes, give me the green ribbon." I tied one end around Allen's wrist and had Kathie tie the other end around my wrist.

"Now what?" asked Allen.

"Get up with me and walk twenty-three steps."

So we walked as I counted one, two, three. . . . We ended up back at the davenport as I counted up to twenty-three. "Now take the ribbon loose from my wrist," I said. They untied it. I took my end of the ribbon and tied it to Anne's wrist. "Now you go together," I said.

"How many steps?" they asked.

"From twenty-three to seventy, or as many as you say," I said.

"Anne says count to one hundred," Allen reported. They walked back and forth from the living room to the end of the hall, from the end of the hall to the living room, counting steps.

With this ceremony I was saying, "For twenty-three years I have been the woman who had first place in Allen's life. Now I give that place to you. Go and be happy together."

Anne joins our family

We arrived in Pennsylvania on a bitterly cold Friday evening, January 27, but our hearts were warm. The wedding took place the next day at Ridgeview Mennonite Church near Lancaster.

A male quartet, with Anne's brother Dick in charge, began to sing, and I was ushered into the auditorium on Eugene's arm, with Grant following behind. During another song, "O Perfect Love," Paul Landis, a Lancaster bishop, and Truman Brunk Jr., walked in from the front left door and stood at the front. Soon Allen and Donald Pellman (son of Mildred and Hubert, who had been *our* wedding attendants) came from the right. Anne entered on her father's arm. He stood with her during a short message by Paul Landis. Then the quartet sang our wedding song, "Two Hearts Are Joined," and Truman Jr., asked, "Who giveth this woman to be married to this man?"

Anne's father said, "I do," and went to sit beside her mother.

Anne stepped up beside Allen, and Truman Jr., married them. Grant reached for my hand. When they were pronounced husband and wife, Allen lifted Anne's veil and kissed her. Then they kneeled as Truman led in prayer. As the quartet sang "O Father Lead," they walked out the aisle.

When we returned home, I wrote to my brother Truman and his wife Ruth, "The sentiment around our family was, we're glad Allen is married to Anne. We're encouraged by the fact that Allen asked Bishop Paul Landis to give a message on the Christian home, and that they were married in a Mennonite church."

We were also encouraged when Professor Smiley from Union Theological Seminary called on January 30 to say that Grant had passed his exams.

In February Grant's name appeared with others at the bottom of a full-page message in the local paper protesting the war and loss of life in Vietnam. The ad provoked some criticism from people we respected.

"All that evil needs to succeed is the silence of good men," I wrote in my diary.

Chapter 20

The Best and Worst Summer

Europe
June–August 1967

Planning for our family trip to Europe prolonged the joy we had experienced at Allen's wedding. But the summer of 1967 proved to be, as Ruthie said later, "both the worst and best summer" of her life. On July 28, Ruthie and I finally arrived in Amsterdam, where the other six were waiting for us. We were in Europe, but under different circumstances than we had planned.

In early June, Ruthie, a beautiful, apparently healthy seventeen-year-old, had complained of soreness in her upper left arm. I had a doctor check it twice, but he thought it was only a bruise that would clear up. Before long a lump developed, and I called Dr. Myers at the hospital. He gave us an appointment that day and had x-rays taken immediately. We soon knew that Ruthie had a bone tumor.

Dr. Myers sent the x-rays to Charlottesville and the doctor there asked us to bring Ruthie down. Dr. Frankel checked her, then talked to Grant and me in his office the way you read about in books, the way you think always happens to someone else. He said of Ruthie's x-rays, "When I saw them, I felt like leaving town. I hope I'm wrong, but I'm afraid it is malignant and that it might be a matter of life or amputation."

Quickly we made plans to take Ruthie to the Mayo Clinic in Rochester, Minnesota. Dr. H. H. Young did a biopsy there and indeed, found malignancy. He called Grant and me up near the operating room and said he, along with two other surgeons and two pathologists, thought it urgent to amputate. My heart welled up and I felt I must let loose a flood of tears, yet I felt a strength and support I could not describe. God's presence was near and his grace sufficient.

After the surgery Dr. Young said, "We hope we got it all." He advised us to stick to our travel plans as much as possible. "It will be good therapy for her," he said.

Ruthie had no idea of the possibility of an amputation until twenty-four hours before she was taken to the operating room. She showed courage, and also frustration, fear, and some depression.

We received many long distance phone calls and caring letters. Flowers, gifts, cards, and letters poured in to Ruthie. "God grant her strength for each task, grace for each trial, healing for each heartache," I prayed.

When Ruthie and I arrived in Amsterdam, the other six met us with the new Volkswagen bus and took us to an apartment where Grant, Eugene, and Helen were staying during Mennonite World Conference. I was in the same room as Ruthie. One night, when the lights were out but sleep escaped us, Ruthie said, "Mother, say the 23rd Psalm to me."

"Yea, though I walk through the valley of the shadow of death, I will fear no evil: for thou art with me."

We attended the final sessions of the conference, where we saw people who had heard about Ruthie's condition and were concerned. Before leaving Amsterdam I went through the Anne Frank House and saw my first movie, *The Sound of Music.*

We drove our van to Germany, where we pitched our three tents for four days near Marburg, where Allen had studied in 1964, and where Kathie would study just two years later. Grant was especially interested in visiting Kaiserslautern, to trace the Stoltzfus, Brunk, and Hess ancestry. We crossed over the river Rhine, which our ancestors had also crossed on their way to Rotterdam for the voyage to America.

In Switzerland we visited Erlenbach, the native village of Jacob Amman, founder of the Amish, and the area where Mennonites lived. In Zurich we visited the church where the Reformer Ulrich Zwingli and the young student Conrad Grebel had their debates in 1524 before Grebel and others broke away and began the Anabaptist movement, which grew into the Mennonite and related churches. We saw the river where Felix Manz, the first Anabaptist martyr, was drowned.

During the trip Ruthie grew stronger and gained a little weight. One evening, when the eight of us played kick ball, she caught a fly ball with her one and only (awkward) arm and put the batter out. Another time she bounced the ball toward first base and gave it a final punch toward Grant, who caught it and put the runner out.

She said she felt better as the day wore on, but depressed in the mornings. She said her phantom pains (painful positions of her missing arm and hand) were worse at night, when she went to bed. Just before and after sleep were her worst times. She was cheerful during the day, but admitted that she dreaded beginning college.

"Her most difficult adjustments will be emotional," I reflected.

Chapter 21

In God's Hands

Harrisonburg, Virginia
September 1967–March 1971

Back home after the trip, Ruthie uncomplainingly tried to do all the tasks of a two-armed person. When I saw her hanging out clothes, I thought, "She is braver than I am."

Pictures taken of Ruthie at age seventeen show the hurt and strain in her face. She had just entered the fascinating world of dating, but after the amputation she said, "I guess I will never marry." After telling her steady date of her slim chances for survival, they decided to quit. As she sat on the edge of her bed crying, I sat beside her, trying to say how people admired her courage. She sobbed, "But mother, I don't want to be noble. I want to be normal."

She didn't stay in the sobbing and self-pitying stage. She broke through to real adjustment and a healthy view of herself, including a genuine optimism that seemed to issue from within. During her college years, she wore an artificial arm much of the time, but for cosmetic purposes only. She got through heavy doors by carrying a leather book bag slung over her shoulder so that her one arm was free.

When she said, "I know a lighter, more comfortable arm should be on the market," Kathie's friend John Fairfield said, "I'll make one." He did. Dr. Charles Frankel at University Hospital in Charlottesville, Virginia, called in other doctors to see her walk back and forth to model the arm (and to have them see someone who had an osteosarcoma and was still on the scene).

She had to learn all over how to write so she could keep up with the note taking required for college work. It was a shock to see her bravely sitting on the platform at church with the chorus, wearing a pink suit and letting her empty sleeve hang against her body.

Faith

Allen and Anne's daughter Laura, our first grandchild, was born in May 1968. When we went to see her, I recorded her baby voice on tape and played it while I was preparing a meal or at my reading table in the living room. I even took it along to the Concord Associates office. It was the next best thing to having her near me.

In April 1969 I traveled to see baby Laura and her parents. On Easter Sunday we went to the morning service at a Unitarian church in Burlington, Vermont. The minister spoke of faith and hope. There was mention and singing of springtime and new life in the sense of new resolve, but no mention of Christ's resurrection. In the message he said, "Personally, I do not believe in the resurrection of the physical body of Jesus, that his dead body came back to life." In his prayer to "Almighty God," he thanked God for Jesus—his life and death!

After the service, as he was shaking hands at the door, I said, "I would enjoy dialogue with you some time. You thanked God for Jesus' life and death. You know, he told his disciples that he would rise the third day, and he was honest!"

"Oh, no," he answered, "that was written later . . . scholars do not believe he rose."

I said, "Scholars need faith."

In November 1968 I wrote to a pastor who urged me to accept a speaking engagement:

> Grant seems to be greatly improved, enjoys his college teaching more, and he seems to be less of a shattered man, although neither he nor I are completely healed, I am sure. Yet I can testify to special strength and grace from the Lord during and since the three family crises we have experienced over the past three and a half years: Allen's statement that he is an agnostic, Grant's nervous breakdown, and Ruthie's serious bone cancer and amputation of her left arm.
>
> I have been taking some speaking engagements, telling the Lord that I am available according to His will and purpose even if things in our own family have turned out so vastly different than I had dreamed, hoped, prayed, and worked toward for fifty solid years. (You can detect at least a little bitterness in that statement and I admit that I struggle with the tendency to be bitter.)
>
> However, I have felt that I must not put even an ounce of pressure on Grant to accept speaking engagements in the area of family life talks. But I will say that just recently he consented for us to participate

Shucking corn with my first grandchild, Laura Stoltzfus, in 1968.

in a special family life retreat for delegates from our churches in the Virginia Conference.

Please pray for God to give Grant special grace and strength in this experience. To speak on family life with feelings of personal failure presents insurmountable problems unless God can somehow perform a miracle and use it all for His purpose.

I must give you my definition of faith that has been hammered out upon the anvil of my own painful experiences: "Faith is not only believing in God and appropriating Jesus Christ to one's life, but it is believing in God and His purposes when almost everything is going backwards and almost everything else seems impossible."

On May 20, 1969, Grant received his Th.D. (doctor of theology) degree from Union Theological Seminary. Later that autumn, when I gave workshops on family life at a Christian education conference in Greencastle, Pennsylvania, Grant chose to attend a historical meeting in the Lancaster area.

Kathie is married

Kathie was engaged to be married on September 27, 1969, to John Fairfield, who was also a senior that year at Eastern Mennonite College (EMC). Three days before the wedding I slipped and fell on our newly waxed floors. I could not move my left leg without pain or even lift my left foot. I dragged it as I walked backwards to the phone to get help. After my cracked left kneecap was put in a cast, I got around without crutches or a cane, but slowly and clumsily, because I couldn't bend my knee.

With my knee in a cast, I hobbled down the aisle of Park View Mennonite Church, next to Grant and behind Kathie, John, and pastor Moses Slabaugh. John's parents, Jim and Norma Fairfield, walked behind us, followed by both sets of siblings, except for Eugene, who was still in Europe.

We stood together around the pulpit for the beautiful, simple ceremony. Moses said one opening sentence and led in prayer. This was followed by a Scripture that Kathie and John had selected from Deuteronomy 15. After we recited the Lord's Prayer, Moses read instructions from the New Testament about the husband's role, then the wife's. This led to the vows. In the closing prayer he called them man and wife. Then the bride and groom turned and walked out, followed by John's parents, Kathie's parents, and the rest.

Kathie was beautiful in the floor-length, off-white dress Mrs. Fairfield had made. Now *she* was Mrs. Fairfield. I remembered my mother's tears when I moved away, and I was glad that Kathie and John were going to be living in the apartment above my office.

Struggling in public and in private

A week after the wedding, Grant and I enjoyed a before-breakfast Sunday morning husband-wife confab. He told me about a minister who had prepared what Grant called a "race hatred" article for a Mennonite research journal. Grant had a one-hour argument with him on the question. At the same time, Grant was participating in planning EMC's controversial observance of the antiwar campaign, Moratorium against the War in Vietnam. In addition to the division in the country at large, there was much division in the church over how involved Mennonites should become politically, as well as over the race issue.

Grant said to me, "To some people, God is a tribal God, to be believed in if he goes along with our politics, protects our wealth, gives us health, wins our wars. If he doesn't do these things, then they lose their faith. Their whole concern is to have God on their side. It's time they know the real question is whether we are on

God's side. It seems their concept of God's business is that he keep us comfortable."

I gave him an account of a person who informed me, "If and when the blacks take over the country, your ideas on civil rights will not save us from suffering any more than any one else." As if our comfort was the main consideration, and not the doing of God's will.

I remembered the comment once thrown in Ruthie's face: "You're a rebel just like the rest of your family!"

That fall, Howard Zehr and Art Smoker spoke at EMC's revival sessions, sharing freely about their own struggles. Howard told of losing his father at age thirteen and how the fear of being hurt again must have been one reason he feared building relationships with people.

Grant commented after the service, "That spoke to me. It is hard to be enthusiastic about anything again, because the things I was sure of did not turn out the way I thought."

Eugene's return

On November 15 Eugene arrived home from months of work with Grant's twin sisters Ada and Ida in an orphanage in Palestine, followed by travels in Europe. Kathie, John, and Ruthie were at an anti-war march in Washington, so Grant went to pick him up at the airport and we had a good reunion. He was reacting strongly to American militarism and materialism.

"He is *so* likable," I wrote in my diary. "With his beard and mustache, he looks for all the world like pictures of Christ. I hope and pray he will find his way—the Way—God has in mind for him. I want to talk with him more about avoiding extremes and about the values of our Mennonite heritage."

He left a few days later for school in California.

Grant's depression

On New Year's Day 1970, I wrote in my diary, "I enter the new year with some fear. I need deeper faith to leave matters in God's hands." A few days later Kathie and John and Grant and I had what might be called group therapy. Kathie and I had noticed that Grant was not well. We told him he should express the way he felt and not the way he thought he should feel. When one of our children or someone else did something that distressed him, he would say, "Oh it's all right," even though he felt hurt.

The next morning Grant said, "I feel cleaned out after our family talks." He admitted that he had been feeling tense, and he made an appointment with Dr. Robert Showalter, a psychiatrist and member of our church. Grant returned from the appointment feeling better, even before he took the anti-depressant medicine Dr. Showalter had prescribed.

Dr. Showalter said Grant needed diversion, so I tried, even arranging to go bowling with the children. But despite our efforts and heavy medication, Grant could not overcome his depression. All his past conflicts kept flashing up in his mind, making it impossible for him to sleep at night or relax in the daytime without medication.

His condition worsened. Even the carefully prepared college lectures that he ordinarily enjoyed were too much for him. He said he couldn't shake off depression because he felt he was a failure. Dr. Showalter encouraged him to enter the psychiatric wing of Rockingham Memorial Hospital in Harrisonburg. Perhaps a break from routine would help.

Before we left for the hospital, we discussed how Eugene had told him a year earlier, "I respect you because you always respected me." I also recalled what Eugene had written after Grant's previous hospitalization, "A boy couldn't have had better parents than I had."

Grant broke down and cried, saying, "I know he meant it."

I bought him a paint-by-number set and took along the TV to occupy him. I thought maybe it would help for him to write out his feelings, but the doctor said, no, introspection would not be good at this point. "We will try to get you over this depression," the doctor told Grant. "Then we will tackle the underlying problems."

The healing process

"How unfair can life be?" I asked myself. "How many crises can one family or one person take?" I knew the answer of faith was, "As many as God allows, as many as God gives grace to bear." I told my sister Stella, "The Holy Spirit is my sleeping pill, and prayer is my tranquilizer."

"What is it all about?" I wondered when a local pastor and a seminary student came to me for advice about counseling. Our family's problems seemed to show that we did not know how to manage family life ourselves.

Myron Augsburger, president of EMC, visited Grant in the hospital while I was there. "The last chapter is not yet written," he said.

After a couple of weeks of rest, Grant began meeting with some of his classes. I picked him up from the hospital and took him back after class, to get him gradually back into teaching. One evening as I was leaving him at the hospital, he said, referring to his work at EMC, "I have things to live for."

"Here is one," I said, pointing to myself.

Earlier in the evening he had said, "I think I could meet my Maker. Not that I did not have my weaknesses. But I tried."

I felt sorry to see how he had lost his self-confidence. When I picked him up after his class, he seemed so tired and looked so thin, I could hardly keep back the tears. I could only moan, "O my God."

In early March, after Grant was released from the hospital, we visited Washington, D.C., for a few days of diversion. He showed signs of being more interested in things, but watching the news depressed him, and he continued on his medication. Kathie and John took him for drives in the countryside.

Slowly Grant's mental health improved and he resumed his normal teaching schedule. We watched as he recovered his sense of humor, his ability to read, study, and make notes for classes. He began to take interest in household tasks like servicing the mower and setting the table and resumed his former practice of jogging around the house before bedtime. By the end of March he didn't need a nap in the middle of the day and he was making arrangements to spend the summer working at the Mennonite Information Center in Lancaster.

Dr. Showalter told me Grant's progress was slow but significant. "Thank God for the healing process," I thought.

Not perfect

One day when Ruthie came in with friends for supper, I noticed that the appearance of unexpected guests did not worry me as much as it used to. I was more confident in my cooking and less concerned about making everything perfect.

In February and March of 1971, Grant traveled in the Middle East. When he returned, he began planning a trip to Russia in June.

I told him, "Our marriage can never be perfect. You will never enjoy concerts as I do, so I will go to them alone. I will never relish historical meetings and travel to far away places, so you will go without me. But we have most of our good times together. Our love is deep and enduring."

Chapter 22

Defending Freedom

Harrisonburg, Virginia
April 1971–April 1974

On April 15, 1971, Grant and I wrote to the Internal Revenue Service (IRS) that we conscientiously refused to pay the portion of federal tax that goes to war. Instead, we enclosed a separate check, representing the forty-one percent we withheld, and made it payable to Mennonite Central Committee.

We explained that we were committed to abiding by the laws of our country except when they asked us to violate a higher law.

In June I called the offices of Senator Byrd and Spong to say, "I urge you to vote for the Hatfield-McGovern Amendment to stop this disgraceful war."

We resist war taxes

An agent from the local IRS office responded in October 1971 to our April letter about withholding a portion of our taxes to protest the military. He said he would enforce the war tax portion by taking it out of our bank account.

We met with others in the community who were also resisting war in this way. In December we hosted the first of several meetings at our house, and in January Bob Hueston, the tax service man, met with our group to discuss the implications for those who could not conscientiously pay war taxes.

John Howard Yoder, a respected Mennonite theologian, spoke at Eastern Mennonite College (EMC) in March 1972. He cut through the objections we had heard. "The telephone tax has been designated by the government as a war tax," he said. "The levying of war taxes is another form of conscription. Jesus did not say, 'Give everything to Caesar.' War taxes are more than what we owe the government. Over half of our tax money goes to war."

In June my brother George was in the area, holding evangelistic meetings called "Encounter 72," and I prayed God to lead me and promised that if he made it clear that I should, I would ask George about whether Christians could support the Vietnam War.

Two evenings later, after a meeting at the tent, I felt moved to ask him, "If this were 'Encounter 42,' and you were preaching in Germany under Hitler, would you remain silent about the human butchery? What about the United States' human butchery?" Then I said, "I think we need an invitation for preachers to confess their silence on the war question."

Although war tax resistance was a minority position in our church—and our church's peace position was a minority position among American Christians—some Mennonite Church leaders spoke out. John Drescher, editor of *Gospel Herald*, wrote several editorials raising questions about paying war taxes. I called to thank him and encouraged him to speak to the issue when he came to Virginia.

About this same time I began to limit my insurance business, which was a matter of talking with people I knew and keeping up the paperwork. I bought and managed rental properties instead. Buying rental property was not only an alternative way to keep food on the table, but it was also a way to lower our taxable income and, therefore, a way of unburdening our consciences and limiting our aid to the United States for the killing business.

Defending freedom

On June 17, 1971, I received a letter from Mennonite women in Lancaster County, Pennsylvania. They were critical of talks that Lois Gunden Clemens, Helen Alderfer, and I had given at a meeting of one thousand women in April on "Women's Liberation and the Christian Woman's Response." All three of us received a copy of the letter, signed by twelve women. They wrote that they "were disturbed by many of the thoughts each of you expressed." They followed with a statement of arguments against women in leadership.

When I showed the letter to Ruthie, she wrote a carefully reasoned reply, answering each of their points and stressing the need for children to have strong relationships with their fathers as well as their mothers. She concluded with words that warmed my heart: "I come from a close family that we consider a roaring success. We did not pick one family member, mother, to do our share of the work so that we could go out and serve in the world. Rather we all share the work that each of us causes by living and this frees us all to contribute to others outside the family."

Planting seeds

In August Grant and I were invited for Family Week at Spruce Lake, a Mennonite camp in the Pocono Mountains of northeastern Pennsylvania. We led discussions with thirty-three families on "Being Persons," "Being Married," and "Being Parents." I pointed out that the gifts given by the Holy Spirit are to be cultivated *and* used, that being a mature Christian means being happy to see other persons use the gifts God has given them.

The resistance I met to these ideas was similar to the letter Ruthie and I had answered in April. A young father said wives shouldn't achieve if their achievements threatened their husbands. I asked if that idea would apply to a man like my brother George. If someone was threatened by him, should he quit his ministry? "No, but it's different with husband and wife," the young father said.

I tried to show that the husband needs to work toward maturity that not only allows, but seeks, his wife's fulfillment.

Another person said, "If the wife helps her husband with the work and helps him to be what he ought to be, she is doing an important thing." That seemed to rule out anything she did apart from family duties as a person on her own.

After trying all week to crack open the "unliberation" of women, in the last meeting we spoke to the question of "the Christian family in the war economy." When we told of our convictions against paying war taxes, all comments but one from the audience repeated the old line of "paying whatever Caesar asks" and, presumably, for whatever human butchery Caesar planned.

At the end of the discussion, while we were still seated at the table in front, I said, "We love you." We realized that we probably changed no one's mind, but we hoped that we had planted some seeds.

Amazing grace

I carried my concern for my family's spiritual health with me wherever I went. One day when I heard the Eastern Mennonite High School chorus singing "Amazing Grace," my heart cried out at the line, "I once was lost, but now I'm found." I prayed, "O Spirit, find Allen, Anne, Laura, Eugene, Kathie, John, Ruthie, Helen, Grant, me!"

During the school year of 1971–1972 Grant had a leave of absence—a sabbatical year—to study at Haverford College, near Philadelphia. Kathie and John were teaching in Zaire with the Teachers Abroad Program of Mennonite Central Committee. Ruthie, who had graduated from EMC in May, moved to Boston.

Helen was away the next school year, taking her junior year at Lancaster Mennonite High School in Pennsylvania. When Eugene began moving his things to a house he was renting with two other young men, Grant and I were left alone. For the first time in twenty-nine years we were without any children at home.

I awoke early most mornings and enjoyed reading and planning at my cozy corner in the dining room. Grant moved his mother's old chair there, so we could watch educational TV programs together in the evening. I wrote in my journal, "Now that we're just the two of us, I'm grateful that I have interesting things to do, and that I still like my man!"

Success and failure

That fall the symposium "Conscience and Society," dreamed, planned, and executed mostly by Grant, was a huge success at EMC. Lawyers, professors, news reporters, and others came from long distances to discuss the Wisconsin vs. Yoder case. The case, before the Supreme Court, was about the rights of the Amish, on the grounds of religious conscience, not to send their children to high school. The success of the symposium brought Grant recognition for his work in the study of religious liberties.

A week later, while I was talking to EMC president Myron Augsburger, he affirmed me in the work I was trying to do. "I want you to know your work does not go unnoticed. I'm thinking you ought to be commissioned and put on the road more. Maybe EMC can do this if Virginia Conference does not." He mentioned the recent ordination to the ministry of Emma Richards in Illinois, the first woman to be ordained by any conference of the Mennonite Church.

I wept as I wrote his comments in my journal. I reflected bitterly, "Unless my own children all come to faith in Christ and a life of usefulness for Him, I will always have to do my work with a deep sense of failure, if indeed I can keep on."

Men only?

In May 1973 Eastern Mennonite Seminary graduated its first woman. During the commencement exercises it was explained that several women were enrolled in the seminary, "but we're not about to ordain them to the ministry this afternoon." Some laughed. I did not. I thought, "Too bad that church leaders are puzzled to know what to do with women who take seriously the call to salvation, commitment, and service that they have heard all their lives. Poor women. They do not realize that the preachers meant 'men only.'"

A visit to Jamaica

On June 19, Grant and I flew to Jamaica with my sister Katie and her husband, John Shank, for a ten-day visit. They brought us to the home of our niece Audrey, daughter of Stella and Ward Shank. Katie and John had lived in Kingston with Audrey for most of the twelve years they were missionaries in Jamaica. Audrey worked in book rack evangelism, with twenty-nine locations on the island. In each location she and her helpers kept book racks filled with Christian books.

Katie and John took us to a basket market and a handicraft shop, where I bought some small gifts, including a hat for little John Reuben, Allen and Anne's baby boy, who had been born on May 23.

We attended several worship services and prayer meetings and visited Robert and Louise Henry in their home outside Mandeville. Louise, the oldest girl in the Peggy Memorial Home when Katie and John were administrators, brought Katie up-to-date about the welfare of the girls they had rescued from a high-crime neighborhood in Kingston.

Welcome

In July, Kathie and John Fairfield arrived home from Zaire. The whole family, including seven-month-old John Reuben, was at our house to welcome them—except Grant, who was studying that summer at Union Theological Seminary in New York City, and Helen, who was traveling with the cast of *These People Mine,* a Mennonite play.

A month later we welcomed the news that Eugene and Pat Baer had decided to get married. Grant and I had had a good talk and prayer with Russell and Gladys Baer, Pat's parents, while they were in Harrisonburg for the General Assembly of the Mennonite Church.

Speaking up for women

Friday, August 10, was a day when God overruled in my life and in the structure of the General Assembly programs. The day began well, with a women's prayer breakfast at Park View Church. So many came that they asked if I would conduct a group while they waited. We introduced ourselves and shared concerns and prayed for each other. In the early afternoon I met with a small group that had formed at the beginning of the week and had encouraged me throughout the Assembly. I felt prepared when the official meeting to discuss "the woman question" began at 3:30 p.m.

Don Augsburger, moderator, introduced the discussion by saying that Percy Gerig, a delegate from Illinois Mennonite Conference, had written a paper attempting to work toward change by recognizing and making use of women's gifts. Comments and suggested changes for the paper were called for from the floor by delegates and non-delegates alike.

My brother George said, "I believe Mennonite men have sinned against Mennonite women and an apology should be included in this document." He went on to say that when it comes to ordaining women, we should study the Scriptures and be careful and prayerful in working through the question.

A delegate up front said, "My wife is home with our seven children and her work is as important as mine here at this Assembly."

I felt moved to say:

> I appreciate the expression that a minority should not have to ask for its rights. But we women are not a minority. We are just treated that way. Just as white people need to exercise a little courage to come to the defense of black people, so men need a little courage to speak up for women. That is why I did not speak until now. I was waiting for my brothers to speak.
>
> I want to say that children in the family need the bodily presence of the father, not just the things his money will buy. The little boy needs close association with his father so that he can say, "That's the kind of

man I'm going to be." And the little girl needs the close association so she can say, "That's the kind of man I'm going to marry." We are told that this has something to do with her ability to get along with a member of the opposite sex later on.

I would like to suggest that it might be appropriate to include in the document under consideration on the role of women, that since children do need to have their father with them some of the time, this could release the mother to spend some time in the work of the church or other activities.

Our ministers often lament our sex-saturated society. But when they say woman exists only for her husband and children, they themselves relegate her to just the body functions. Woman has a mind, too, that needs to stretch and grow, and abilities that need to be developed.

In Romans 12 and 1 Corinthians 12, the Bible speaks of differing gifts that the Holy Spirit has given and teaches that the church is to discover, encourage, and use these gifts. So, rather than assign roles, let us pause, be careful and prayerful, and look at what God has done in the giving of gifts. Then if we are not frustrated or threatened ourselves, we can see each other's gifts, encourage their development to the fullest, and give each other the freedom to become all that we can be, according to God's will and purpose.

Afterward many—as many men as women—thanked me for my comments. This assured me I had not said too much. Unlike many wives, I had the strong affirmation of my husband. "That was the best talk I ever heard you give," he said.

Women's role and women's freedom

Six months later Lois Gunden Clemens, author of *Woman Liberated* and editor of *Voice*, the Mennonite women's magazine, was in Harrisonburg to speak at EMC on "The Christian Liberation of Women." I invited her to my favorite Chinese restaurant, where we talked for hours.

We knew that our views were ahead of the times. When I was asked that year if I would let my name go on the Park View Church slate as congregational chair, I said, "I guess I'm willing to embarrass myself to make a point. I don't think the congregation is ready to elect a woman." It wasn't.

Typical of the attitudes we were dealing with was an article in the *Gospel Herald* by the columnist, "Menno B. Hurd," against women in leadership. I expressed my views in a response that appeared in the April 9, 1974, issue. After my article appeared, I received an anonymous letter saying, "I picture you as counseling girls to have abortions, seeing no harm in divorces, and stomping down any man's authority you don't like."

Years later Hurd wrote a surprising column in another church publication:

> How would [God] personally address us today? God's word in Micah 6:3-4 for me goes as follows: "What is your complaint against me? Why do you tire of me? Itemize where I have short-changed you. I brought you out of poverty, sin and ignorance. I provided H. S. Bender [Mennonite Church leader], J. C. Wenger [Mennonite scholar], Ruth Brunk Stoltzfus to lead you, but you, donkey-like resisted. For shame."

Yet, after this apparent confession, in the April 5, 1983, *Gospel Herald*, Hurd named "advocates of women ministers" in a category of "terrible" things written about in that periodical: "Those of us already awake and vocal about what we consider normal and correct, read with shock about homosexuals, social drinkers, advocates of women ministers, and the warlike among us."

Chapter 23

Together

Harrisonburg, Virginia
September 1973–June 1974

Sunday, September 23, 1973, began with breakfast and the wedding ceremony on the lawn of Eugene and Pat's house. Then the two families came to our house for dinner.

Grant, Helen, and I had been preparing for days. We washed windows, Grant outside and Helen and me inside, with Helen running the sweeper to clean sills, then washing the kitchen window venetian blind in the bathtub. We took an upstairs door off its hinges and placed it between the dining table and breakfast table, put the extended table in the living room and dining area, and set it with twenty-five places. Over the west picture window I hung pictures of Pat and Eugene from childhood on up.

After an 8:30 buffet breakfast, Eugene and Pat appeared in their wedding clothes. Pat was dressed in a gown and veil she had made, and Eugene in a white silky shirt (without a tie) given to him by his Palestinian friend Issa and a pair of dark blue sailor pants he had bought for fifty cents. Everyone gathered on the lawn and sat on folding chairs. Eugene sat between Grant and me and Pat between her parents.

Kenneth Brunk began playing his guitar while seated at the end of the front row, and we sang "Morning Has Broken." Eugene's brother-in-law, John Fairfield, while seated, read from the Bible and Kahlil Gibran's *The Prophet*. Moses Slabaugh rose from his seat on the front row to stand on a mound under a tree (a nice platform) in front and gave a message of about ten or fifteen minutes, including an invitation to everyone to offer advice to the bride and groom. Then he asked Pat and Eugene to come forward if they were still of the mind to be married. After they were married, Pat and Eugene turned to face the audience.

Russell Baer said someone asked him why he was not marrying his daughter. (He was a Lancaster Mennonite bishop.) On this day, he said, Pat wanted him to be her father. When he sat down, Pat came down from Eugene and the preacher and kissed her father. Then Gladys Baer said a few words.

I was next: "Eugene told me to keep it under half an hour if I spoke," I said. I gave the points on what married love is: physical attraction, admiration, friendship, and God's kind of love. Then I hugged and kissed Eugene and Pat.

Grant spoke next, quoting that, "Love is not so much gazing at one another, but both looking out together in the same direction."

Allen said, "I think I'm speaking for every Stoltzfus when I say that we welcome Pat into the family. We think Eugene exercised unusually good judgment in selecting her."

The service was closed with the song "The Lord Bless Thee and Keep Thee," led by Pat's brother Conrad.

New beginnings

All twelve of us were together for Thanksgiving 1973. Ruthie came from Boston, where she had enrolled in law school; Kathie and John drove from Durham, North Carolina, where John was doing graduate work in computer science at Duke University; Allen, Anne, Laura, and Reuben journeyed from Charlottesville, Virginia; Eugene and Pat came from their house two miles from ours. After Ruthie's bus arrived at 4:00 a.m. Thanksgiving morning, we sat in the living room and talked until daylight. It was good to know the children were home, that they would come home, and that they were hooked on seeing each other and us.

Priscilla Muganda, an Eastern Mennonite College student from Tanzania, was renting the apartment upstairs. One day in March 1974, she knocked gently on my hall door, visited awhile, and then said she was having labor contractions. I took her to the hospital, carrying her suitcase as we went along to the maternity floor. When I saw the sign "No visitors except husbands," I told the nurses I was the "husband." They were sweet about it because Priscilla's husband was in Africa. I stayed from 11:00 a.m. to 5:00 p.m., and returned when a nurse called to say that Priscilla was in the delivery room. She delivered a baby boy at 8:15 p.m. This was the beginning of my long and close relationship with the "Muganda babies," as

Priscilla's children became known to our family. They called me "Bebe," which means "Grandma" in Swahili.

My third grandchild, Kathie's son, Joshua Allen Thompson Fairfield, was born later that same month, on March 26, 1974, weighing five pounds, fifteen ounces. John was with Kathie the whole time, and Kathie herself picked up the baby and carried him out of the delivery room. I drove down to Durham, arriving at 8:45 p.m. on April Fools Day. I tapped at the door, met the new mommy and daddy, and made my way to the bassinet, where a little light-haired, blue-eyed, fair-skinned baby boy lay, looking like Kathie. The baby's head barely filled John's hand.

In between doing laundry, cooking, washing dishes, cleaning, resting, and reading the paper, I had the pleasure of holding or changing the precious little baby. He looked so much like Kathie, I said to him, "Couldn't you be a little more original?" He even had her cowlick on the right side in front.

That spring was a time of new beginnings for others in the family. In April, Allen and Anne moved to Lancaster County, Pennsylvania, where Allen began a new job as a real estate salesman, and Anne worked as a medical technologist at a local hospital. Eugene bought a tractor-trailer truck and began a hauling business. Pat completed a truck driver's course so they could drive as a team.

Grant was doing research for a pioneering book on the United States government, conscientious objectors, and the quest for alternatives to military service. He received a grant from the Eleanor Roosevelt Foundation to study Mrs. Roosevelt's support of COs' work in mental hospitals. After spending some time in Hyde Park, New York, in June, he continued his research at Swarthmore College, near Philadelphia. On June 15 he gave me a beautiful pot of green plants for our thirty-third anniversary, since he would be at Swarthmore on the seventeenth, the actual day.

All the children were home that weekend. They bought two apple trees and two linden trees for our anniversary, and John, Allen, and Eugene planted them. We took pictures of the planting, of Reuben crawling up and sliding back on the slide in the backyard, of Kathie and the new baby, and everyone except Grant near one of the new trees.

Journal entry, July 21, 1974

How can I bring myself to write the words, Grant died on this day?

PART FIVE

HEARTBREAK
1974

Chapter 24

Grant's Death

Harrisonburg, Virginia
July 1974

Journal entry, July 26, 1974

Grant died five days ago, on Sunday morning, July 21, 1974. The shock is new each time I get awake, but the Bible says that God's mercies are "new every morning."

Just the day before, on Saturday, Grant came home from three weeks at Swarthmore College, where he was doing research and writing for his book on the U.S. government and alternate service. "It was to be the crowning work of his life," said James O. Lehman, a colleague at Eastern Mennonite College (EMC).

Grant arrived at 2:30 p.m. with his brother Ivan and Ivan's wife, Alice, from Pennsylvania, and his sister Ada, who was home on furlough from work as co-administrator of a boy's orphanage in Hebron, West Bank. As he came to me eagerly from the car and I rushed to meet him on the lawn, I saw that he still had the beard and mustache he had let grow earlier in the summer to please and surprise the children. (His whiskers felt so soft when we kissed.)

It suited all five of the children except Allen to come for the occasion—Kathie from Durham, Ruthie from Washington, D.C., Eugene, who phoned from truck-hauling in the west to say they hoped to get back before the weekend was over, and Helen, who was already at home.

After several hours of visiting in the living room, I went to the kitchen to prepare supper. Grant followed, came near me, and, in one of those moments I liked to call "blooming and blossoming," said, "I did a lot of writing on my book!" Then, seeing me peeling potatoes, he said, "Let me peel those things and you do something else." Afterwards, he put leaves in the table, set it for the meal, and said, "Now I believe I'll do some mowing." He mowed the level front lawn but when he came in to eat, his face was red. (Oh, how I wish I had not left the mowing for him to do!)

Grant sat at the head of the long supper table and led the prayer. During the meal he was affirming other persons, as usual. As he often did, he said, "Good meal, Mother." Ruthie remembers how he asked about her law studies and summer work. He turned down pie, saying he'd like to take it but shouldn't. Then followed an evening of family fellowship.

At about 9:00 p.m. Grant went to EMC to check his mail. He came back with an exciting letter about his book. He stood at the end of the living room and read it to us. Then he was absent from the living room, which was not unusual since he often checked his walls of books or used the phone in our bedroom.

Helen came to me, saying urgently, "Daddy wants you to come to the bedroom. He isn't feeling well."

I found him moaning with chest pains and rolling from side to side, trying to get relief. This was a shock, for as far as we knew, he had never had any heart trouble. What should I do? My mind seemed to go blank for a moment, but I called Dr. Helbert's home and the rescue squad. An efficient team of two young women and two young men quickly arrived, gave Grant oxygen, put him on a stretcher, and rushed us to the hospital in the squad vehicle.

Dr. Helbert met us at the emergency room. We soon knew it was serious. Was it mowing after being away from such activity for three weeks? Dr. Helbert was helpful and kind. "This might mean being in the hospital eight weeks or so," he said.

Ruthie and Helen soon came to the hospital with Kathie, John, and baby Joshua. Allen was called and he, Anne, Laura, and Reuben got in the car and came from Lancaster, arriving here at 3:30 a.m. Sunday. Eugene and Pat got back from truck driving at 7:00 that morning.

Our three daughters felt they had to go to the intensive care room to their Daddy's bedside one at a time, rules or no rules. Each one treasures those last twenty seconds with him, as each in her own way told him she loved him, kissed him, and held his hand.

I stayed by Grant's side until 11:00 p.m. It was our first time alone in three weeks.

He said, "I'm ready for anything."

I bent over him and said, "I love you so much. I should have told you more."

He said, "No, you did."

I said, "You have been a good husband and father."

Oh! How I wish I had told him that more, especially during those rough times when Grant felt he was a failure as a father. It pains me now to think how he had taken comfort earlier in the "maybe" when he said, "Ruth, I remember how you said, 'Maybe it isn't our fault.'"

Lord, he is in your presence now. Could you tell him that one of the children just said, "We children are lucky to have had Daddy for a father"? Or does he already know?

We said how thankful we were that we had always kept a good relationship with each other. He suggested that we pray together and we each led a short prayer. He had gotten relief from some but not all of the pain through shots.

I cannot adequately describe the feeling I had as I left his side— a deep hurting feeling, yet a certain satisfaction because of our words together and the relationship they represented. I still have that feeling of satisfaction even though I weep as I write.

At home I could not sleep. In the night I called the nurse in charge and learned there had been a change in Grant's heart rate a little after midnight. I told her, "I will feel better if I come to be close to my husband."

She said, "I wouldn't blame you." It was more proof that the situation was serious.

At 4:30 a.m. I drove to the hospital, sat in the intensive care waiting room, and tried repeatedly to go to Grant's side. But they said, "No, he's sleeping."

Finally, at 7:30 that morning a nurse said, "He's awake. You can come in and talk to him.

I went to his side and asked how he felt.

"Some of the pain is gone," he said, "but not all. I may not make it." He told me to cancel some appointments. He was to be in an Ohio church the next Sunday and at Elizabethtown College for a three-hour lecture on August 12. I was standing by his side, making notes and waiting for his next words when he made a loud snoring sound and became unconscious.

Hospital personnel, alerted by monitoring equipment, came running. A nurse asked if I would like to leave. "No, I would not," I replied. "Whatever it is, I can take it." But they ushered me out. Imagine living thirty-three years, one month, and four days with the man in your life, and you must leave him when he is dying! At least I was standing beside him at his last conscious moment.

In the adjoining waiting room I could only pray four words: "God, overrule, undertake, enable."

I phoned for the children to come. I tried to phone our pastor, Harold Eshleman, and Don Augsburger, our pastor-designate, but they were both out of town. I phoned my sister Katie and asked her to call the other brothers and sisters. The shock was too great for her to comprehend my words until I repeated that Grant was in the hospital because of a heart attack and had taken a turn for the worse.

Our five children soon came to the waiting room, also Eugene's wife, Pat, Kathie's husband, John, their baby, Joshua, and Grant's sister Ada.

Dr. Helbert arrived and rushed to Grant's side. After some time he came into the waiting room, shaking his head and saying, "We worked with him for twenty minutes, but he did not respond."

"Is he gone?" I asked.

"Yes," he said.

Chapter 25

Grant's Burial

Harrisonburg, Virginia
July 1974

Journal entry, July 26, 1974

Dr. Helbert stayed by us quite a while and helped us with plans. When we said we did not want an expensive funeral in an artificial setting, he said he and his wife felt the same way and expected to donate their bodies for medical purposes. He said he would try to find out which funeral director offered the simplest funeral plans.

He asked our consent for an autopsy so they could learn more about what had happened, since eighty-seven percent of those having their first heart attack recover. We also consented to the donation of Grant's eyes to enable some person to see. We felt this would be in line with Grant's wishes.

A nurse came in and asked if we would like to go to Grant's body. As we surrounded the bed, I kissed him for the last time, placed my hand on his chest, and, weeping, led a prayer of thanks that we had had him for the years that we did, that he lived the kind of life he did, that he loved and affirmed all of us as he did—asking God to help us to think deeply, to live nobly as he did, and to follow him as he followed Christ.

That was the only viewing, just as it happened naturally. We could not bring ourselves to plan for the usual display, formality, and artificiality of a funeral home and a corpse-centered funeral service. We did not want to judge others, but it was not for us. We wanted to take care of his body ourselves.

Our children were the first to make plans for a different kind of funeral and burial, deciding to dig the grave and build the casket themselves. Grant's ideas had gotten across to them during informal table conversations.

Beginning on Sunday morning, my nephew Truman Jr., and his wife, Betty, arrived and took over—Betty managing the meals and Truman Jr., advising on building the casket, both entering into our pain and supporting us at every turn.

Pastor Harold Eshleman soon came, giving words and prayers of strength and planning the burial and memorial services with us. Eugene Souder followed through on our suggestion that at the memorial service a sheet of notebook paper be passed to each bench for signatures, to avoid having people wait in line to sign in a book. Many friends came to visit and thought of ways to help us in our loss.

The children building Grant's casket. From the left: Kathryn, John Fairfield, Ruth, Eugene.

Digging Grant's grave.

The funeral director, known for the simplest funeral accommodations in the area, said, nevertheless, that he would not be involved unless we consented to embalming, so we decided to have no funeral director.

By calling the medical examiner in Richmond, the commonwealth attorney, and a pathologist, Allen and Eugene found that, contrary to the opinion of many, embalming and a vault were not required by law, except in cases involving death from certain diseases or transportation of the body out of the state.

So they, along with Kathie's husband John, dug the grave. When they built the casket, we all helped with the staining and rubbing, even with inner sobbings. We then placed the foam and a favorite pillow and draped the sheet material inside. The children said it was better therapy than sitting around.

Dr. Helbert got a death certificate at the Health Department and told us to register it there after he filled out information, including the cause of death—acute myocardial infarction. He had arranged for Grant's body to be kept in the hospital morgue until burial. The children and Grant's brother Mahlon, who had flown in from

Alaska, put the clothes on Grant's body, placed it in the casket, and transported it to Lindale Cemetery in Kathie and John's station wagon for the burial service at 5:00 p.m.

It was a simple, private burial with family and relatives present, including the relatives of our son-in-law and daughters-in-law, also Moses Slabaugh, our preacher-friend who had the service, and his wife.

The children and I, and Grant's brothers, Ivan and Mahlon, carried the casket from the car to the grave.

Then followed the burial service. I can only describe my feelings as continued shock and numbness, interspersed with waves of terrible hurting. As our Allen and Eugene, Ivan and Mahlon, John Fairfield, and Truman Jr. lowered the casket into the grave, and with brother-in-law John Yost and nephew Gerald Brunk, took turns with shovels to fill in dirt, our daughters and I moved up as close as we could. My brothers George and Truman came and stood with me.

Chapter 26

Grant's Memorial Service

Harrisonburg, Virginia
July 1974

Journal entry, July 26, 1974

The women from church who had been providing food at our house, provided for us again between the burial and memorial services.

Park View Church was crowded when we arrived a little before 7:00 p.m. Our children, grandchildren, and I walked down the left aisle along the wall and occupied the second bench. Grant's relatives and mine sat behind us, a few across the aisle and back. Nephew Gerald Brunk was on the front bench with a cassette tape recorder.

In the memorial service three people spoke about ten minutes each from the pulpit, as planned: Harold Eshleman, pastor of the congregation; my brother George, dean of the seminary; Daniel Yutzy, dean of Eastern Mennonite College. President Myron Augsburger was out of town.

Then followed what we intended to be a time of meditation with an occasional word from anyone in the audience. People wanting to speak were standing up as many as two and three at a time, I was told later. As we were planning this part of the service with Harold, I suggested that the closing time be flexible, letting everyone who wanted to speak an opportunity, but the children said "No, Mother, Daddy was always particular about promptness. When it's your funeral, it can be late!"

We did have such times of laughing at the same time we were crying. We had a similar session with Grant's brothers and his sister Ada after the service, as they told favorite stories about Grant. At certain points in the service Grant's humor was acknowledged and the audience responded with restrained laughter. Near the close of sharing time, I felt led to speak a few minutes to pay tribute to Grant and to testify to God's strength in time of crisis.

Those who spoke mentioned many aspects of Grant's work and spoke with appreciation of him as a teacher, writer, scholar, and committee member, including Francis G. Brown's appreciation for his contribution to the National Committee for the Conference on Religious Liberty. It was a revelation to us all. I knew he had touched a lot of people deeply, but I did not know how many or how deeply.

It is a comforting thought to know that Grant invested his life in so many others. He had a knack for surrounding people with esteem. Rather than being threatened, the more he could help others to learn, grow and be, the better he felt. This theme has been repeated to us in letters, notes, and private conversations. A pastor: "He encouraged me in the ministry." A counselor: "He made me feel important." A student: "We lost a hero." An attorney: "He encouraged me to go into law." A medical doctor: "He wrote me an encouraging letter when medical school was the roughest." The list goes on.

Judging from the flood of letters from his students and colleagues and comments at his memorial service, what Grant planted in the lives of people will continue to yield fruit.

Chapter 27

Grief

Journal entries

August 20, 1974

I find I am often caught unawares, thinking I hear Grant's step, or catch myself thinking of something I will tell or ask him when he comes. Fresh pains come daily.

We have tapes and transcripts of the burial and memorial services. Moses Slabaugh is writing an article about the burial for the December 1974 issue of *Christian Living*, along with a *Mennonite Community* editorial Grant wrote years ago on expensive funerals.

The mail has been heavy with hundreds of cards and letters. Many confirm us in the type of burial and memorial services we had. I received further confirmation in a strange way—by remembering how it shook me years ago when I learned that Grant did not believe in embalming and the use of a vault. In his characteristically gentle but effective way, he brought me, and later the children, around to his way of thinking.

Several weeks after Grant's death we found in his "famous files" a folder on funerals, in addition to the one on death. You would think we had read it and followed in detail the things he had clipped, underscored, or copied. The gist of the materials must have gotten across to us in family conversations.

My only reservation is that Grant's approach might have been to try to help the whole brother/sisterhood to change from expensive funerals, and he might not have been so radically different if I had died first. The children thought he would have, after family discussion. I don't know. I do believe we followed in line with family conversations according to the way Grant believed and the way the children and I had come to believe.

A funeral director told Moses Slabaugh (who had a talk on

179

funerals at Virginia Conference two days after Grant's burial) that a vault is for the comfort of the survivors who hate to bury a loved one's body in cold or wet weather. Dan Yutzy says he thinks embalming preserves the body for about one week.

I read last week that the average U.S. funeral costs $1,975.00. We didn't feel we could have honored Grant more than by caring for his body ourselves and by paying the $40.00 cost of materials for the casket in line with the way he believed. (Not long before his death he quoted to the family, "If there is a lower class I am in it.")

August 28, 1974

I am experiencing fresh hurts as I see the stirrings of a new school year beginning at Eastern Mennonite College and Seminary without Grant. He taught there for seventeen years. But I must believe his influence will continue to be felt and God's mercies will continue to be "new every morning."

September 1974

Oh, how it hurts to think I am no longer married to Grant. After thirty-three years of our lives being intertwined, I cannot soon become extricated in my mind and emotions. A part of me seems gone. A part of him will always be with me.

Sometimes I think I have made little progress in the grief process as I have not felt able to move his shoes and other clothing from our bedroom, or move his glasses and books from his reading chair.

I think of our dear friends and know they must suffer, too. May we experience the comfort of God's presence and promises, and somehow carry on with faith and courage until he brings us also to our eternal home.

Grant often said in times of stress, "We have much to be thankful for." With an aching, hurting heart I thank God for the quality of Grant's life and our life together for thirty-three years, one month, and four days. I would rather have lived with him for thirty-three years than with any other man for more years.

Even so, I have bitter moments when I think how our children were raised and we had just begun our less stressful years together, rejoicing in the fact that we both had interesting work to do and still liked each other! His book lies unfinished, and I have moments of fantasy when I think of something to tell or ask Grant. Waves of lonesomeness and hurt come over me as in my mind I often see him in different poses—sitting in his reading chair, mowing the lawn, leaving for classes, returning home, standing with hands in hip pockets as he hashed over ideas, or snapping his suspenders as punctuation.

Mental companionship was half of our marriage. As I returned from a women's retreat in Alabama on September 23, I thought I could not bear the pain of Grant's absence. He had helped me plan my talks. Now he would not be here to ask "How was your trip?" or to discuss his and my latest ideas and experiences.

But God seems to bring comforting thoughts to my mind. Lately it was the thought that Grant's love, influence, and help are like a great storehouse of grain that I can draw from personally. I will always benefit from the way he affirmed me and my work. (He was big enough in his thinking and secure enough in his work to do this.)

What a moment it was when Al Keim and Gerald Brunk drove back from Swarthmore College with Grant's car, clothes, files, books, and attaché cases. I cannot describe the sick feeling. Among the things were neatly organized folders and tapes—resource materials for the book he would never complete.

To the friends giving a gift of Gideon Memorial Bibles in memory of Grant, I wrote:

> He was a student of the Word, often sitting in his special chair reading from one translation or another or from the Greek, often remarking about some deeper meaning he had discovered. One night recently, when the evening news was less than reassuring, he got up in the middle of the night and spent a long time reading from the Bible and meditating.
>
> Most thrilling of all, and this causes me to rejoice, even in my tears, Grant lived the teachings of the Bible, as he understood them, to show the price of true discipleship, as he sought to follow Christ.

October 22, 1974

I got awake with a sick, lonesome feeling for Grant. I did not know fully what I had when he was living. But I will not beat myself. We both knew we had a good marriage.

What are the priorities for my remaining days?

October 25, 1974

I hang on every word from friends who express appreciation for Grant. Jean Snyder wrote these words: "Grant was a very special person to me, too. I can concur wholeheartedly with those who say, 'He made me feel important,' as though my opinion on a question mattered to him. His interest in me and in what I was doing was a real affirmation. I miss him."

February 2, 1976

To Grant's brothers and sisters:

> This morning I got awake with tears in my eyes. I had been experiencing such waves of lonesomeness for Grant. I feel something like a vine that has had another vine intertwined with it for thirty-three years, then it is torn away leaving the remaining vine ruptured and hurt.
>
> Enclosed is a sample of the bookplate I had printed to go into the books (2,000 or so) from Grant's library that are donated to Eastern Mennonite College and Seminary.
>
> Grant had written five chapters of his book on the U.S. Government and Alternate Service. Our family has consented to the plan that Al Keim will use Grant's chapters as research, write the rest of the book, and be shown as co-author with Grant.

June 18, 1985

Grant, you are there and I am here. Yesterday, June 17, was the 44th anniversary of our wedding in 1941. I'm experiencing inner sobbings and at the same time rejoicing in our years together, in the contribution of your life to me, to the children, to the church.

In *Up the Golden Stair*, Elizabeth Yates says best what I've felt since your death: "Often I ache for our days of dear companionship . . . the endless talking and the listening, the philosophizing." Yates goes on to say, "They that love beyond the world, cannot be separated by it. Death cannot kill what never dies. . . . Death is but crossing the world, as friends do the seas; they live in one another still." That is how I feel about you.

Chapter 28

Helen's Journal on the Death of Her Father

Helen was asked to write an article for *With,* the Mennonite youth magazine, about Grant's death. It appeared in the July 1975 issue as "Journal on the Death of My Father."

July 21, 1974, morning
Dad dies unexpectedly of a second heart attack Sunday morning while we, his family, wait for word outside his room.
FLASHBACK: *Sat. night, July 20* We are awake most of the night awaiting news. I fight with the instinct of hope and energy of life itself against the possibility of death. Hope is so powerful. And so important. I think it is what keeps us going in this life.

July 21 and 22, afternoon
My brothers and sisters and I dig the grave and begin building the casket from pine boards.
I want to pound in nails; I want to help dig the hole that will hold him. I must participate concretely in this long difficult process of taking care of my father's body. As we work, we realize our sweat works off some of the tremendous tension and weight of the situation, as well as making us the caretakers of our own loved one.
FANTASY: Dad will be delighted at our joint effort to produce what has become a beautiful piece of workmanship. He'll soon drop in and see us all working together on this project.

July 22, night
We are finishing the casket. We have laughed and cried all day, realizing with sorrow that he is gone but with thanksgiving that the noblest of him—his concerns, beliefs, attitudes—are within each of us, manifesting themselves unconsciously in a thousand ways.
It has become important to us that our hands and finally our

minds know the reality of his death. So we all want to help carry the coffin when we bury him. We take turns lying in the coffin so we can practice carrying it. I am carried by my family in this box of death, staring up at the sky and their faces, alive and marveling at the trust that develops. They will not drop me. They will take care of me.

FANTASY: My family carrying my body after my death in the same gentle, loving way as we did practicing for my father. And later, as at his funeral, singing my favorite songs, rejoicing at my life.

July 23, afternoon

Many people have been in and out all day Sunday, Monday, and today. They bring what they can: food and sympathy. I am amazed at the possibility of community. Must it take such monumental events as marriage and death for us to hold one another's hands and look into one another's eyes?

We eat lunch.

FLASHBACK: Complaining when Dad says he has to eat supper now and can't wait. Didn't I realize how precious words were?

July 23, afternoon

We take Dad's cold body from the morgue and place him in our homemade coffin. I stare at Death. And Death—its ugliness, its withering away of all that is vibrant and joyous—thunders its silence and finality.

FLASHBACK: Dad patting me on the cheek as he walks by, a little clumsily and too hard, but with such affection.

July 23, evening

We stand in the rain and I watch them lower my father's body into the ground for final rest. It is our last physical duty to him.

FANTASY: It is a dream. It must be a dream, for there is no reason to this grief. Why am I dressed in black? We are pretending. We are dressed up and pretending.

July 26

I read the hundreds of sympathy cards and letters and wonder how wide and profound my influence is.

I am overwhelmed with opposing emotions when I contemplate

Dad's death. At times, I sense as never before in my life, that there is a Source, a Comforter, One who sows the seed of life and harvests it in due time. I crave more of that peace that settles over me when I resign this small, frantic life to that greater purpose.

At other times, it seems there is no reason to our dance on earth; we are brought here and torn away again at random. Fate, like nature, is indifferent and impersonal. Can life have meaning if death seems to have none?

O God, I am expected to trust You and accept this thing I cannot understand. Is this blind faith? What is faith?

FLASHBACK: Dad reading in that deep reverent rhythm: "The Lord is thy keeper: the Lord is thy shade upon thy right hand. . . . The Lord shall preserve thy going out and thy coming in. . . ."

July 30

My friends do not know what to say to me. Some mysterious and untrodden territory has been spread out between us. They do not know how to talk about this that has uprooted me and left me too thoughtful and sad. I feel older.

FLASHBACK: My last trip with Dad. Riding along Interstate 81 on a sunny day discussing the concept of community, Mennonites, etc. Picking up an Amish man who knows our Stoltzfus relatives. Dad and I were two of a kind on that trip. Our relationship reached a new and better plane the past few months before his death. I am grateful.

August 1

Bitterness fills me at times. Suddenly, for no reason, sadness has replaced joy. My trip abroad this summer has dissolved, and I feel cheated that all of my life must change now.

FLASHBACK: Dad describing his luck with research on conscientious objectors. He is so eager and enthusiastic about his book. How cruel and unfair that he will never finish his most exciting project.

August 15

Now, for me, beneath all of life, beneath the joy and the boredom and the rush, there is a deeper dimension, an older ring to everything.

Now I know there is a conclusion to it all. A seemingly random cutoff, but somehow a necessary—an integral part—of the mysterious arrival and departure of all our lives.

FLASHBACK: Saturday night, July 20. My sisters and I walk to his hospital room despite the rules. It is the last time I see him alive. I hold his hand and in those few seconds allowed, tell him I love him. There is nothing more to say. I could have held his hand all night.

August 16

I miss Dad in concrete ways. I want to ask his advice on my future plans, my college courses, theological issues. He's missed the impeachment proceedings he would have enjoyed so much.

DREAM: Dad and I were in a public place—church perhaps. All I remember in the dream is that I laid my head against his chest and heard the sweet, sweet holy music of his heart pounding, thundering in my ear in perfect, faithful rhythm.

March 15, 1975

My baby nephew Joshua inspires me with incredible joy and hope. I watch him and realize: time moves on. A new generation, exhilarated with life from the start, has arrived and brought new hopes and possibilities. We will carry on.

FLASHBACK: Dad playing with Joshua his last afternoon on earth. Something of his life, his future, has been passed on to the new little one.

April 17, 1975

I am thankful my father lived so vigorously to the end. I think on my own life and death and I want my life to be full of energy, hopes, dreams, joy, because life is so precious, so rare. It may be asked back again at any time.

I want my death, and the activities involved in returning me to the earth, to be worthy of my life. And as personal as my life.

FLASHBACK: Dad snapping his suspenders after telling a joke. We joke about the fact that we buried him wearing his suspenders.

April 18, 1975

The move from fantasy to acceptance must occur, not only within myself but among those around me as well. We must discuss death. We must talk of the practicalities, like how costly we want our burial, and our emotional reactions of bitterness and guilt.

FLASHBACK: Why did I—we—let him mow the lawn the night before his first heart attack until he was totally exhausted?

Sometimes we will stop pretending, stop fantasizing, and in discussing the practicalities and realities of death, discover that if we fear it, we are conquered. But knowledge, including the knowledge that recognizes the source of knowledge, will make us conquerors.

PART SIX

PAVING THE WAY
1974–1981

Chapter 29

A Loyal Critic

Harrisonburg, Virginia
September 1974–April 1976

Sunday morning, just weeks after Grant's death, I had the morning message at Park View Church. "God, help me to feel sent, not just tolerated, as a Sunday morning woman speaker," I prayed.

My topic was "Homes would be happier if . . . " I made five points, all wrapped up in loving God, neighbor, and self. Enough warm comments came to encourage me. Other people were apprehensive about a woman preacher, and some stayed away that morning. I prayed, "God, help me to work for necessary changes, but in a right spirit."

At the end of September, Priscilla Muganda and baby Kenneth moved into an apartment next to my office in the Concord building. I knew my children and brothers and sisters were glad that Priscilla and her baby needed me, but when they returned to Africa in February, I felt more alone than ever.

In May 1975, while Helen and I were at Allen's in Lancaster, Anne gave birth to their third child, Kathryn Ann (Katie). I cried as I walked down the hospital hall to see the new grandbaby without Grant.

Task force on world hunger

Pastor Don Augsburger appointed me to a task force on world hunger that was formed at Park View Church in late 1974 and remained active through 1975. When the task force led the morning service in February 1975, I had the Scripture and prayer. I spoke of our expensive, extravagant, showy ways at home and in our church, our worship of the American gods of success, money, power, and prestige.

191

Priscilla Muganda and me.

As a follow-up we showed a film on hunger in Niger, West Africa. During the discussion afterward I said I was frightened at our ability to talk much and do little about the little children with arms that looked like thin sticks, with flies at the edges of their eyes and mouths—little children the ages of my grandchildren.

In September the task force presented recommendations to the congregation: population control, wise land use, agricultural assistance to developing nations, and practical suggestions for the simple life. I was chair of the committee but thought it best for Kenton Brubaker, professor of biology at Eastern Mennonite College (EMC), to lead the discussion, because he had a good grasp of the issues and because the congregation would be more comfortable with a man as leader.

The issues raised by the task force did not go away, and neither did my urgency about simple lifestyle. I was concerned about the affluent living by people who professed to follow Christ. We needed to be consulting with each other, curbing each other, being accountable to each other. There was too much of the American idea of success and not enough of the idea of the suffering servant.

Commissioned

In May 1975 I experienced a feeling of being commissioned for some task not yet clear. Soon afterward I received a request from Daniel Hertzler, editor of the *Gospel Herald,* asking me, among others, to write a brief article to stir thinking before the Mennonite Church General Assembly.

In my article I wrote:

> I speak as a loyal critic of the church I love, and with a desire to be faithful to God's urgings within. We have many strengths but many needs.
>
> Governments with all their benefits make demands that violate our higher allegiance to Christ. We will continue to be asked to lay our bodies and dollars on the altar of the god of war. We will have painful decisions to make and positions to take on the question of our part in the killing business. More of us should face these things together.
>
> In a world with many persons starving in body, mind, and spirit, we ought to be conscientious objectors to the expensive, showy ways of the "successful"—ways that reinforce a system of injustice to the poor. We must call on each other to live simply, give generously, and seek first the kingdom of God and His righteousness (right treatment of others).
>
> Unfortunately, we have battles between brothers. Rival power instead of servant power is killing witness power. The old question of who is greatest is still asked.
>
> We are little credit to our foremothers. In early Anabaptist days when men and women were baptized, it meant they were also ordained to preach, teach, and baptize others. (It was more important to get the Gospel out than to fuss about which sex does it!) In Bible times women were wives, mothers, prophetesses, judges, managers, sheep tenders, employers, builders of cities, buyers of real estate, salespersons, teachers, deaconesses, co-laborers in the Gospel. . . .
>
> We must consider customs in Bible times, reconcile different passages, not latch onto one to prove a pet theory. Jesus and Paul radically broke custom in their treatment of women. Some customs need breaking today and it will happen only with some mind stretching and Spirit-filling.
>
> Are we citizens of Christ's kingdom? Let the concept strike deep into

our hearts and minds, into the very marrow of our bones, so that God may accomplish DEEP changes within us, between us, and through us, for the advancement of His kingdom in our time.

That summer I flew to Youngstown, Ohio, for four talks with the Berean Mennonite Church. Friday evening, Saturday evening, and Sunday morning I spoke on family life. On Sunday afternoon, responding to an invitation to speak what was on my heart, I talked about world hunger, the U.S. military budget, the military tax, and the Christian conscience—1.5 billion dollars for food aid, 80.5 billion dollars for the killing business.

On July 13, after my final message, pastor Fred Augsburger asked if I would stand so that he and others could lay hands on me. Some put hands on my shoulder and arms and back while others prayed. It was a thanking, commissioning ceremony. I could not keep back the tears. I felt then and later that I was being ordained for further service.

Reaching young people

In January, at the invitation of the men, I taught the combined men's and our women's Sunday school classes. Apparently, it was a first for that class of older men to have a woman teach, but none of the women spoke a word.

Those days I felt closer to the EMC students, speaking in chapel and preaching and teaching Sunday school at campus church. The women students often came to talk about the role of women and the church.

In February I met with Myron Augsburger and shared with him how Allen was becoming active with a Mennonite church in Lancaster, Pennsylvania. Myron said he'd like to make a suggestion for my next fifteen years: that I think of going to school a year or so to get a master's degree, then teach at EMC.

I told him I was sixty. He said he had not realized that. I told him I did not have a bachelor's degree, only two years of college, plus summer school. He still wanted me to turn in my credits for him and Dean Dan Yutzy to review. He said, "What you have been talking about for twenty years we now need someone to teach about."

I told him I had plenty to do with my broadcasting and writing and publishing, plus the children and grandchildren.

When I spoke at Broad Street Mennonite Church in April, I felt more comfortable speaking on the subject of spiritual training in the home than I had for eleven years because of changes in Allen. He and Anne were blossoming as adult Christians.

Tribute to Truman

Kathie was teaching junior high school science in Durham when she decided to go to law school. She passed her exams and was accepted at Duke University, where John was studying computer science. Kathie and Ruthie began to make plans for working together in a law and counseling practice.

One day when my brother Truman stopped by, he was surprised to see Ruthie, who had come to Harrisonburg for an interview with a local law firm. "I'm proud of you," he told her. Then, turning to me, he said, "We must have a celebration when she graduates. This is the first lawyer in our family."

Truman Brunk Sr.: No nicer brother. [Truman Brunk family album]

On April 25, Stella and Ward drove me to Warwick River Mennonite Church, Newport News, for a meeting honoring Truman for his thirty-five years as bishop. Lloyd Weaver Jr., the new bishop-overseer, invited people who had been baptized, married, or ordained by Truman to come forward. Twila Brunk read a tribute to Truman's wife, Ruth. Young people sang "A Ballad to T. H."

After time for telling stories about Truman was cut off, I felt moved to speak. I prayed, "Lord, if you want me to say anything, you'll have to make a way." Sure enough, near the close of the meeting Lloyd Weaver said, "Is there anyone else?"

I sprang to my feet. (My nephew George Brunk III said he noticed it didn't take me long!) "I would like to speak from the standpoint of the family," I said. "Truman has the kind of Christianity that wears well in the family. When he was in the hospital some years ago I wrote him a little poem:

> No better bishop
> No nicer brother
> No more-loved uncle
> To those I mother.

"He wrote a letter in response, saying, 'When a man is down on his back, I guess you are justified in stretching the truth a little.' When our daughter Ruthie had to have her arm amputated, she asked to be anointed and said, 'I'd like Uncle Truman to do it.' He had her kneel in our living room and he had a beautiful service there. Exactly one year after my husband's death, the telephone rang. It was Truman, who remembered and said, 'Ruth, we're thinking of you and praying for you.' "

Chapter 30

"We Need a Pastor to Our Pastors"

Lombard, Illinois
April–May 1976

In 1976 I saw this announcement in the *Gospel Herald:*

> Women in Ministry Seminar is to be held at the Lombard Mennonite Church, 528 East Madison St., Lombard, Ill., April 30 to May 2. The seminar is for women of Mennonite churches who are a part of a team ministry, co-pastors, ministers, chaplains, seminarians, or in any way directly related to pastoral or ministering services. Purpose of the weekend will be that of mutual encouragement, study, and sharing. For more information write: Women in Ministry, Lombard Mennonite Church, at the above address.

I felt sure I was to go to the seminar even though I had no official assignment in the ministry of any one church. Dave Augsburger, former speaker on the Mennonite Hour and Choice radio spots, called before I left, confirming that I would stay in their home and requesting that I come a day early in order to speak to his class at Northern Baptist Theological Seminary.

When Dave introduced me to the class, I was surprised that he said, "If she had not done broadcasting and writing, I doubt if I would have."

My theme, by request, was "Death, Burial, and the Grieving Process." I told the class I had mixed feelings about circulating pictures of our family digging Grant's grave, making his casket (how can it be true that I am writing those words?), carrying the casket to the grave, standing during the burial service, etc., but I would do so if they paused for a moment of silence.

At the seminar Emma and Joe Richards spoke of their ordinations and work as co-pastors at the Lombard Mennonite Church. "Joe is the freest and the most creative. He does more committee work and hospital visiting," said Emma. "Emma is one of the best Bible preachers I have heard," Joe remarked.

During times of large and small group discussions, women told of their sense of calling, their joys and frustrations. After one of these discussions, Emma Richards met me in the hall, called me aside, and said, "We wonder if you would consent to being ordained by this group."

"What responsibility would it mean?" I asked.

"How would you feel, for example, being a listener to me?" she asked.

"I do that kind of thing all the time," I said. "The regular kind of pastorate may not be for me."

The meeting was starting. It seemed a hurried time to decide anything. Emma said we could talk more later. "I'm willing to give serious consideration to the idea of such an ordination," I told her.

At the Sunday noon meal, approaching the time to get my things together for the flight home, I took a chair beside Emma and thanked her for her morning message.

She said, "About the idea of your ordination we talked about last night—we discussed it in our Findings Committee last night and it was decided that we should not do anything that would alienate us from Illinois Conference. But I have not given up the idea. We need a pastor to our pastors."

Chapter 31

Standing Up for Justice

Harrisonburg, Virginia
May 1976–October 1978

In May of 1976 I spoke to an Eastern Mennonite Seminary class on "Home as an Educational Agency." I lamented the misinterpretation of Scripture that supported the view that men do not need to adjust and adapt in marriage. I was pleased and surprised at the number of men who thanked me for my talk. The one woman in the class said with feeling that she had prayed about the missing emphasis on the woman question.

At a church in Ohio where I was speaking on "Family Life Enrichment," a man called me aside after I had given four of five talks and said, "I want to make a confession. After your first talk I said to my wife, 'Do we have to have a woman speaker for the weekend?' Then, what got me to change my attitude was that you had Scriptural backing for what you were doing. The teaching we had in church years ago was negative toward women speakers in the church."

Later that year Myron Augsburger surprised me by bringing up the question of ordaining women to the ministry. "We will have to look at this, since women are graduating from our seminaries," he said to me. "Just be patient."

"Do you realize I am sixty-two?" I answered, meaning, "How long does a person need to wait?"

Standing up for justice

On September 23, 1976, Ruthie called from her work at the Hoover law firm. "This is Ruth Carol Stoltzfus, attorney-at-law," she announced.

When she opened an office on the fourth floor of the Rockingham County Court House, Ruthie was the only woman attorney working in Harrisonburg or Rockingham County. In

January 1977 she became the first attorney for the newly opened Harrisonburg-Rockingham Legal Aid Society.

The Equal Rights Amendment (ERA) narrowly missed being passed in the U.S. Senate that year, so in October, Helen, Kathie, John, Joshua, Ruthie, and I participated in a local demonstration. We walked in the rain down Main Street from James Madison University to the courthouse, chanting, "Hey, hey, what do you say, ratify the ERA!" and "No, Virginia, don't wait—ERA in '78!"

I wrote an open letter to our state representatives, urging them to "help Virginia to join the 20th century on the ERA, also to be as up-to-date as the first century, when Paul in the Bible taught the equality of male and female. Please do not give support to the notion that we cannot take a stand for equal rights because this or that (partly conjectures) will happen down the road. Let us stand for what is fair and right and meet the consequences as they come. Can fair-minded and courageous people do anything else?"

As a member of Amnesty International's Urgent Action Network, I began in 1977 to write letters to heads of state and of the military and information organizations on behalf of persons who were not being treated with justice.

The appliance company, General Electric, once sent me a refund of seventy-five cents on some product. The check had on it the statement, "We bring good things to life." I wrote them that they also bring good things like human beings to DEATH, by their involvement in the business of producing instruments of death for the United States.

Memories

With Ruthie living in her own apartment in Harrisonburg and later sharing a house with Helen, it made sense for me to leave the big house on the hill. I moved to an apartment in my office building at Mt. Clinton Pike in January 1977. I made plans to sell the house and, with Allen's help, had it appraised and put on the market. But while I was showing it to people I realized I was hoping they wouldn't buy it. After two years I sold the house to the children.

In October that year I had a meditation at the wedding of my niece Nancy Yost and Robert Eberly, at Hershey's Mennonite Church in Lancaster, Pennsylvania. At the reception I was called aside to sign the wedding certificate (my first experience) along with the ministers. I remembered the time in 1960 that a Lancaster County bishop had refused Jim Burkholder's request for me to give a message at their wedding.

The bitter and sweet memories were mixed. In Ohio, when overseer Richard Bartholomew introduced me before a Sunday morning Mother's Day message, he referred to talks Grant and I had given years earlier and the effect they had had on him, his wife, and their marriage. When I began to speak I could only say, with tears, "It is amazing the way God can use our poor, feeble efforts. Just amazing."

Servanthood

Pastor Don Augsburger asked me to have the message during a service of foot washing and communion at Park View Church in April 1977. It was the first time I knew of any woman doing so. I spoke of how Jesus, in washing the disciples' feet, was performing the task of a slave. "As we wash one another's feet in this service today," I concluded, "we express our willingness to be servants doing lowly tasks for each other, and our intention to follow the example of Jesus in love and servanthood."

I was involved in the lives of many Eastern Mennonite College (EMC) international students, especially Priscilla Muganda and her two babies, who had recently moved into the apartment above my office since returning from a brief time in Africa. In November 1977, after helping a Palestinian student buy a car, taking another to his driving test, and putting the Muganda babies to bed, I wrote in my journal, "I'm beginning to think I am running an international office of some sort. It feels right. Maybe it is in the divine plan for me."

Priscilla and her children became such a part of the family that I grieved when she announced in November 1978 that she was leaving Harrisonburg. I arranged for EMC students to help move her things and for Eugene to drive Priscilla and the children to New York City, where she earned a master's degree while working as a nurse at Columbia University hospital.

Esther Brunk Shenk

My sister Esther Virginia Brunk Shenk died on March 8, 1978. Helen called to tell me the news and offered to come and stay with me, but I said I thought I would be all right. I was alone that night with my thoughts and memories and did not sleep well. I shivered with shock, not with cold. Just that morning I had talked to Esther on the phone. "Ruthie, I'm sick," she had said. Her last words were of concern for her family.

I remembered how Esther had gone along with me to teachers' meetings when I taught in the public school system. I was the only plain Mennonite and she went to keep me company. I thought of the many times she packed my lunch to take to school. My mind went back to the times I brought college friends home to a house she had cleaned and decorated with flowers.

Speaking for the poor and powerless

When Ross Bender from Goshen Seminary came to Harrisonburg in 1978 for EMC Ministers' Week, he told me I should be ordained before I retired, if for no other reason than to help pave the way for younger women. I told him that perhaps women with the gift of preaching should ordain each other, but I would hesitate to be ordained and perpetuate a system of hierarchy. I was feeling that being a pastor of a church was not my niche.

Speaking for the poor was one of my niches, and I had many opportunities. One was at an evangelism seminar sponsored by the Mennonite Christian Leadership Foundation at Smoketown, Pennsylvania, in 1978. Messages by church leaders called us to be involved in programming, supporting, and doing evangelism.

After the first session and throughout the seminar, I felt a warmth of affirmation and a freedom to participate that I had not anticipated. I felt that even though I had not always been given recognition, freedom, or fair treatment in the past, I must sweeten my attitudes, by God's grace. In private conversation, I was reconciled with a church leader I had felt hostile toward.

In the closing moments of the last session I had a strong impression that I must speak out. Different ones were sharing visions for evangelism. Feeling strongly that evangelists tend to be insensitive to social injustice and that little was said about this aspect of Jesus' concern and our mission, I opened my Bible to Luke 4 and read to myself verses 18 and 19. Then I breathed a prayer that if God wanted me to speak, he needed to tell Don Jacobs, the chairman. Just then Don looked at me sitting at the back and said, "Ruth, do you have something to say?"

I stood up and said, "I just told the Lord, if he wanted me to speak, tell Don."

Don said, "He just did."
After giving some illustrations, I said:

Jesus preached and he healed. He cared about the body and soul
both. According to his words in Matthew 25, the test of guilt or
acquittal in the last day is whether we fed the hungry. Today thousands
of people have starved to death. Thousands starved yesterday.
Thousands will starve tomorrow. At this very moment people are being
tortured in prison simply because of their political or religious belief.

I want to read some verses from the Bible, Luke 4:18-19: "The Spirit
of the Lord is on me, because he has anointed me to preach good news
to the poor. He has sent me to proclaim release for prisoners and
recovery of sight for the blind, to release the oppressed, to proclaim
the year of the Lord's favor."

I cannot explain away these verses and say that they do not refer to
those who are literally poor, in prison, blind and broken. I guess my
question is, whose job is it to minister to social needs? Is this something for someone else to do in line with what we believe about differing gifts? Or is it our responsibility?

Later that year I attended a seminar at EMC on abortion. The
medical, psychological, sociological, and ethical aspects were discussed by a Mennonite psychiatrist, a Mennonite medical doctor,
and EMC faculty members. The theological viewpoint was left out,
I felt. I listened until the psychiatrist made the statement that a
woman faced with a particular dilemma may justify getting an abortion "because she could make better use of her time."

It was near closing time, but I could keep still no longer. I said:

It is not for us to say when life begins. Let's let God be God. I have
problems with the idea that the forty-four-year-old pregnant woman,
married and with three children of college and high school age would
decide to have an abortion because it would be determined by modern
techniques that the child would be Mongoloid or otherwise handicapped and because her time could be better spent in other ways.

I gave birth to five children, the fifth when I was forty-one. The
child was more intelligent and more beautiful than I am. We learned
later that it was a risk because an old egg could have been fertilized,
but my husband and I were responsible for that life. I still believe that
terminating a pregnancy is taking a life. I could no more do that than
stand by the child's crib and decide to terminate the life because the
child was handicapped or because I could make better use of my time.

Here is where the brotherhood/sisterhood, the caring community,
should surround such families with support.

A psalm of praise

In May 1978, I visited Allen and his family in Lancaster and went along with them to First Deaf Mennonite Church, where Paul Zehr gave a spiritually nourishing sermon on "Confidence in Prayer." I wanted to respond to his message, but I just thanked God in my heart that Allen and Anne were in the orbit of Paul and Mary Zehr and others at the church. I felt in the core of my being that God had answered Grant's and my prayers for Allen.

I expressed my feelings in a psalm that I wrote for Virginia Conference Assembly that year:

Personal Psalm of Praise, Petition and Commitment

Oh, God, I thank you
for my parents and grandparents
and all those persons of the past
who made it possible for me
to believe in you and your Son.
I thank you, God of the generations.

I thank you
for bringing into my life
the other part of me—
my spouse who loved you, your Word,
your work, your people.
I thank you, God of love.

Your Spirit gave us gifts to use,
kingdom work to do
in our home
and in our church.
I thank you, Giver of gifts.

You gave us children
to love and to teach
but not to keep,
for they belong not to us
but to you,
not to our generation
but to theirs.
I thank you, Giver of life.

You sustained us
when crises struck.

With tiny infant in my arms
I knew I might not live.
You gave me grace to say
your way is best,
and then you snatched me back
from the gates of death.
I thank you, God of strength.

When a son's intellectual approach
to life was a hindrance to faith
and all things seemed to go awry,
you heard our cry. In time
you answered our prayers and his.
You honored our tiny
mustard-seed of faith.
I thank you, God of salvation.

When crippling disease took its toll—
the best arm of a teenage daughter—
and tormenting tallies
said she would likely die,
your servant, a loved uncle,
anointed her with oil,
with tears and prayers,
and you spared her life.
I thank you, Destroyer of death.

When you allowed death
to take the other part of me
and every morning I awoke
to crushing grief anew,
you comforted me with your Word:
"The steadfast love of the Lord
never ceases, his mercies
never come to an end:
they are new every morning."
You gave me strength for each day.
You gave me caring family and friends.
You made the resurrection hope
come alive in my heart.
I thank you, God of comfort and hope.

I thank you for forgiving
the sins of my youth,
of my middle years,
of my older age.

*You gave me freedom
from worry and guilt.
I thank you, God of forgiveness.*

*You brought me in a new way,
into the fellowship of your
called-out ones,
members of the body of Christ.
I thank you that my gifts are
used in the church,
and that where I am limited,
my brothers and sisters are gifted,
so that we might be a whole body
in the mission of the church.
Help us to work together with courage,
with caution and with charity.
We implore you, Lord of the church.*

*Enable us to love you first and best
and to cast out all other gods—
the god of money and things,
the god of intellectual knowledge,
the god of sinful pleasures,
the god of prestige and power,
the god of nation and military might.
Cast out anything and everything, Lord,
that threatens to take your place
in our affections and in our trust.
Help us, O God of peace.*

*And teach us, Lord,
that we are not gods or rulers.
We are but men and women, brothers and sisters,
servants of you and of each other,
followers of your Son, our Savior.
Your Spirit has gifted, called,
and commissioned us to serve
in a world of physical and spiritual starvation.
Heal our eyes that lust for luxury
and do not see the plight of the poor.
Tune our ears to their cries
for they are the cries of your own heart.
Help us, O God of justice.*

*Teach us how to be poor.
Take our purses and possessions.*

Like the cattle on a thousand hills
they all are yours.
And take us, Lord,
take our whole personalities
for your service.

Take our hearts and love through them.
Take our minds and think through them.
Take our voices and speak through them.
Take our hands and help through them.
Take our feet and walk through them.
Lord, take even the pains we have suffered
and make them do their creative work in our lives
all for your purpose and for your praise.
Amen.

Women's gifts

I was scheduled to read my psalm on the day when a resolution was going to be presented to the conference, urging the use of all gifts in the church regardless of age, sex, class, or race. An example of the problem: mine was the only female name on the program of the whole Virginia Conference Assembly that year.

During the morning session Bruce Yoder, a young pastor from Richmond, came to me with a copy of his statement to the resolution committee. The day before we had discussed the use of women's gifts and the resolution, which said, in part, "We resolve to encourage the stewardship, celebration, and commitment of all gifts of all persons for all ministries of the church regardless of age, race, sex, or economic status."

In the afternoon session an edited version was presented to the conference by the resolutions committee, but without the words "regardless of age, race, sex, or economic status." I believed it was providential that I had seen Bruce's draft and noted that the words were missing. So when moderator Glendon Blosser asked for discussion, I felt free to suggest that the missing words be restored. Someone objected, saying "the conference is not ready for that."

Alvin Kanagy, pastor at Weavers Mennonite Church, said, "I think that is what Ruth is saying, that the conference has not been ready for it but should be ready. Is that right, Ruth?" Before I could answer, a man farther back said, "Amen!"

I said, "Amen, Amen."

Glendon Blosser was able to satisfy both sides by saying, "This does not speak to the question of ordination." The resolution was passed with the missing words included.

I felt that a little progress had been made even though these words were omitted from the resolution: "to encourage . . . all gifts of all persons for all ministries of the church." I told the conference, "The Virginia conference is not as up-to-date as the Bible on this question." I cited the way Jesus affirmed Mary, who was different from her sister Martha. I said that I had once told my four sisters, "The time I feel good is when I get up to speak," and they said, "You are no sister of ours!" Then I heard myself say (released, I thought, by the power of the Spirit from previous church-inspired inhibitions), "If God gave me the gift of speaking, then I want to speak."

A couple of months later I read an article about Catherine Booth, co-founder of the Salvation Army. After giving her first lecture, she wrote, "Indeed I felt quite at home on the platform, far more so than I do in the kitchen!"

Ordination?

My friend Angie Williams stopped by one day in September and while we were talking, she raised the question of ordination. She said that Daniel Yutzy, the academic dean at EMC, had raised the question with her. "I told him I wouldn't consider it unless Ruth Brunk Stoltzfus and Grace Jones are ordained," she said.

I wrote in my journal:

> I am sixty-three. The church has not been ready to ordain a woman with the gift of speaking (proclaiming God's message). I have had plenty of work (speaking) to do—in a sense having had to build my own platform in order to do so. It seems God has blessed my feeble efforts. I do not see my role as being that of sole pastor of a church. Maybe ordination is not the best as it has connotations of elitism in spite of the talk that it is servanthood.
>
> Maybe I have more freedom to "speak the truth in love" without being ordained. The $64 question: should a person proceed in a speaking ministry when the church has not recognized and commissioned the gift? Am I on safe ground if after I launched out on my own then individual pastors called me into their churches and many church members and planning committees affirmed my gift?
>
> Can we say that ideally the church calls out the gift, but if it does

not, then the person follows a personal sense of calling without the blessing of the church originally and without the call of the local church ever? I wonder.

Who killed woman's gift?

At a Women in Ministry Conference held that October at Akron (Pa.) Mennonite Church, I spoke on "Women in ministry among Mennonites in my lifetime." I had unusual audience response. It was like a good movie as we laughed and cried together. I shared my poem *Who Killed Woman's Gift?* a paraphrase of the classic nursery rhyme *Who Killed Cock Robin?*

> *Who killed woman's gift?*
> *"I," said the man of terror*
> *With his mix of truth and error.*
> *"I'd rather not hear the word of truth*
> *"Than to hear it from a Jane or Ruth.*
> *"I killed woman's gift."*
>
> *Who saw her gift die?*
> *"I," said the woman who only knits.*
> *"These ministering women give me fits.*
> *"Why can't all women be of the same mold*
> *"And just look out the window*
> *"When they are old?*
> *"I saw her gift die."*
>
> *Who'll be chief mourner?*
> *"I," said the freeing man*
> *"I never favored the put-down and ban.*
> *"Women should not wait till they're 63*
> *"To see if the church will set them free.*
> *"I'll be chief mourner."*

I received more affirmation than at any other time in my life, and it felt good. I saw divine prompting and timing at work again and again. The best part of the conference was being in the midst of women who knew what I meant when I talked about a speaking ministry for women.

After I returned home, I sent my list of Bible references that spoke to women's work, worth, and role to conference leaders and offered it to readers of *Gospel Herald*. I had compiled the list to show that heresies start by building a doctrine on one or two verses while ignoring the many other verses. This, to me, was not only going against the main thrust of the Bible, but responsible for the heresies in our church that restricted the use of women's gifts, particularly the gift of proclaiming God's message.

Chapter 32

Paving the Way

Harrisonburg, Virginia
November 1978–July 1981

My brothers and sisters in the church and in my biological family didn't know what to do with me and my God-given gift of speaking, which I now openly acknowledged. I spoke of my father's encouragement of my gift at the annual meeting of the *Sword and Trumpet*, the journal my father had founded, where the new biography of Papa was officially released.

Our family had commissioned Mennonite theologian and historian John C. Wenger to research and write the biography of our father, and Hubert Pellman, my nieces Audrey Shank and Emily Shenk, my brother George, and I did editing and rewriting. *Faithfully, Geo. R.*, was published by the *Sword and Trumpet* on October 1, 1978, in time for their annual meeting at Lindale Church, where Papa and Mama first met.

I wrote in my journal, "It was the nearest thing to looking into the face of a new child when I saw for the first time the book about my father."

Legacies

Allen and Anne's fourth child, Susanna Joy, was born on December 1, 1978. Her big sister Katie told me, "Grandma, it came out today!"

On January 17, 1979, John Fairfield called and said, "Grandma, I'm holding a baby boy in my arms." I was concerned that the baby had come early, but John said he was "well done." They named him Nathaniel James Stoltzfus Fairfield.

Our children and grandchildren were one legacy of Grant's life. Another was the Grant M. Stoltzfus memorial scholarship, set up in January 1979 at Eastern Mennonite College. With money from investments I established a fund for a student to do studies and write a paper in an area of Grant's concerns: church-state relations, peace issues, social concerns, or male-female issues. This would be a way to continue Grant's work and influence. I felt commissioned to champion the causes he believed in and worked for.

The family likeness

An issue close to Grant's heart and mine was simple living. Music in worship at Park View Church became a point of contention when some of us objected to having a paid music minister and the purchase of a pipe organ. I also raised questions about making decisions by majority vote rather than consensus.

I hoped and prayed that the plans would be thwarted, but the organ was approved by a vote of sixty percent of the congregation. The minority was being treated as if their objection was opinion, and not conviction, I said, and the spending of $35,465 for a pipe organ was extravagant when 12,000 to 15,000 people were starving to death daily.

I expressed my convictions in a response to Doris Longacre, who had asked me to contribute to *More-with-Less Living,* a sequel to her best-selling *More-with-Less Cookbook:*

> I need not claim to belong to the Lord unless "being saved" includes being saved from affluence and insensitivity to children who suffer— unless I engage in concrete ways to help. 1 John 3:17 hits home. "If anyone has material possessions and sees his brother in need but has no pity on him, how can the love of God be in him?" That speaks to me as a parent. If my child sees other children of mine in need and does not help them, he need not come home, kiss me, and say, "I love you, Mother." He need not bother.
>
> God means for me to bring my thinking and helping down to personal terms. Suppose my grandchildren were among the thousands starving to death today? (Each day most of the starving thousands are children, victims of an unjust world system.) These are some of my thoughts that back the regular donations for food and projects for the hungry channeled through Mennonite Central Committee. There are regular donations for spiritual food, the distribution of the Bible, so that my efforts are not "all in one basket." I am a member of Bread for the World, a Christian citizens' movement advocating legislation favorable to the world's hungry. This means writing letters to a man by the name of Jimmy Carter and other U.S. officials, asking support for specific bills or issues. Small efforts, but I would want someone doing

them for me and mine. (If I am starving, forget the arguments, PLEASE, about voting and speaking to governments.)

Again, in personal terms, suppose it were my daughter arrested in the Philippines while working (with peasants) toward a master's degree in rural sociology? Suppose she were reported missing and torture was suspected? As a member of Amnesty International's Urgent Action group, I wrote letters to the President of the Philippines, his wife, and the Secretary of Defense. Among other things I felt moved to say, "I have a daughter about the age of Jessica M. Sales. . . . May we all work for her to be treated as a person of dignity, just as we would want our own daughter or son to be treated." In some such letters I felt led to close with the words, "In the name of the Father, and of the Son, and of the Holy Ghost. Amen."

What I do is so little. God help us to be His faithful sons and daughters showing the family likeness.

We start a shelter

In a survey of domestic violence in the Harrisonburg area, 158 out of the 327 women that responded reported abuse. They said shelter and counseling were their greatest needs. They knew, and their husbands knew, that they had nowhere to go. Intervention was needed so the battering cycle would not be perpetuated into another generation. Ruthie's Legal Aid office and a local task force got involved. Ruthie and I decided that the apartment above my office could be made available, for a few months at least, in order to get a shelter started in the community. So for three months in 1979, thirty women and children took refuge in the Shelter for Abused Women, as we called the two-bedroom apartment.

The project was a community effort. An organization was formed called First Step: A Response to Family Violence, Inc. This group coordinated the operation of the shelter with support from local churches and civic groups while planning for a permanent location for the shelter. Women who needed help were referred through a telephone hotline and the Community Services Council. Volunteers screened applicants and helped them connect with legal aid, welfare assistance, and other social services. The address was kept confidential and the sheriff was alerted to patrol the area regularly.

Twelve women and eighteen children took refuge in the apartment, as many as thirteen people at once. Most of the women who came had been beaten by their husbands. They stayed only two or three weeks, just long enough to relocate or get assurance, sometimes through the courts, that they could live safely in their own homes.

After both bedrooms in the shelter were occupied, plus the living room which we had quickly converted into a bedroom by placing mattresses on the floor, a woman and her four children needed to come. The women already in the apartment knew that these new arrivals would mean uncomfortable crowding. They also knew what it was like to be beaten, so they said yes, let them come. The five new arrivals slept on the floor in the kitchen and hall until private homeowners opened their doors. To the newcomers the women said, "You are free here. Don't worry. You will get help."

There were many late-night therapy sessions upstairs as these women, belonging to a sisterhood of pain, talked and listened to each other. Each of the women told me her painful story bit by bit as I checked things upstairs or they came down to talk or use the telephone, washer, and dryer. More than one was abused in both her childhood and marriage. Most of the abusive husbands and fathers had a drinking problem. Most grew up in homes where the father beat the mother. I was never more grateful for my secure childhood and good marriage.

Another call for shelter came from an unexpected source. While I was visiting Allen and Anne in Lancaster in March, we heard the news of an accident at Three Mile Island, the nuclear power plant near Harrisburg. It was decided that I should take the four grand-babies home with me: Baby Susanna, four months; Katie, three; Reuben, five; and Laura, ten. I drove back with them on Saturday, March 31, and they stayed through Wednesday, when Anne's sister, Sally Jo Hess, drove them back to Lancaster.

Even though the grandchildren's visit was exhausting, I was glad to help. But what could be done for the little ones and their mothers upstairs in the shelter, whose needs continued?

Rough road ahead

At Mennonite Church General Assembly 79 in Waterloo, Ontario, I was elected to the Council on Faith, Life and Strategy, a long-range planning and listening committee for the church. At that assembly I also participated in workshops and led responsive readings during worship sessions. As people affirmed my leadership, I felt certain that I was a minister who just happened not to be ordained.

In November I attended the fourth Women in Ministry conference, held at Elkhart, Indiana. Between sessions Lloyd Weaver Jr., a Virginia Conference leader, said he was open to change in the conference on women in ministry, not as sole pastors, but as members of a team.

Conversation about women in ministry with other leaders alerted me to the rough road ahead for women with a call to a speaking ministry. I prayed to God for strength to work for necessary change with caution and with charity.

Paving the way

In May, after I gave a series of talks in Ohio, Sue Clemmer Steiner of Kitchener, Ontario, a seminary student who was in the audience, wrote, "I want to acknowledge that we younger women (I'm 33) could not be doing what we are if people like yourself had not gone on before. We have few enough models!"

I acknowledged my role as one who was paving the way for younger women, and then I told her, "We need each other in the struggle for more necessary change."

Later, in 1982–1983, when I was interim pastor at Grace Mennonite Church, Pandora, Ohio, I promoted Sue's book, *Joining the Army That Sheds No Blood*. In the book she challenges teenagers to consider what Jesus said about violence, war, and enemies. In 1987 Sue Clemmer Steiner was ordained to the ministry in Eastern Canada Mennonite Conference.

Saying no

I was part of a group at Park View Church that supported Andre Gingerich and Luke Hurst Jr., in their conscientious objection to registering for the draft. Some people, including my nephew Gerald, thought the constitution prohibited conscription in peacetime. Gerald told me about a discussion at Weavers Mennonite Church in which several young men asked the older people, "We have been discussing the question of giving our bodies for the military. What about giving dollars for the military?"

In July 1980 I participated with a local group called Christians for Peace at a presence at the Harrisonburg Post Office. I stood at a pick-up truck displaying a banner about fifteen feet long that said "Questions about registration?" I gave out literature and entered into conversations with passersby and participated in a service of singing and Bible reading on the steps of the post office.

One day my friend Gail Nardi, a reporter for WSVA radio news, came by with a tape recorder, and at her invitation I said for the broadcast audience, "Registration always leads to the draft, and the draft always leads to war. I want to read a poem on war written by my father, George R. Brunk, in 1931":

> *A strange delusion blinds the public mind*
> *Having long forgot the angels' Christmas song*
> *They dedicate their sons to the god of war.*

Another day a young woman came for literature for her boyfriend, saying, "He recently became a Christian and I told him, 'I don't see how you can be a Christian and go into the military.'"

When I asked Kathie what I should say if some of my disapproving relatives drove by when I was with the non-cooperators, she said, "Tell them, 'Hi, come on in the fiery furnace with the young men. This is where the Lord is.'"

That summer Kathie was studying for the Virginia bar. She got her law degree preparation done before the baby came, had weekend guests who left October 19, and on October 21, 1981, Peter Baskin Brunk Fairfield was born.

In July 1981, I had met with Christians for Peace to help plan another witness on the steps of the post office, where young men were being called to register for the draft. In between rounds of babysitting the grandchildren, I made a poster to carry in the march. On it I wrote, "Grandmothers of All Nations Say No to War!" and added pictures of babies and small children.

After a time of talking to passersby and giving out literature, we marched to the cannon in front of Harrisonburg High School. I felt uncomfortable, as I had the year before, but being faithful was more important than being comfortable.

Saying yes

The gifts discernment committee at Park View Church asked if I would serve as an elder for a term of three years, and after prayer and consulting with my family, I agreed. On July 11, the dated page of my devotional book seemed directed at me as I weighed the matter:

> Don't be afraid, for the Lord will go before you and will be with you; he will not fail nor forsake you. . . . God has said, "I will never, never fail you or forsake you." That is why we can say without any doubt or fear, "The Lord is my helper and I am not afraid of anything that mere man can do to me. Our only power and success comes from God."

Chapter 33

"For Such a Time as This"

Bowling Green, Ohio
August 1981

I never thought I would live to see what happened at Mennonite Church Assembly on August 13, 1981. A motion passed requesting that "General Board appoint a committee to study and facilitate the process of full participation of women in leadership ministries of the church."

During the week-long assembly at Bowling Green, Ohio, Thursday afternoon, August 13 was set for the report on the study guide, "Leadership and Authority in the Church," with discussion to follow. As a member of the Council on Faith, Life and Strategy, I was part of a listening committee sitting near the front. I placed myself not far from one of the mikes on the floor, in case I would feel moved to speak on the question of women in leadership.

My nephew George, chairman of the Council, had reported to us on the pre-assembly sessions, including the expectation that there would be some rough times the day the leadership study was discussed. When Marlin Miller, president of Goshen Biblical Seminary, and the rest of the committee who had worked on the leadership study were called to the platform, photographer Mike Hostetler, sitting next to me, said, "You should be up there." Later I knew my place was near a floor mike.

A number of women and men spoke on the question of women's role in the church. After waiting, praying, jotting a few notes, and leafing through some sheets from my quote book, taken along for use in a later workshop, I felt the time had come to go to a microphone. While waiting for the young woman to my far left to finish, I begged the Lord to guide my words. They came out thus (as near as I could remember later).

I do not agree with the statement by Adela Rogers St. Johns, "God made man, took a good look and said, 'I can do better than that.'" I believe in equality too much for that.

The statement is something to laugh about, but if women plastered it all over the world, taught it to all their children, saw to its teaching in all the books, schools, and churches over the land, it would be no worse than the heresy of the superiority of men that has cursed the world and the church for centuries.

A heresy begins when a doctrine is based on one or two Bible verses and violates the teaching of other verses on the subject. The way some verses in the Bible are translated tells more about the sex of the translator than about the role of women. In both the King James and Revised Standard Versions, Genesis 6:1 says that men began to multiply on the earth and daughters were born to them.

I get the feeling that somebody left something out. Today's English Version uses the term mankind, which seems a little better.

It is interesting that the verse Ephesians 6:4, "And, ye fathers, provoke not your children to wrath: but bring them up in the nurture and admonition of the Lord," is interpreted in such a way as to exclude men from home duties, and Romans 12 and 1 Corinthians 12 are interpreted in such a way as to exclude women from the use of their gifts in the church.

For their best emotional development, children need the close association of their fathers, their actual care, not just the things their money will buy.

In 1 Corinthians 12 on the use of gifts, verse 15 talks about "I am not needed," and that sounds like an inferiority complex. Verse 21 talks about "You are not needed," and that sounds like a superiority complex.

There is so much to be said on this. I do not ask the Lord what to say, but what to leave out.

Women are no greater ministers than when they are wives and mothers. Men are no greater ministers than when they are husbands and fathers. But women's work should not be limited to the home any more than men's work should be limited to the home. "Man does not live by bread alone," and I say that woman does not live by baking the bread alone.

Some people think that woman exists to serve man. The Bible teaches that she is to serve with man. There is a big difference. Both men and women are needed to share responsibilities in both the home and the church.

As soon as I sat down a female reporter from the *Toledo Blade* came and got my name and address from the tag I was wearing.

After a number of men and women had spoken, the assembly

delegates voted to accept the study document, "Leadership and Authority in the Life of the Church" as printed in the assembly workbook. A separate motion was then brought and passed by majority vote "that the General Board appoint a committee to study and facilitate the process of full participation of women in the leadership ministries of the church."

At the close of the meeting, something seemed to break loose. The newspaper reporter was at my side asking for an interview. People came to me, men as well as women, with strong affirmation. From that Thursday afternoon until the last assembly session on Sunday morning, some eighty-seven people (more men than women) came to me at mealtime or stopped me on the sidewalk or talked to me before, during, or after sessions.

I said to some of those who commented, "I do not ask the Lord what to say. I ask him what to leave out." But I had prayed *hard* for guidance.

My critics did not approach me. I was to learn of some of their comments later. A Lancaster Conference pastor told me of one critic who spoke to him while still upset. "But that is the tail of a snake that is dying," the pastor said.

In the Saturday morning session the motion on women was clarified. Conference and congregations could recognize the preaching gifts of women if they were ready to do so, was my interpretation. But they could block things if they wished.

On the ride home, Virginia Conference leader Samuel Weaver said, "You are forty years ahead of your time."

PART SEVEN

INTERIM PASTOR
1981–1983

Chapter 34

A Nice Surprise

Harrisonburg, Virginia
August 1981–January 1982

I would not know until later the significance of going to give talks at Elida, Ohio, in April 1981. "You could fly to Toledo," the planning committee advised, "and then travel by car with women driving to Elida for our annual meeting of the Ohio Women's Missionary and Service Commission (WMSC).

After the WMSC sessions were over, we returned to Toledo, and on Sunday morning I went with my host and hostess, Clayton and Wilma Bender, to their church, Bancroft Mennonite. Inside the church door I was greeted warmly by veteran churchman A. J. Metzler, who was serving as interim pastor.

"You should be in the pulpit this morning," he said to me. When I declined, he asked me to lead a responsive reading and a closing prayer. At the noon meal, Clayton mentioned that A. J.'s term as interim pastor would soon end and the pastoral search committee on which he served was looking for another interim pastor.

"Do you want a woman preacher?" I asked, half joking.

"Would you consider it?" he wondered.

"I would be willing to think and pray about it," I said.

"I think the congregation would accept an older woman as pastor better than a young woman," Clayton said.

It seemed that God was springing a nice surprise on me. A few weeks later, Jay Martin of the ministerial search committee asked if I would consider coming as interim pastor to Bancroft Mennonite.

As I pondered the request, I read on the dated page of my devotional:

Be glad for all God is planning for you (Romans 12:12). Because of our faith, he has brought us into this place of highest privilege where we now stand, and we confidently and joyfully look forward to actually becoming all that God has in mind for us to be (Romans 5:2).

My brothers and sisters respond

I felt sure of God's leading as friends and family and church officials confirmed my call. The Park View Church elders said I could take a leave and continue as elder when I returned.

My nephew George said, "Judging by what happened at Bowling Green 81 (Mennonite Church General Assembly), the church seems ready for women to participate more fully in leadership ministries."

My niece Audrey Shank was concerned that I do more than speak on the woman question. "It would go over better if you were a co-pastor, not sole pastor," she said, "not managing things too much. Do Bible preaching. Preach Christ."

"Most of my spoken and written messages have been on Bible themes," I replied, "and I could hardly give every sermon for six months on the use of women's gifts—though that was an important teaching in the Bible!" We both laughed.

As to being sole pastor and "managing things too much," I would be part of a team of elders and council members.

My sisters loved and respected me in spite of our differing viewpoints. One said, "Papa would not want you to be a pastor."

I replied that Papa, a conservative who was progressive for his time, had groomed me to be a public speaker, but admittedly he did not think a woman should be a pastor. Could not my service in the church be a speaking ministry?

Another sister said, "Call yourself deaconess or something else besides pastor."

I answered that we must first look at what gift God has given to be used in the church, not whether the person is male or female, and I would not call the role something other than what it was.

A third sister said, "Yes, go."

Three of my four brothers (all preachers) gave differing answers.

Truman said, "If a congregation calls her and she feels the conviction, I approve of a woman being a pastor. These days a pastor is under the elders or other church officials anyway." He continued, "Twenty-five years ago in Sicily I ordained Franca as a deaconess, but she was really the leader of the church." He also advised,

"Don't go to Ohio and make a lot of the woman question."

"I had already decided not to do that," I told him.

I knew that Menno would say the opposite. My daughters advised, "You should go and talk to him. He's your brother." I went.

"You have gone in a wrong direction, and you know it," he said. "I don't believe God gives the gift of leadership to any woman."

I asked if he knew about the women in Old and New Testament who were leaders despite the fact that women were considered far inferior to males, and I named them.

He cautioned me strongly to never get up and speak in a pulpit unless it was under the authority of a man. We parted knowing that love was not destroyed, but differences were sharp.

My brother George called me about another matter and then said, "A little bird told me you have been approached about being an interim pastor in an Ohio church." He went on to say that "prophesying" in church was all right, but that the New Testament pattern does not include ordination of women.

"Does it include the ordination of men?" I asked.

"Yes," he said.

"Where?" I asked.

"Timothy would be an example," he said.

"Paul had a lot to say about women's work," I said. "The title for Phoebe [who held office in the church] was translated *servant* in the Bible, while the same word in the original language was rendered *minister* for a man. Women had such a low status in that time that Paul had to cater to it rather than to split up the church. But he still did an incredible thing to teach equality in that time and culture. And he expected that principle of equality to bring about changes, just as he did for slavery."

George said he had a book I ought to read. "The author is an active church woman who does not believe in ordination," he said.

"I'm reading a book better than that," I told him. "It tells about women in Old and New Testament times who were leaders even when the status of women was shamefully low."

"I think the time will come when you will change on this question," George answered. "Even if I do not agree with you, I appreciate you and your gifts. The Lord bless you."

The call

When Jay Martin called on September 23, I said I would be open to serving as the church would decide. I would be reluctant to accept if the vote was less than eighty percent.

That night I prayed, "O God, lead in clear ways." On the dated page of my devotional guide I read:

> Moses said to the Lord, "guide me clearly along the way you want me to travel so that I will understand you and walk acceptably before you." And the Lord replied, "I myself will go with you and give you success."

The voting at Bancroft was heavy on my mind, but my heart was not heavy. I prayed, "O God, take over the voting. Your will, not mine be done. And not the will of my (biological) brothers and sisters, though I love and respect them and would not trade them for any set of brothers and sisters in the wide world!"

The congregational vote was eighty-four percent affirmative, forty-three favorable out of fifty-one. When Jay Martin reported the results, I said, "At the risk of seeming to take myself too seriously, I do feel a mandate to consent, among other reasons, to help bring about necessary change for other women in the church."

A conversation with Ward

My brother-in-law Bishop J. Ward Shank and his wife, my sister Stella, were able to express a differing view in the spirit of love. About this time Ward and I had a conversation that I recorded in my journal:

> *Ward:* You definitely have the gift of speaking—more than I do. Our daughter Audrey has it also. But there is to be a limitation of the use of gifts.
> *Ruth:* What chapter and verse in the Bible would support that idea of limitation?
> *Ward:* The verses on silence for women.
> *Ruth:* I do not know of any teaching in the Old or New Testament to the effect that gifts are to be limited. In 1 Corinthians 2, Paul gave instructions to prophesying women in those verses having to do with propriety in public worship. Then in 1 Corinthians 14 (in the very same letter) he spoke about "noisy women needing to be silenced." I believe these were two different sets of women and one set had nothing

whatsoever to do with the other. Yet, men have built a doctrine of silence on the one or two verses on silence while ignoring all the other verses in the Bible on prophesying and leading. And they push "headship" so far that not only is God male but male is God!

Ward: It is the feeling in the family that this question has become an obsession with you.

Ruth: Audrey intimated that to me. I have made a special study of the question for forty-four years. At age twenty-two I came home one evening from teaching in the public school and read a column in a Presbyterian paper about the Bible verses on silence for women, and how they need to be reconciled with the many verses on women in leadership. That was the beginning of a long study, and it has been a specialty with me.

Ward: We think that you are being used as a tool by the liberal element of the church.

Ruth: Ward, a member of the pastoral search committee at the Bancroft Mennonite Church contacted me before Bowling Green. You must understand that it has been a long pilgrimage. I see my going to Bancroft Mennonite Church as a time of service to the people and, as my daughter Kathie says, a time of growth for me. I also see it as a part of the process for necessary change in the wider church. I think there is a kind of bereavement that men experience when they find out that there is no biblical basis for their superiority. I think that is the core of these problems.

Ward: Now you are getting impassioned.

Ruth: Let me ask if you would get "impassioned" if you knew God gave you the gift for a speaking ministry and you were not allowed to use the gift because of some physical characteristic like your eyes being the wrong color, if you were asked to bury your gift, to quench the Spirit. It is a law of mental and spiritual health that we should use the gifts God has given us. We should look at what gift God has given a person, not the sex of the person.

Church leaders respond

James and Arlene Stauffer, pastoral leaders at Weavers Mennonite Church spoke words of encouragement about my going to Bancroft. At the same time, James told me, "You come on strong."

"I feel that men have been acculturated to prefer women to act weak," I told him, "and even strive for incompetence. I need to be careful that I do not threaten them. At Bancroft I want to have males and females serving together and have a man as worship leader each time I have the message, not because of any superiority or special sacredness of the male sex."

I made an appointment with Glendon Blosser, a bishop in Virginia Conference. As former moderator of General Assembly, Glendon had a view of the wider church, and as former moderator of Virginia Conference, a view of things nearer home. He said, "Just go and do it. You do not have to prove you are right." He said we needed to rethink ordination, that it was not positional (illustrating by his hands held vertically) but functional (illustrating by his hands held horizontally).

My daily devotional book that day had the paraphrase, "They began to argue among themselves as to who would have the highest rank." In the margin I could not resist writing, "Who is the greatest? That question is still being asked—which man is the greatest and which sex is the greatest."

My nephew Truman Jr., said, "You will have to look to the younger generation for most of your affirmation. With people who say, 'You have gone in a wrong direction and you know it,' you must forgive them before they even start to talk. Don't let them spoil this exciting part of your life. I'm as sure of this for you as I am of my own ministry. In the Bible, whenever there was any change there was always conflict."

Helpful advice

At the December monthly meeting of Christians for Peace, Eastern Mennonite Seminary professor Ed Stoltzfus said to me, "Maybe you will be interim pastor at other places, too. You are sixty-six? You have ten more good years."

When I confided to him my secret ambition to be the Grandma Moses in the art of preaching, Ed counseled, "Do good preaching, do visitation, be involved in church administration—not in a bossy way."

After I got home, I called Ed for more help. "Over the years I have spoken many times on Christian family relationships. What part could that theme have in my sermons at Bancroft Mennonite?"

"Use your strengths in your messages," he said.

I told him, "For months before Bancroft Mennonite contacted me, I was working on sermon outlines, not knowing where I would be using them. But what counsel do you have on whether to take a topic or a passage for a message?"

"Use both methods," he suggested. "If it works out that you can use a passage, fine, but I have no problem with using topics."

I explained my method and asked for advice. "With topics I use passages, for example, Ephesians 5 and 6 on family relationships. What about tools? I have studied different versions of the Bible and have had the Tyndale commentaries for years. The family has Grant's four-volume set of the *Interpreter's Dictionary of the Bible.* I have *Halley's Bible Handbook* and other study books. Do I need to invest in other tools?"

"You might buy a book now and then," he said, "but no, don't make any big investment."

"What a lift it is to get this counsel from Ed, a seasoned, warm-hearted, loyal pastor and seminary professor," I wrote in my journal, "especially since I am not free to ask those who do not believe a woman should be a pastor."

At the December 15 elders meeting at Park View, I sought more advice, asking what material I should have for a wedding or funeral or taking in members. Pastor Owen Burkholder showed me his *Worship Manual,* a binder with five booklets: "Planning Congregational Worship," "Baptism and Church Membership," "The Celebration of the Lord's Supper," "Celebrating Christian Marriage," and "Funerals and Funeral Planning." I went to the Eastern Mennonite College book store and bought the whole set for $14.10.

Sam Weaver, executive secretary of Virginia Conference, affirmed my calling and asked what the conference could do to recognize women's gifts.

I said they could confront men who needed to change. I thought I spoke for a lot of women when I said, "We did not want status, but freedom to speak what the Spirit tells us to speak. I have been a church woman since age fifteen, and something is wrong, either with Virginia Conference or with me, that Virginia Conference officially has nothing to do with me."

In a kind way Sam said I threatened men. I answered that I refused to strive to be incompetent, and that the men would have to grow up.

"Can I give you a little advice?" he asked. "Don't say a lot about the woman question when you are at Bancroft."

The next day my nephew Paul Brunk said to me, "Only one thing is wrong, Aunt Ruth. You were born thirty years too soon."

"I was born for such a time as this," I said, "to be a part of the process of necessary change that is to come in the church. I realize I am saying this at the risk of sounding like I take myself too seriously. But I thank God for his providential hand—and I am having a good time! Male preachers have had a greased highway," I told him, "and I have had briers and brickbats and obstacles along my preaching path. But if people meant it for harm, 'God meant it for good.'"

Ruthie's wedding

On January 2, 1982, Ruthie and Timothy Jost were married at Weavers Church. My brother Truman performed the ceremony. Timothy's brothers, David and John, provided the music. I preached the wedding sermon, as Ruthie had requested when she told me in October that she and Timothy were planning to marry.

"Timothy is unassuming, like Daddy," she had said. "You and Daddy had intellectual and spiritual stimulation and companionship in your marriage." Timothy was a law professor at the Ohio State University School of Law, and, like Ruthie, he had worked in legal services.

The commissioning

On Sunday evening, January 17, 1982, a service was held at Park View Mennonite to commission me as interim pastor at Bancroft Mennonite. Owen Burkholder gave the invocation and greeting. My nephew George gave the meditation.

In his opening comments George mentioned that this was the first commissioning of a woman to pastoring in Virginia Mennonite Conference. He said, "If God enabled a man to be both father and mother to God's people, can he not enable a woman to be both father and mother?" Addressing words directly to me, he said, "'Know how to conduct yourself in the household of God.' This was the first text of your father at Virginia Conference. We have the distinct impression that this is not a new commission. It is a recognition of achievement in ministry already made and encouragement for future ministry."

When Owen called for my "Response and Vision," I reviewed the steps leading up to this commissioning and spoke of feeling as never before a need for my brothers and sisters in the church. Then Harold Eshleman, Harrisonburg District overseer, gave the charge:

This congregation, the Harrisonburg District, the Virginia Conference, and indeed the church at large have these many years greatly appreciated your ministry, a ministry that has also been a blessing to many Christian congregations and groups of other denominations. We see your ministry in the Bancroft Mennonite Church as a continuation of that ministry. You have in past years ministered on occasion to this congregation.

Your responsibilities during these coming months will be somewhat different in nature, but as you serve in response to the call of the Bancroft congregation and under the leading of the Holy Spirit, we want to assure you of our prayers as you seek to be a faithful witness in declaring God's eternal truth and in ministering to the needs of God's children and all whom the Lord may call.

We charge you to be a faithful servant in using the spiritual gifts God has given you as you minister to the Bancroft congregation, assuming such spiritual responsibilities as the congregation is calling you to assume.

Ruth, do you in the presence of Christ, in the presence of Kenton Miller representing the Bancroft congregation, and in the presence of this your home congregation, promise to accept faithfully this charge?

I answered, "I do." The congregation responded, and Harold invited my family and anyone else from the audience to come up for the laying on of hands. The hands on my arms and shoulders felt wonderful.

Harold called on me to pray first. I felt moved to pray, "O Father, it is in you that we live and move and have our being. Thank you for your love that sent Jesus to be our Savior. Thank you that he loved us enough to die for us. We just want to give your message."

John Martin, Paul Yoder, and others led in prayer. Then Harold laid his hand on my shoulder and prayed. He mentioned Grant, thanking God for his contribution to my life and to the church. After his prayer he shook my hand and put his arm around me and I put my arm around him. I then turned and hugged my family and about everyone else who had come up front.

Chapter 35

Interim Pastor, Bancroft Mennonite Church

Toledo, Ohio
January–June 1982

Letter to my family and friends, January 25

I am well settled in a nice, clean, tight, warm, well-built, well-furnished, two-story, two-bedroom parsonage just eight steps from the Bancroft Mennonite Church, Toledo, Ohio. Stan Nickel, a pharmacist and chairman of the church council, helped me unload my car, and then he and his wife took me out to eat. I learned from them that the widow of Bancroft's first pastor had died and there would be two funerals the next day, one at a funeral home in Toledo, and one at Lockport Mennonite Church, thirty-five miles away. With their encouragement I attended both. At times I was introduced as "the new minister at Bancroft."

After consulting the elders, I decided to change the sermon I had planned, in accordance with what I had been feeling and teaching, that when a death occurs it would be good to speak on death and life after death. From 2:00 to 4:30 a.m. Sunday I added to and subtracted from my notes on "Death, Burial, and the Grieving Process" that I had used just days earlier at the Keystone Bible Institute in Lansdale, Pennsylvania.

The benediction was from Romans 15:13 and inspired my own heart: "May the God of hope fill you with all joy and peace as you trust in him, so that you may overflow with hope by the power of the Holy Spirit!"

I can hardly wait until next Sunday!

Journal entry, January 26

I must learn to say "Bancroft Mennonite Church" when I answer the church phone in the parsonage office. Toledo Hospital, one of many in this city of 500,000, called yesterday to report a man in intensive care. At the hospital I found a man who seemed to be in his seventies with an oxygen tube in his nostrils. I read Psalm 91, then prayed while holding his hand. Can a woman my age get by with this, or should I use the cold approach? He is beautifully black.

Journal entry, January 27

I can hardly wait until time to preach again next Sunday, even though the preparation is hard work. Since I am now interim pas-

At age 67 I became the interim pastor at Bancroft Mennonite in Ohio.

tor at Bancroft Mennonite, I have mustered up the courage to use the word "preach" once in a while, instead of the word "speak," but will need to be careful where I use it.

Journal entry, January 31

I was working to finalize my sermon—God, is it wrong to call it a sermon?—when Myron Bollman, chairman of the elders, called to say that church is canceled on account of the big snow.

Journal entry, February 1

This was to be my day off, and I treated it as such, except for two counseling sessions by phone—one made by me, one by a school teacher who feels beneath two other women because her house is not as spick-and-span as theirs. I could identify with her. I said, "Your specialty is teaching school. Respect that. If their specialty is keeping a perfect house, give them that freedom. But don't feel that every woman must have the same specialty."

Letter to family and friends, February 1

I came down to earth quickly this morning after calling Stella for a telephone visit. She told me that the *Sword and Trumpet* is coming out against ordination for women. Aunt Stella and I are always able to express love in spite of this difference. Ward was on the phone when I said, "No one has ordained me but the Lord. Human beings have commissioned me twice."

Flower Hospital called about a woman who gave Mennonite as her church affiliation when she was admitted. She is not a member here but I called her three times, prayed with her over the phone, and gave her a Bible verse to claim. She is a cancer patient who has had a lung removed.

A husband and wife came for counseling Thursday. A woman, age twenty-three, came to talk Friday afternoon and brought along her little daughter, age one.

Next Sunday my sermon will be entitled, "As It Is Written." I can't wait.

Journal entry, February 5

I called Myron Bollman to ask about the plowing of snow at the church. He said it would be taken care of and thanked me for thinking about it. It's easy to think about it because I want to give a message (preach) tomorrow. May the Lord forgive me if that is a sinful desire!

Letter to Harold Eshleman, February 5

You said something before the commissioning that I appreciate: "She came and talked to me about it and I approve of her going." That helps me bear the pain of coming here without the approval of most of my siblings. Truman and Edna in Denbigh approve, as do lots of nephews. Although George, Ward and Stella, Katie and John do not think a woman should be a pastor, they are magnanimous in affirming me and keeping up family connections.

Journal entry, February 7

Got awake at 3:30 a.m. Could not go back to sleep because sermon thoughts were on my mind.

Letter to family and friends, February 7

Before my sermon yesterday, I spoke to the children up front, some on the benches, some on the floor. I sat on a chair to be near their level. I said they reminded me of my seven grandchildren, and talked about Bible stories as the best stories. A little four-year-old boy piped up, "My daddy reads the funnies."

While I was reading the first story in book one of Eve MacMaster's *Story Bible Series*, little Aaron Plank, age three, came up to me, took hold of one side of the book and leaned against me. So dear. I put my arm around him and read on. To help the littlest ones sustain interest, I had them make the four rivers with their fingers and join into one big river in the middle of the Garden of Eden.

The elders and I stated in the bulletin that Friday, Saturday, and Sunday will be my half-time for the church; Monday my day off; Tuesday, Wednesday, Thursday my half-time for desk work for Harrisonburg responsibilities. "Only as a guide," we said, and I added, "Call on me any day and any time, day or night, if you need me."

I have never been happier in any kind of work.

Letter to George R. Brunk III, February 10

Thanks for the outline I requested of your meditation, "The Full

Humanity of Pastoring," given at my commissioning January 17, 1982. A complete article for the *Gospel Herald* would be of inestimable service to the church. You would know what *not* to say about me.

I am settled here in the parsonage just steps away from the Bancroft Mennonite Church (80 members, 120 attendance), a convenient arrangement, especially during these heavy snowfalls. Except for working with elders as the pastor, doing visitation in hospitals, and counseling more than usual, my work is little different from before. Giving messages in this one pulpit is much like what I have done since 1950. I enjoy it in spite of the hard work of preparation and see the giving of messages in the churches as a speaking ministry to which I have been called these thirty-two years.

Your approval has helped me bear the pain of coming here as interim pastor without the approval of all who love me.

Journal entry, February 11
I went over to the church at about 11:15 a.m. to take in the Women's Missionary and Service Commission (WMSC) program and eat the noon meal with the women who were working on quilts. Karen Rupp, president, said, "Sit down and quilt beside me."

I said, "I will watch you." My gifts are not in the quilting line. Her gifts are not in my line. I have long since stopped feeling bad about it.

Letter to family and friends, February 15
Mercy! I had an awful time finding the Mercy Hospital to visit a new mother and her baby. I had not expected that after the ten-mile trip the receptionist would say that maternity visiting hours would begin three hours later. When I told her my church connection and answered the question, "Are you of the clergy?" she let me go to the room. The beautiful two-day-old baby boy was in a bed beside his mother's. It felt good to be a pastor who knows the experiences of new motherhood and old.

That visit, and others totaling eighteen in person or by phone, reinforced in my mind what George said at my commissioning about "the full humanity of pastoring," both male and female ministry to the men and women in the church. Also what Ira Miller said before I left: "Preaching may be the least important thing a pastor does."

I miss everyone but am happy here. I know this is the work for me at this time and in this place. I feel deep thanks to God for his providence.

Letter to family and friends, February 26
At 4:00 p.m. on Monday, the neighborhood Bible study group (usually nine people) met here at the parsonage. I served doughnuts, tea, and orange juice. I'd rather serve the kind of diet that is from a pulpit!

Tuesday morning I made the one-hour trip to Archbold for a breakfast meeting of Northwest Ohio Mennonite ministers. Fourteen of us were men, one a woman. I knew a good many of them by being in their churches, and most went out of their way to say a friendly word to me.

Letter to family and friends, March 7
Attendance at church this morning was larger than usual, 112. My message was "Before the Child Arrives," one in a series on the

In the pulpit.

Christian family. The babies were quiet today, but last Sunday they all bawled until I stopped, and then they stopped.

I wanted to visit a mother and her new baby in the hospital, so I called for visiting hours and had the phone conversation of the week:

RBS (phoning Toledo Hospital): "What are the visiting hours on the maternity floor?"
Male Information Person: "Except for the father and grandparents, 7:30 to 8:30 in the evening."
RBS: "How about a pastor?"
MIP: "Anytime after 9:00 a.m. for the pastor, but not his wife."
RBS: "I am the pastor. I don't have a wife."

Letter to family and friends, March 21

Thursday I made the three-hour trip to Columbus and enjoyed being with Ruthie and Timothy. Also, Kathie, John, Joshua, Nathaniel, and Peter came from Harrisonburg. Friday morning, before leaving for Ohio Conference meetings at West Liberty, I consulted Kathie, John, and Ruthie about my worship meditation. They said, "Don't bring in the woman question." John said, "Just have worship." It was good advice. The audience responded well, and I felt the brothers and sisters were worshiping with me.

Journal entry, March 27

I worked with books and papers for a few hours, then took off at 8:15 a.m. for North Clinton Mennonite Church, Wauseon, Ohio, for a weekend of messages on the use of all gifts.

Journal entry, March 28

Early Sunday morning I was making final notes on my message, "Your Gift, Your Brother's, Your Sister's." I had put together two sets of triple statements about the Spirit giving gifts TO EACH ONE: "You are gifted, you are limited, I am needed. I am gifted, I am limited, you are needed." I felt free and comfortable during the presentation. Toward the close I led a verse of the song, "God is so good, he's so good to me," then improvised other verses in line with the theme.

Following the Sunday afternoon discussion, a father said that he told his young daughter, "There's your model," while I was speaking in the Sunday morning worship service.

As we chatted together afterwards, Pastor Bob Schloneger said a man had told him that he had not thought a woman should be in the pulpit, but after the Sunday morning service, "I had my eyes opened."

There were encouraging comments about my talks, but I never feel fully prepared before a talk or fully satisfied. Before a talk I ask God to take my heart, mind, voice, hands, feet—my whole personality—for his purpose. I am overwhelmed by his plan to use us poor humans, male or female, in his scheme of things. I believe he answers our need, enables and blesses in spite of our human weakness.

Journal entry, March 31

I feel guilty that I am not keeping up with visitation. To keep track of people I need to check on, I have made a list of names at the back of my journal.

A letter from daughter-in-law Pat tells about operating on a white mouse in physiology lab in her nursing classes, about Eugene's fixing the roof, and his architecture work and dreams. At the close she says, "I think you are going to have plenty of writing material when you get through with that experience. I hope my life will be as exciting as yours when I am sixty!"

Letter to family and friends, April 7

It's eleven degrees outside and we have nine inches of snow, with more predicted. Before the snow there were furious winds, "The beginning of the twister season," a radio report said. Branches and tree limbs were hurled to the ground, and since the parsonage yard is beside the church, I gathered up the debris before the Sunday service. Several times while driving I felt my car was about to lift off.

At last I am getting my fill of speaking engagements. I was able to say no to one church when two in the Archbold area asked me for the same evening!

So far I have kept a record of forty-two visiting or counseling sessions in person or by phone. More are needed. Like woman's work, it's never done.

Journal entry, April 9

Communion and foot washing service is Thursday night. My first—and probably last—experience in conducting such a service. I once conducted a communion service at Laurelville Mennonite Church Center, with mostly women (two ministers present), and had a communion message at a women's retreat.

Journal entry, April 14

Pastor Emma Richards called to ask what happened on the woman question at Ohio Conference annual meeting. She is chair of the committee appointed by Mennonite Church General Board "to study and facilitate the full use of women's gifts in the leadership ministries of the church."

She said several weeks ago Illinois Conference passed a resolution that persons in ministry will be chosen according to gifts and not according to sex! I thanked her for calling and said, "We radicals need to support each other."

Journal entry, April 25

I was at Lester and Martha Miller's for a hospitality evening. After the meal I washed the dishes while Martha put away food and dishes. Not all pastors feel guilty if they do not do dishes after dishing out a sermon.

Journal entry, April 26

Phoned Martha at St. Vincent's Hospital and told her I would visit her soon after she is out of the hospital. Phoned Alice, who returned recently from the Toledo Hospital and said I would call Wednesday to see if it is suitable to visit. Phoned Bonnie, whose grandmother died Saturday.

Journal entry, April 27

I went with Marge Grieser to the Central Mennonite women's salad supper and meeting near Archbold. Marge stopped to see her mother before the meeting. "She has read a lot of your writings and wants to meet you," she said. Marge's ninety-one-year-old mother reads, does handwork, and some work in the kitchen.

Of the 200 women at the meeting, half were guests from the community, many from other denominations. My assigned topic was "God's Promises." I spoke of having a balance between preaching and protesting (military madness of the nations, world hunger, torture, etc.), though I did not use the words "preaching" and "protesting." I said I had sent that day a letter to a man by the name of Ronald Reagan and read it to them: "Dear Mr. President, I send you the enclosed one dollar bill, no strings attached, to express my support for the Kennedy-Hatfield Senate Joint Resolution 163, calling for an immediate nuclear freeze by both the U.S. and the USSR."

Toward the close I came back to the theme of God's promises and said I felt led to make, in return, a promise to God. I invited the women to make their own promises as they felt led during a few moments of silence, and then I closed with this prayer of commitment:

> *Take our minds and think through them.*
> *Take our voices and speak through them.*
> *Take our hearts and love through them.*
> *Take our hands and help through them.*
> *Take our feet and walk through them.*

Many people came up to meet me afterwards. I got home late because the speaker was long-winded!

Journal entry, April 28

At 10:30 a.m. I left for the funeral of the grandmother of a member at Bancroft Mennonite. At 11:45 I went to Sveden House for the noon meal. At 1:30 p.m. I visited Alice, recently home from the hospital. After a nice conversation I read Psalm 46 and had prayer with her. At 2:15 p.m. I phoned ahead to Martha and went to visit her. At 3:00 p.m. I got back to the parsonage for a nap, a little time to take and make phone calls, write in this journal, and sweep the walks. Then I visited two motels and selected one for my last 15 days here, when Phil Ebersole, the permanent pastor and his family will occupy the parsonage.

Journal entry, April 29

Toward evening I drove to West Clinton Mennonite Church to have a ten-minute devotional at the Northwest Ohio Ministers' and Wives' Fellowship meal and meeting. (The group should be called Ministers' and Spouses' Fellowship.) On the way I thought that in addition to reading Psalm 46, "God is our refuge and strength, an ever present help in time of trouble," and testifying to the personal security I feel in God, I should confess the questions that haunt me about my (our) responsibility not to be silent on the military madness of our time if I love God and my neighbor.

At the meeting I said God would not let me have just a comforting devotional. That, in view of widespread hunger, torture, and military madness, I felt helpless to know what one person can do. I heard affirming and sympathetic groans by about three people at my end of the banquet table.

I told a parable of one snowflake that fell and broke a branch after 3,741,952 flakes had fallen, showing that one effort can make a difference. I read the letter I had written to Ronald Reagan, expressing support for the nuclear freeze. I gave the analogy of two angry men in a small room, both doused with gasoline, brandishing matches and threatening to strike and throw them on each other. "Arguing about who has the most matches is irrelevant," I said. "So it is with the superpowers."

After my closing prayer, Ellis Croyle, overseer of Bancroft Church, asked me, "Do you have a strong heart?"

I said, "Sometimes."

He said, "In line with your talk, some young people are waiting outside the door to speak with us about the nuclear weapons situation."

Three young people came in and spoke of their concerns for taking a stand against the military. They suggested that three people from the ministers' group be selected to meet with them. I enjoyed witnessing a good exchange between the young people and the ministers.

Journal entry, May 6

Today I spent five hours in Reynolds Corners library with a stack of books about as high as my head on the question of women and sexuality, in preparation for an article on inclusive sexuality, requested by the editor of *Daughters of Sarah* [a Christian feminist magazine edited by Reta Finger, a Mennonite].

Journal entry, May 8

I spent most of the day working on precisely made and precisely typed plans for the reception on Sunday of members transferring from another church and dedication of their six-month-old baby. This is my first experience of being in charge of transferring members and dedicating a baby. Was I ever glad I bought the booklets from the worship manual!

Journal entry, May 9

Preceding the sermon, David and Ann Weldy were received as members, transferring from the Mennonite Church of Aurora, Ohio. Then we had the dedication of their baby, John Isaac, six months old. It was incredible the way the baby looked at me when I gave him the words of blessing! Likewise, his brother Steven, four (standing by), when I also gave him words of blessing!

Journal entry, May 18

Josie Bollman came for me about 5:00 p.m. and we rode to the Mother-Daughter Banquet at North Leo Mennonite Church, Leo, Indiana, where I was to speak. After the salad supper, attended by 200, I prayed and weighed and decided to leave my notes in my purse and give a message from my heart on the question, "What is a woman's work?"

I opened by saying, "I should warn you that traditional-looking persons sometimes have untraditional ideas, even radical ideas—as radical as the Bible." At the end I called for those who mostly do housework to affirm those who do not, and for those who do not do mostly housework to affirm those who do.

Journal entry, May 25

As a kind of pastoral call I took a young couple out to eat for supper at Sveden House. He wanted to talk with me about "where you are coming from" on the question of a woman being a pastor. He wanted to know how I could reconcile "those Bible verses about women." He felt he should tell me that he voted against my coming and did not expect much from my messages but was surprised on that score.

I should not have been hurt, but I was, a bit. Intellectually, I know the struggle for the free use of women's gifts is not over.

He is sincere, with an open attitude. He is a dedicated husband and father, a convinced first generation Anabaptist Mennonite who has been chairman of the evangelism committee. He thinks my "sanctified commercials" (as I call them) do not help men in the church with the woman question.

I said the problem is that men think with their emotions.

Journal entry, May 30

My message was part two of "Gifts of the Spirit . . . and Us." There were more encouraging comments than usual. Only sixty-three were present, as some were away for Memorial Day weekend. I announced the plan for churches to celebrate Peace Pentecost and called attention to the June 12 march and rally in New York City to support the United Nations special session on disarmament, call for a freeze on nuclear weapons, and the transfer of funds from the military to human needs.

In the afternoon I drove to Ruihley Park, Archbold, for a Peace Pentecost service in a United Methodist church, planned mostly by Mennonite young people. They called it "a time of prayer, singing, sharing for people concerned with peace in a nuclear age."

Journal entry, June 12

I packed the last of my things in my car and moved to room number 18 at the Bel-Air Motel, as previously arranged.

Letter to Pastor Emma Richards, June 15

I'm pecking away at a too-high typewriter on a motel dresser and have stacks of paper and books all around, not only for church responsibilities, but for trying to manage Harrisonburg rental units (owned by the bank and me), and orchestrating the Family Life Series in newspapers by remote control.

I was to be half time for Bancroft, but shaping up a message for Sunday morning and doing visitation and counseling exceeds half time, as you know. I have enjoyed every day here and continue to feel that this was and is supposed to be.

Journal entry, June 16

I went with a church member to court, where she appeared before the judge for not yielding right-of-way and getting hit by another car. The duties of a pastor are varied! I would not take the ten dollars she offered, but she insisted on taking me out to eat.

Letter to family and friends, June 22

Last Sunday morning I persuaded Phil Ebersole to be worship leader even though, as taught in the seminaries, he wanted to sit in the congregation several weeks before his term as pastor begins July 1.

We met with the elders last evening. I said I have enjoyed every day here in spite of the work and responsibility. Affirmations have been more than ample. There are flies in the ointment, but my rating of the Bancroft experience overall is ninety-nine percent.

Journal entry, June 27

Sharing time this morning began with Myron Bollman, chairman of the elders, and Stan Nickel, chairman of the council, coming into the pulpit and giving words of appreciation, naming the messages they liked best and some things they remembered from them.

They said they had wanted to choose a gift for me and had asked elder Wilma Bender to find out from one of my daughters what would be appropriate. She reported that Helen had said, "If you give her money she'll give it away. And don't give her anything for her apartment because she's trying to get rid of stuff." So they called Centerpoint Bookstore in Harrisonburg and arranged for a $150.00 gift certificate account. I got up from my chair in the pulpit and shook their hands.

During sharing from the audience, Wilma Bender said, "She helped me and prayed with me over the phone."

Clayton Funk, Bowling Green University student, said, "Several times I called her in the evening and said, 'What are you doing in the morning?' and she said, 'I think I'm eating breakfast with you.'"

Myron Bollman said, "To poke a little fun, if you think her sermons were long, you should have been at the elders' meetings!"

At the farewell potluck meal folks were gracious. I stayed at the church until the last ones left. Then I picked up the big impatiens plant from the parsonage, took a last look, and drove away.

Chapter 36

A Welcome, Open Door

Harrisonburg, Virginia
July–September 1982

On July 20 at 9:30 a.m. a phone call came from Phyllis Suter, a deaconess on the board of elders of Grace Mennonite Church, Pandora, Ohio. She and her husband had been at Bancroft Mennonite my last Sunday. Their daughter, Joanna, had recently moved to Toledo and attended Bancroft while I was there. The call was an invitation to consider being interim pastor full time for four to six months, beginning September 1.

I said I would give the matter careful and prayerful consideration. She said she would call back in a week.

I decided that if a definite call came, before answering I would consult a list of people who knew what the Mennonite Church was about and what my life was about. I would request at least an eighty percent vote of the people. I didn't want to be allowed to go. I wanted to feel called and sent.

My brother Truman phoned on July 21, the eighth anniversary of Grant's death. When I told him about the possibility of a call to Grace Mennonite Church and my plan to consult a list of people, he said, "Save your twenty cents. If you have a call, go."

When I told the Park View Mennonite elders about the inquiry from Grace Mennonite, one said I need not accept the call, that there would be plenty of times to be an interim pastor. I told him there weren't many opportunities for women. Another encouraged me to accept the call while also saying there would be interim opportunities in the future. "I'm sixty-seven," I said. "In three years I'll be seventy."

Conversation with Audrey

I took my niece Audrey Shank to lunch. "What can I do to keep peace with my siblings who do not approve of my being a pastor?" I asked her.

"They are plenty proud of you," she said. She thought I should downplay going again as an interim pastor.

"No," I said, "I have to be out front about it. But these days the pastor is under the elders and there is less elitism and more of the servant-leader idea in being a pastor. Since the time of Christ, women have been concerned more with service and men with status."

Audrey encouraged me to take the next interim call, whether from a congregation of our Mennonite Church or, like Grace, from a congregation of our sister denomination, the General Conference Mennonite Church. She did add that my siblings thought I spoke too much about the woman question and peace and hunger concerns.

The call

On the evening of July 28, as the Grace Mennonite elders were meeting to decide whether to give me a definite call, I prayed, "O Lord, may your will be done. Move them to not call me, or move me to say no, if I am not to go."

At 9:30 the phone rang. A man's voice said, "Mrs. Stoltzfus? This is Walden Hilty at Pandora, Ohio. Our elders have met and decided to extend to you an invitation to be our interim pastor for a minimum of six months."

Another elder, Russell Suter, came on another phone and said they hoped I could begin September first. They wanted me to preach on Sunday mornings, meet once a month with the elders, meet once a month with the council, help plan Sunday evening services, and conduct Thursday evening Bible study. I would be expected to do visitation in two hospitals. A church secretary would be available one or two days a week. I would not be expected to do the newsletter. I would be expected to help with planning the annual meeting of Central District, to be held in April, at Grace Mennonite.

This sounded like a setting where none of my gifts would be wasted. "O Lord," I prayed, "please make your will clear." I asked them to send the call and job description in a letter and told them I would need to consult the Park View pastor and elders.

Seeking counsel

A few days after our phone conversation, I sent this letter to fourteen church leaders, seeking counsel on the call to serve as interim pastor at Grace Mennonite Church:

> I think of you as being among those who understand best what my life is about. May I ask you for a few words of counsel in the next possible mail? On June 28 I returned from five busy but enjoyable months as interim pastor at Bancroft Mennonite Church, Toledo, Ohio. It was one of the best chapters in my life.
>
> On July 20 I received an inquiry from Grace (General Conference) Mennonite Church, Pandora, Ohio (near Bluffton College, 70 miles from Toledo, 20 or so miles from Elida) asking if I would consider being their interim pastor. I said I would give it careful and prayerful consideration. On July 28 a definite invitation was extended to me for a minimum of six months beginning September 1, 1982, if possible.
>
> Personally, I feel favorable toward accepting the call but sense the need to consult my brothers and sisters in the faith. Do you think my going to Grace Mennonite would have any detrimental effect on the progress we are trying to make in our MC denomination toward the full use of women's leadership gifts?
>
> I hope I am not magnifying this matter unduly. I feel the need for sufficient support, I confess, before deciding to go to Grace Mennonite—support comparable to that which I had before going to Bancroft Mennonite. It was enough to help me bear the pain of going against the wishes of some dear ones who did not approve.
>
> My profound thanks for any words of counsel, pro or con. I want only the will of the Lord to be done.

Myron Augsburger, former president of Eastern Mennonite College, then pastor at Washington Community Fellowship, responded by telephone. "This is a wave of the future, to work with the General Conference," he said. "It could be that your interim is significant for the church as a whole."

My nephew George said my interims could help congregations not yet ready for a woman pastor on a permanent basis. My brother Truman said, "You should accept the call as you feel the call of the people and the inner voice of the Holy Spirit."

Marlin Miller, president of Goshen Biblical Seminary, wrote:

> I encourage you to accept the assignment. It is true that serving in a General Conference Church may be seen by some in the Mennonite Church that women in leadership are a symbol of liberalism. It may

also remind people that God may call capable women elsewhere if the Mennonite Church is closed to them.

Ross Bender and Glendon Blosser, former moderators of Mennonite Church General Assembly, Ernest Martin, former president of Ohio Conference, Wilmer Hartman, Ohio Conference minister, James and Arlene Stauffer, Ed Stoltzfus, Sam Weaver, executive secretary of Virginia Conference, Joe and Emma Richards, and my nephew Truman and his wife Betty also encouraged me to go.

Call and acceptance

On August 5 I received a letter officially inviting me to serve as interim pastor. The letter described Grace Mennonite as "a General Conference Church located in the village of Pandora, Ohio, population approximately 900 augmented by surrounding Riley Township. Our church has a membership of 374 with an average attendance of 200 at Sunday school and worship service. Our constituency is rural, the majority farmers or farm related with a generous reservoir of talents for music and teaching."

I replied, "In spite of the heavy tasks involved, I have inner urgings of the Spirit and reminders of his sufficient enabling, so I accept your invitation to be interim pastor of Grace Mennonite Church."

One evening around that time I ate supper at Katie and John's, along with my sisters Edna and Stella and Edna's husband, Arthur. Edna told me later that she said to the rest after I left, "Ruth looked good and seemed happy. Whatever it is she is doing, let her do it."

Chapter 37

Interim Pastor, Grace Mennonite Church

Pandora, Ohio
September 1982–June 1983

Journal entry, September 2, 1982

This is my first night in the Grace Mennonite Church parsonage. It was a 100-mile trip from Columbus. By 6:30 p.m. I had all boxes of books and all clothes and bedclothes carried in from the car, but not unpacked. I knew I had to rest before the elders meeting in the parlor room at the church at 7:30 p.m., so I put a fitted sheet and pillow on the bed and flopped down for half an hour's rest.

Walden Hilty chaired the elders meeting. (I am to chair it each month hereafter.) He called on me for opening prayer, and then we had a time of getting acquainted and discussing church procedures and duties. I asked questions about sermon themes in the recent past, whether to announce hours for people to see me, responsibility for weeknight Bible or course of study beginning in October, visitation expectations, and more.

Each congregation has a personality all its own. Here, I am told, the people are not comfortable sharing personal blessings and concerns. The bulletin shows "congregational concerns," but they are announcements about people in the hospital.

Journal entry, September 3, 1982
Walden Hilty brought the mail, which is to be picked up daily. He talked about living in New Jersey for over forty years. They joined a Presbyterian church and he served as an elder. Seven years ago he and his wife moved back to Pandora and Grace Mennonite, where they grew up and were married.

I said my main problem with other denominations is the military question.

He has respect for conscientious objectors to military service, he said. He mentioned wars in the Old Testament and asked, "What about defending our country?" Then he said, "I guess you noticed that there is a flag in the church. It's a bone of contention. Some say it's an idol. One man said he will leave the church if it's taken out."

I had not been told about the flag or the controversy before consenting to come. I told Walden I appreciated that we could "speak the truth in love" to each other. But I was pointed in saying that Christ never said a word to encourage anyone to kill. He only taught us how to die.

Journal entry, September 5, 1982
Today I had my first message, "As It Is Written." As Tom Schumacher, worship leader, walked with me to the pulpit, I saw Ruthie and Timothy in the audience. Attendance was 201.

Ruthie and Timothy were invited with me to Dwight and Phyllis Suter's. Suter's daughter, Joanna, and sons, Bob and Bill, were there, also the Mildred and Roy Lugibihls. Good fellowship and good food were the order of the day. On their 240-acre farm Suters grow corn, soybeans, and 2,000 pigs.

In the evening there was a salad supper, well-attended, and a get-acquainted time. Each family introduced themselves and I was asked to speak a few moments. I included some family stories.

Letter to family and friends, September 14, 1982
I live in the three-bedroom parsonage (one floor) near the church and meet people in the study here rather than the one in the church. This study is convenient, since my days start early.

The people are friendly, many of the same extraction and with the same convictions as mine. The attendance at Sunday morning worship averages about 200. A U.S. flag in the church is a source of conflict. Pray God to give me wisdom. The worship is more formal than at Bancroft Mennonite. A choir sings with and for the rest, instead of the four-part a cappella singing by the congregation that I am used to.

Yesterday afternoon I drove over an hour to Bancroft Mennonite for the licensing of Phil Ebersole as permanent pastor and enjoyed seeing the people who are on my heart. They literally received me with open arms.

On the way I stopped at St. Luke's Hospital to visit a member here who was having surgery to clear blockage in an artery in her neck. On the same day, her double first cousin had the same surgery, and I was with her before and after surgery and stayed during the two-hour operation at Lima hospital half an hour away.

Pandora is a storybook village with a hardware store that has the atmosphere of 1900. The post office window is closed over the noon hour. I'm at the east end of Main Street. The sidewalk leads into the parsonage lawn and up to the front door! There is little traffic (population 900), also few accommodations when I want office supplies, smorgasbord, or laundromat. I pick up these services to or from visitation duties at the hospital and Mennonite Retirement Home in Bluffton, seven miles away.

There are two lawyers in the congregation, one medical doctor, teachers, bankers, and librarians, but most are farmers, averaging 200 acres each farm. There are big farms as far as the eye can see. I saw a field of sunflowers bowing to each other, tomato fields with Mexican migrants bowing to the ground with their tomato baskets. I was told that they are paid thirty-five cents for each bushel picked and that one whole family is able to pick 150 bushels in a day. I fear living conditions are wretched in the shacks I see as I travel. An elder here says, "Our migrants are happy."

Journal entry, September 21, 1982

I received a note from Don Diller, who was here on Sunday. He has mixed feelings about the flag, said he had his eyes opened at [Mennonite World Conference in] Amsterdam about the Anabaptists and advised me to tell stories about them to change things at Grace. "Use the back door approach," he said.

Letter to family and friends, September 30, 1982

I am about ready to go to Bluffton Electronics to have an AM/FM cassette player put in my car, run off copies of this letter at the Bluffton College library, and visit two church members at Mennonite Memorial Home.

The cassette player is pure pleasure. All my trips seem shorter, and when I stop the car I am reluctant to stop the music!

Journal entry, October 2, 1982

After my message, a prayer, and a hymn, I went from the pulpit to the floor, and the deacons and deaconesses joined me for distribution of the communion elements of bread and grape juice. My own heart was "strangely warmed." God seems to have answered my prayers for a meaningful service.

Many indicated that they had been blessed. Some comments as people shook hands at the foyer: "It was the most meaningful communion I ever attended." "Your messages are so practical. I don't know if it's because you're a woman or because you are you." "It was beautiful." "Your message reached us."

I was enjoying these comments and would have enjoyed more, but the next woman said, "Nice day, isn't it?"

Journal entry, October 4, 1982

Sunday evening Bill Suter, acting for the peace and service committee, conducted a meeting on draft resistance. We divided into groups for discussion. Some in my group said "Yes," some said "I don't know," and I said "No," when asked if we would register if we were required. Bill asked me to have the closing prayer, which was not easy.

When I visited Madeline Bixel today, I had in mind to read from Isaiah 43, and before I read it, she mentioned that the verses in Isaiah 43 mean much to her. As I was leaving, her friend Helen, who had come in while I was there, said, "Here you are at the right place at the right time." I wanted and needed that affirmation.

Journal entry, October 6, 1982

I feel more accepted here than ever before. Church secretary Shirley Sommer said a woman asked, "Why can't she be permanent pastor?"

Journal entry, October 8, 1982

Last evening my heart was warmed when thirty-three people showed up for the congregational study of *Justice and the Christian Witness.* I had told the congregation I like to study the Bible alone, but I don't want to study it alone on Thursday nights. I said, like Jacob on the night he wrestled with the man of God, I expect to be both bruised and blessed in the study, and "Come and be bruised and blessed with me."

Journal entry, October 14, 1982

More people came to the Bible class! We need to order more study booklets! The elders had said at first, "Order twenty-five booklets if the publisher will let you return unused ones." We were eight short the first night, and after buying ten more, were still eight short the second night. About 43 are in the class and interest seems high.

Journal entry, October 15, 1982

No doubt there will be enough upsetting experiences to keep my head out of the clouds, but I'm finding jewels among the members at Grace Church. Herman Hilty stopped by today to discuss his part as worship leader on Sunday. He told of his born-again experience in 1975 as a result of his children asking him over and over, "Daddy, are you saved?" They had gotten "warmed up" (my term) at Youth for Christ meetings.

His spirit and attitude are beautiful. He told me how he helped an older woman in Mennonite Memorial Home who called for him (a maintenance man) to come and help her spiritually. She wasn't sure she could get down on her knees, but he said, "I can put down a pillow for you to kneel on," and he helped her to kneel and pray.

What a preparation for my Sunday message on "Gifts of the Spirit . . . and Us."

I prayed hard for God's help. He answered and I do not wish to take credit for anything more than my surrender to his will (and he even helped me to do that) in regard to comments after the service like: "I was never in a meeting where I felt the presence of the Holy Spirit like today." "You speak and pray out of the depths of your heart instead of the top of your head."

Two church members took me out for a meal after church. We rode in their Cadillac. Must I rebuke them or work more gently on responsible lifestyle? Can I bite the hands that fed me?

Journal entry, October 21, 1982

I got a call from Ron Kraybill, director of Mennonite Central Committee Conciliation Services, asking me to participate in a conference for pastors and lay leaders on marriage reconciliation. Would I be a resource person for two talks?

I asked what gaps I would fill that would not be filled by him or Abe Schmidt, a psychologist.

He said, "We need your empathy and warmth." He said some of the others are "clinical and cold." He said, "Reflect on the church as a reconciling community, the roles and resources of congregational people. A woman is needed."

Letter to family and friends, October 25, 1982

I drove three hours northwest to attend the Great Lakes Bible conference held Sunday evening to Tuesday evening October 17–19 at Goshen College Church. A bonus was meeting people who know what my life is about. Dorsa Mishler said, "I'm glad for your courage in being an interim pastor. You probably have more experience (as a traveling preacher) than most pastors. I believe if your father were living today, he would come to hear you."

As I drove home to Pandora with beautiful stereo music on the cassette player, thinking of the contacts at the Bible conference and the circumstances of my life, I thought, "It is almost wrong to be so happy when there is so much suffering in the world."

Journal entry, November 11, 1982

I studied five hours for this evening's study on justice and the Christian witness. Afterward someone commented on how people are sharing freely. I thank God. May he please make something good come from this evening.

There is sympathy here for participating in the military. Walden Hilty brought up the U.S. military keeping peace in Lebanon after the refugee camp massacres. He mentioned the U.S. role in defeating Hitler's Germany. I said it's a tough question, there should be a way to control evil without taking a life, but if the government decided to take lives for any reason, I could not participate. I read selections from John Drescher's book, *Why I Am a Conscientious Objector.*

Someone said, "People ask what would you do if someone came to harm your family?"

I said, "We are frail humans and can't say what we would do, but if God gave me grace, I would not take a life. As a Christian I can give my life, but I cannot take a life. I'd rather die as a Christian at age twenty-five than live centuries as a non-Christian."

Journal entry, November 14, 1982

A woman from the church called and in minutes came to see me, seeking a deeper faith experience. "I want what you've got," she said. In the evening two young mothers came wanting help in starting a young women's Bible study group. I don't know what to think, except that God is hearing our prayers. May God be praised, and may this be the start of continuing growth.

Journal entry, November 22, 1982

I suggested places for the Grace Mennonite treasurer to send donations from the church instead of the amount going to me as salary. I must keep income down because fifty percent of each federal tax dollar goes for the killing business.

Journal entry, December 2, 1982

A woman from the church came for counseling. We discussed Scriptures and had prayer together. She said, "The church is filling up. We need you. God sent you here."

At noon I went to the Senior Citizens' meal in Bluffton. A good time, including the invitation to tell stories. I told how I brought back Naeim Mohammed's car and was driving it down the main street of Harrisonburg with the sticker Naeim had on the back: "Hungry for love? Follow me." I had been introduced as the minister at Grace Mennonite, and I told them I couldn't tell that story in a sermon.

Journal entry, December 16, 1982

Monday night of this week the seven-member pastoral search committee met at the church and after some discussion called me to join them. They said encouraging words about my work. I'll need to remember them when things get rough on the flag question, but six of the seven want the flag out of the church.

THEY ASKED IF I WOULD CONSIDER SERVING A THREE-YEAR TERM AS MINISTER.

We talked long and late. Yes, I can decide one year at a time, have help with visitation and the church mail. I can ask that the flag be removed. "Almost all of us want it out." (That ratio is not true of the membership.) Yes, I can have a month or more to think and pray and consult family and church people. I can be at

Harrisonburg for periods of time. I can take other appointments with regular Sundays off at Grace Church. (I would be reasonable.)

Mark Weidner, the conference minister, is encouraging. He says it would be appropriate for me to have four weeks of vacation a year. If there is a licensing service, he thinks it should be by both General Conference and Mennonite Church officials.

Could four weeks a year with children and grandchildren make up for the months I am gone? ("Bad Grandma," as son-in-law John Fairfield said with mock seriousness to fourteen-month-old Peter.)

I feel favorable to a longer term here, providing it does not do damage to my relationships with my dear children and grandchildren, my biological brothers and sisters, our Mennonite Church, and the process of freeing the use of all gifts. I have no problem with my relationship with the Lord. He and I both know that I am a preacher.

Journal entry, January 3, 1983
I had lunch with Mark Weidner, conference minister. He was supportive of my idea of offering to continue six months as interim pastor, instead of considering a term of three years, and to assist in a series of discussions on the flag issue that has been a "festering splinter in the flesh" in the Grace Church. He let me know that, while he admired my stand against the U.S. flag in the Grace Church, it might mean that I would not be asked to stay when we reassess the question of my taking a three-year term as pastor.

Journal entry, January 5, 1983
I read this letter to the pastoral search committee this evening:

> I appreciate very much your request that I consider a term of three years as pastor of Grace Mennonite Church. The work has been heavy but enjoyable, the fellowship enriching. The people have gotten in my heart.
>
> I would feel ready to give a favorable reply if it were not for the flag of our nation in the church, a practice contrary to my understanding of the separation of church and state as taught in the Scriptures, as practiced by our martyred Anabaptist forebears, and as the founding principle upon which America was based.
>
> Perhaps those of us who object to the flag in the church do not say enough about the good our country has done: Better provision of housing, food, clothing, than any other nation; more education; oppor-

tunity to people disadvantaged; refuge to refugees and the persecuted (from us as Mennonites to the boat people of Southeast Asia); freedom of speech, political persuasion, worship; foreign aid; attitudes toward progress, optimism, improvement.

However, the realm of the nation and the realm of the church are separate. If the nation did everything well and deserved no criticism, the symbol of the state would still not belong in the church, in my view. The flag issue in the congregation, like a festering splinter in the flesh, did not heal before I came as interim pastor and I believe it will not heal until the matter is brought out in the open and dealt with in a mature Christian way.

For the unity and spiritual good of the congregation and for the leadership you may wish to attract in the future, I would think it necessary to begin immediately with a series of congregational meetings in which the flag issue would be clarified and resolved.

I am willing to remain as interim pastor for a six-month period and to assist in such a process with all the objectivity I would expect from others. At the end of the six months we could reassess the matter of my being the pastor of Grace Church for a three-year term.

I would consider the following to be important in congregational meetings such as those I am proposing:

•A written presentation of the official position of the General Conference Mennonite Church as it relates to the separation of church and state and the question of having a flag in the church. Copies distributed to facilitate discussion and clarification.

• A written presentation of the history of the flag issue in Grace Church with copies distributed for discussion and clarification. Perhaps some communication ground rules should be agreed upon beforehand.

•Those favoring the flag in the church presenting their reasons. Those opposing the flag in the church presenting their reasons. Both sides listening carefully and respectfully to each other.

•No pushing for a hurried final vote at any time but much time taken for guidance (not proof texts) from the Bible, prayer for each other, prayer for God's help, and work of grace in us all.

•Addition of other features as God would lead and according to the consensus of the congregation.

•A study of the attached suggestions on resolving church conflict and use of methods appropriate for our situation. They come from Ron Kraybill, director of Mennonite Conciliation Service at Mennonite Central Committee.

I trust these suggestions to your broad understanding and for your handling as you see best. I fervently pray that we may have God's clear guidance and enabling as something of a miracle in this situation.

After I finished reading the letter, the committee showed overwhelming appreciation. They asked me to read it at the congregational meeting tomorrow night. We expect an eruption because the church council has agreed to a request from Central District to remove the flag during their April conference at Grace Church. Shirley Sommer typed and duplicated 175 copies of my letter for distribution at the congregational meeting.

I left the committee meeting thanking God for his help and the help of my children, nephew George, and others.

Journal entry, January 6, 1983
The audience was deathly still while I read my letter, but there was no explosion when I finished. When I was asked if the flag would be removed during my interim, I said, "No, I want to subject myself to the process of discussion and listening."

After the meeting I heard these responses: "Do you know how the flag first got in this church? The American Legion asked a member at Grace to put it in. That man is no longer here! The Legion had asked my husband to put it in, but he would not do it."

Journal entry, January 7, 1983
This morning a woman spoke angry words to me on the phone: "Why did you take sides? You gave wonderful messages here and we loved you. Now this! There must be a flag at the church where I worship. The attendance at church will dwindle. People will be leaving."

Shirley, church secretary, said I was amazingly calm.

In the evening, Russel and Jean Suter, though they have no objection to the flag in the church, came by to see how I was. They, like senior elder Walden Hilty, love and respect me although our viewpoints are different.

Journal entry, January 8, 1983
Estella Schutz illustrated the above when she called to say, "Gertrude and I are happy you have decided to stay."

Rachel Schutz came this morning, at my request. I needed to discuss whether she would be on the ballot for deaconess. She also is one of the loyal opposition to my position. She came bringing candy. We had a good talk and prayer together. She said she would call me with her answer at 4:00 p.m. She did, and it was positive—a miracle in view of the flag upset. Didn't I ask for miracles?

I went at 9:00 a.m. to the Lunch Box restaurant to see Roland Etter, owner, to ask if he would be on the ballot for deacon. We had a good talk about the flag in spite of differing views. His answer was positive. Another miracle. Roland told me a group of some fifty people asked to meet at his restaurant for church tomorrow, and he told them they should settle things at the church.

In the afternoon Tom Schumacher and wife, Joyce, good old standbys, came by the parsonage. I learned from them that the group threatening to break away had asked Jon Diller, attorney, for legal help but he declined. Another miracle. We had good conversation and prayer before they left.

Conference minister Mark Weidner said, "No matter who the pastor is, the matter must be settled, but whoever is pastor at the time will get the credit."

In the evening, Russel Suter called to see whether Roland Etter had agreed to be on the ballot for deacon and Rachel Schutz on the ballot for deaconess. I told him both consented and I considered it a miracle in view of their positions on the flag.

Journal entry, January 10, 1983

There were 208 at church, ten less than last Sunday, but the woman who said "People will be leaving" was at church with her husband. I invited Loris Habegger, former pastor, who was visiting with his wife, to speak a few moments, lead in closing prayer, and go out with me during the choral benediction in order to meet people. He wished me the best in reconciliation here, saying, "The only appropriate symbol in the church is the cross."

Journal entry, January 10, 1983

NOT a miracle: The words of a church member to elder Tom Schumacher were, "You people's objections to the flag are a work of the devil," and "The church should be doing more important things."

Marj Hilty said I looked tired and without my "spark" Sunday night at the council meeting. I guess the turmoil has been affecting me. And I do wilt in the evening.

Journal entry, January 12, 1983

Today and yesterday I worked with Shirley to get out the newsletter for January. As requested by the pastoral search committee, I included my letter asking for discussions on the flag in the church. What additional explosions will that cause?

I also included a sample letter to President Reagan asking for a better solution to the terrible situation of blacks in South Africa. I expect this to bring yells from the flag people that I am not keeping church and state separate. My answer will be, "Church and state have dealings with and responsibilities to each other without being married to each other." The flag in the church is a sign that church and state are married to each other.

This evening at the board of elders meeting Russel Suter said someone asked, "What do they mean when they talk about separation of church and state?" A revealing question. This church is untaught.

An elder said, "Reading Ruth's letter at the congregational meeting diffused the plan of some to protest the council's decision to remove the flags (both the "Christian" and U.S. flag) during Central District conference.

Journal entry, January 14, 1983

This afternoon I performed my first wedding. I have spoken at three weddings, but this was the first time I officiated. Vernon Bucher, a widower, married Wilma Neuenschwander, his deceased wife's best friend. Wilma's sister and the sister's husband were attendants.

I mailed to the Court of the State of Ohio, Putnam County, the marriage certificate, certifying that I "solemnized the marriage." In the lower left-hand corner of my copy of the certification are the words "to be retained by Minister for his record or file." I substituted the word "her."

Journal entry, January 15, 1983

Another miracle: When I called Ron Kraybill, director of Mennonite Central Committee Conciliation Services, for the name of someone to help us on the flag controversy, as he had suggested, he said he himself would come. He asked for the name and phone number of a pro-flag person, also an anti-flag person, so he can listen to them before the weekend with us.

Journal entry, January 16, 1983

As people came by to shake hands after my sermon, Marjorie Hilty said, "I think you have come to this church for such a time as this." I told her I had just asked the Lord if he is trying to match me with a need here, and that we desperately need his help.

Another miracle: Walden Hilty said, "Someone pointed out that the congregation did not decide at the annual meeting to go through these discussions on the flag." Russel Suter answered, "Tell them the board of elders has the right to do this." Walden said, "I did." The miracle: Both Walden and Russel have had trouble seeing that the issue needs to be discussed!

Journal entry, January 21, 1983

I called Ron Kraybill about coming for a meeting on the flag. The short-range plan is to focus on whether the flag will remain in the church. The long-range plan is to deal with the root of the problem: the question of church and state. If I stay longer at Grace Church, how can I walk carefully on this and be faithful?

Ron has convictions against the flag in the church, but he must be NEUTRAL. He prefers that people not know which side he is on.

I told him that role is NOT FOR ME.

He wants good relationships with both sides and "will set aside personal convictions"! He said some people see their role as prophet.

I said, "THAT'S ME!"

Ron said, "You speak boldly, but with love."

Thank God for that! Was there any servant of God in the Old or New Testament times who was NEUTRAL? Give me the role of the prophet!

As Ron requested, pro-flag people called him on the phone. They feel the flag issue is being forced on them. Ron felt they invested trust in him. They said, "Let's make an effort to talk." As Ron requested, anti-flag people called him long distance also. And also invested trust.

Ron is not worried about a split in the church. That gave me encouragement. But maybe some issues are worth splitting over. He thinks I should be present at the meeting. I'll try to be quiet. He will talk with Russel Suter about people signing up for times of special prayer. He thinks it's best for Russel to promote it, not me.

Russel asked if Sunday school classes could do an exercise on January 30, just before Ron is with us. I have doubts. The question has been explosive. I have no idea if the flag will stay in the church after the discussions, or if I will stay much longer as interim pastor.

Journal entry, January 26, 1983

At the elders meeting this evening we heard that some are asking how the church can rent rooms to Head Start, a government program, if there is separation of church and state. I explained that while church and state are separate, they have dealings with each other. I wish I had said the question is, "Why is the flag necessary for worship?"

Journal entry, January 29, 1983

An insert in the January 30, 1983, bulletin about the February 3 meeting:

> Chairman for the meeting will be Ron Kraybill, director of Mennonite Conciliation Services and a graduate of Goshen College and Harvard Divinity School. He has dealt with both congregational and individual conflict and has spent time training personnel in conflict and management skills.
>
> At Ron's request the Board of Elders selected four people with opposite opinions on the flag issue to talk with Ron beforehand. Ron requested that a committee with diversified opinions be formed. He suggested those four plus two more who are neutral. The committee will form a panel to be interviewed by Ron, with congregational discussion following.
>
> Our aim is to work out an understanding everyone can live with on the question of the flag. We will not be making any decisions on the issue at this meeting.
>
> The Board of Elders encourages all members to be in prayer at least several minutes daily for these concerns.

Journal entry, February 3, 1983

I moaned and groaned in prayer over our meeting this evening. If nothing else comes of it, at least the congregation had the experience of listening to opposing views with respect. People attacked a problem without attacking each other. They were able to disagree without being disagreeable. They could "speak the truth in love."

Ron Kraybill began with a panel of six representing the pro-flag view, the anti-flag view, and the neutral view. The straw vote of the 160 in attendance showed that a strong majority favors continuing the discussions. Another miracle!

One woman spoke critically of my letter and of the fact that in the same newsletter there was information and a sample letter to the government. She knocked the emphasis on justice and said, "Our emphasis should be on growth." I wonder if she has any idea of the importance God places on justice.

Another person asked, "How can we tell the government what to do and not have a flag in the church?"

After the meeting I had a cordial talk with a man who says he doesn't care if the flag is in the church. I said he ought to care.

(It came out in the meeting that the flag was placed in the church in World War II without congregational decision.)

Journal entry, February 10, 1983
Study, study, study for the justice study this evening. With the majority embracing civil religion, it is uphill, but I have enough support to keep me encouraged.

Journal entry, February 13, 1983
Tom Schumacher said (and the others seemed to concur) that he will be disappointed if I decide to terminate at the end of August. Others want me to go.

Journal entry, February 15, 1983
I've been reading John Woolman's *Journal.* His struggle to obey God's call to talk to Quakers about owning slaves is like my call to speak out about the separation of church and state and ask for the issue of the U.S. flag in the church to be brought out into the open.

In the evening I had a pre-arranged telephone conference with Ron Kraybill. We agreed that we should not have a quick vote. He said he is more favorable than before toward my idea of *not* considering a three-year term. He said my letter may take the wind out of the sails of those who feel manipulated.

This is the letter I wrote to the pastoral search committee:

After much prayer, reflection, and consultation with others, I believe I should not consider, as you requested, a three-year term as pastor of Grace Mennonite Church beyond the six-month extension I offered in my January 5 letter, but should end my interim on the last Sunday of August 1983 or before, if another pastor can be secured.

This has crystallized in my mind only recently and I thought it good to let you know now so you can move forward in your efforts to secure a new pastor. It may also be helpful in the current discussions of the flag issue for the question of my tenure to be settled so that this does not cause undue pressure to persons holding either view about the flag.

Whether the flag remains in the church or is removed, I feel strongly that after serving a maximum of twelve months here, I should return to a schedule that would permit me to accept more freely writing assignments and requests for speaking engagements in other places.

My recommendation that the congregation bring the flag issue out in the open for discussion was successfully accomplished, I feel, at our February 3 meeting under the guidance of Ron Kraybill, director of MCC Conciliation Services.

However, not only for the spiritual welfare and unity of the church, but for the sake of any pastor you would wish to call, I think it is urgent that the congregation consider over a period of time and resolve the deeper questions of the biblical and historical (they are the same) meaning and implications of the separation of church and state, the nature of civil religion, and how these questions relate to the biblical doctrine of nonresistance. (I see this as being vitally more important than a hasty decision as to whether the flag remains in the church!)

I am thankful to God and to the congregation for the privilege of being interim pastor at Grace Mennonite Church for this period. I will always value beyond words the rich experiences in the fellowship, the service, the struggles here. For my brothers and sisters in the faith and for me I claim the promise in Romans 8:28: "We know that in all things God works for the good of those who love him, who have been called according to his purpose."

Journal entry, February 16, 1983

Tonight at the meeting of the board of elders I gave my letter to Arman Habeggar, chair of the pastoral search committee. He asked me to read it to the congregation Sunday morning. Three elders wanted to go ahead with a vote to decide if the flag will remain in the church. Others favored tabling the decision and working on issues of nonresistance and separation of church and state.

Letter to family and friends, February 17, 1983

I hate to disappoint those who want me to stay, but the majority do not embrace nonresistance any more than mainline Protestants and are no more inclined to hear about it. Since learning that and since they have heard my view, my messages go harder. If I would consider a three-year term now, I don't think I would get two-thirds support to stay.

I'm in the midst of a storm, but I have a strange peace. I would hold off my decision and take the rejection if I knew it would help the church, but I do not feel led in that direction. One year here is enough.

Journal entry, February 19, 1983

I continued studying commentaries, Bible dictionary, etc., for my message tomorrow, "I am the Messiah." Gene Augsburger, who is to be worship leader, came by to discuss procedures and seemed to want to stay to talk. He did. I decided I should value that and relax about my sermon. I did.

Keith Sommer came by to bring me a copy of the Mennonite Confession of Faith and seemed to want to stay to talk. He did. I decided I should value that and relax about my sermon. I did.

Both men had the flag issue on their minds. Gene seemed in the process of re-thinking his position of not caring one way or the other about the flag in the church. Keith is definitely against the flag in the church and the military-mindedness it represents.

Saturday evening I decided I would not worry about my incomplete sermon notes for Sunday. I have done considerable study. I may even preach without notes!

Journal entry, February 20, 1983

A surprising number came to the meeting during the Sunday school hour to further process the flag discussion. We formed pairs and listened to each other, using guidelines provided by Ron Kraybill. I was paired with a woman who was pro-flag but not hostile. She told me, "I like the flag up front. Our ancestors came from another country, and we have freedom. The flag is not a symbol to me and I don't worship the flag. It's always been there. It's a part of our church. It hurts me to see our church torn apart. The people in Pandora are talking about us and praying for us over this issue of the flag. I want the flag, and I ask, where do we draw the line on separation of church and state? How about the church renting rooms to Head Start? How about speaking to government? We should get this settled quickly and still love each other."

In the worship service I read my letter stating that I terminate as pastor on the last Sunday in August 1983. During the sermon I spoke from John 4:4-42 after deciding to leave my notes in my purse. I was free to look at the passage and the audience. A well-written paper may be more important for a seminar speech than a sermon. I don't know.

Journal entry, February 22, 1983
The board of elders tabulated the results of the interview sheets. On the question, "If I were the only person in this church, on this issue I would probably choose to. . . ." the results were: leave the flag in—33, take the flag out—37, neutral—6.

Journal entry, February 27, 1983
Ron Kraybill came for more conciliation work. His sermon was entitled, "Thank God for conflict!" He was more pointed than heretofore. Afterward someone said to me, "It sounds like he has been talking to you."

In the afternoon Ron met with church leaders as they drew up a recommendation that the council reverse its decision to remove the flags from the sanctuary during Central District Conference. I said the only way I could consent to a recommendation that undercut the authority of the council and rewarded the fussing of the critics was to "hang by my eyelids" on Ron's contention that the recommendation is justified because the congregation is in the process of discussion.

After the evening meeting the elders and I met with Ron. Something clicked in my mind and heart that I felt was of the Lord, and I said, "Since some are clamoring for a quick vote on the flag (which will solve nothing), and since people on both sides have said we need teaching on the separation of church and state, maybe the flags should remain in the church for a period of months (not just during Central District Conference sessions) while attention is paid to these questions."

Both Tom Schumacher, anti-flag, and Roland Etter, pro-flag, agreed. Ron said, "The elders have it together. Let's see if it they can carry the congregation along."

With help from the elders and Ron, I wrote a recommendation to be read to the congregation Sunday morning, March 6. I noted that Ron Kraybill echoed the sentiments of many in the congregation when he said, "A vote on the flags at this time would be a mistake because we would still have the same win-lose situation as before."

Leaving the flags in the church now will be an act of reconciliation. The long-term issue of the flags will be decided later.

Letter to family and friends, March 20, 1983

What I call civil religion is deep with a lot of people here, but most of them seem teachable and well meaning. I do not regret bringing the flag question out in the open. It was a splinter in the flesh with a Band-Aid over it. I have friends here on both sides but think it is good that I do what I can for one year and leave in August, six months before the elders bring to the congregation a proposal about the flag.

The bottom line is the military question. I was told that only ten percent of the eighty men drafted in World War II were conscientious objectors. Three lives were lost in the war. A sweet elderly woman, mother of an elder, said, "One of my sons went into the service. He had a family and no other way of support."

Many do not seem to know that their denominational and congregational constitutions include the doctrine of nonresistance, meaning, among other things, nonparticipation in the military. Historian Evan Suter, of the solid core of COs here, told me that years ago young men of Grace Church who were attending Ohio State University came to the pastor and elders, reporting that university officials called them in and said, "We know you are Mennonites and will excuse you from the ROTC training if you bring us a statement from your church leaders." The pastor and elders said to the young men, "No problem. Take the ROTC training."

Journal entry, March 27, 1983

My heart is singing praises to God for his providential hand and the spirit-led sermon this morning by Doug Reichenbach, Wayland, Iowa, our speaker for Holy Week. Doug thanked the congregation for nurturing him. He said when he went to Wayland Mennonite Church he spoke on peace and justice, and people said, "Preach

Christ!" They wouldn't have said that if they had known it would deepen his convictions on peace and justice, he said. He was clear that we cannot buy such lines as "Peace through (military) strength." He was clear on nonresistance.

During a time for children he had the boys and girls hold up their palms (it was Palm Sunday) and wave them. He said, "God doesn't want us to have any blood on our palms from hurting others." He then had them hold up the left palm and put the other arm around the next person.

Journal entry, April 8, 1983
During the Central District conference sessions I have been encouraged by comments about being at Grace Church. Many in the wider General Conference Mennonite Church, like the minority in this church, object to a flag in church. I told Myron Augsburger, moderator-elect of Mennonite Church Assembly, that any moves toward merging the General Conference and Mennonite Church should deal with this question.

The people here must be the cream of the crop of the General Conference, dedicated saints of the Lord. I doubt if there is much civil religion among them. News of the conference was covered by Associated Press on radio and in newspapers because of a resolution that passed encouraging congregations to "offer aid and sanctuary" (though illegal) "to Salvadorans (refugees in this country) uprooted because of greed, violence, and lack of love and justice." I felt like it was the General Conference at their best and felt one with them.

Journal entry, May 6, 1983
Yesterday I came to Ruthie and Timothy's at Columbus, on my way to Harrisonburg where I am to speak Sunday morning at Lindale Mennonite Church. After a long but pleasurable eight-hour trip from Columbus—feeling good and enjoying good music on the cassette player—I arrived at my Harrisonburg apartment in the early evening. I went to Kathie's for supper, and John was alarmed when he saw me, saying that I was "not pale, but ashen." He called Kathie to look at the lack of redness when he pulled down my lower eyelids. "Get to a doctor," he said.

Journal entry, May 9, 1983

This is the day I saw my doctor. After seeing there was not enough redness when he pulled down my lower eyelids and checked my tongue, he said, "Can you tell me how you could be a pastor with no blood? Your blood may be so low that you need a transfusion. I suspect you might have what we call a silent tumor in your tummy." He sent me immediately to Valley Lab for tests to determine whether to order x-rays and those results could decide if surgery is to be done. I may be in trouble.

I may have to change plans. But I feel good, assured that God knows my day and my hour. I have had a good life. I told Kathie that, and I know it in the depths of my being.

Journal entry, May 10, 1983

I saw my doctor. The report on the tests indicates a lack of iron. My white blood corpuscle count is good, so that rules out leukemia. I have severe anemia.

Journal entry, May 18, 1983

What a week! Many blood tests, x-rays four different times, blood transfusions two days in a row, two pints each time. I had more pep after the blood transfusions and was glad I chose to be an out-patient, so I could go home to check mail and eat what I want. As instructed, today I called my doctor for a report of this morning's x-rays and to find out if I can go back to Ohio. The x-rays show stones in the gall bladder, not the kidneys. This is not an emergency. No tumor was found, but they are concerned about one area of the bowel.

When I get back to Ohio, I must get my blood count done about June 3 and report it to my doctor. I must take two capsules of iron each day. When I return to Virginia at the end of June, the hospital wants to do more x-rays of the area of concern in the colon.

Journal entry, May 20, 1983

After lunch I slept a deep nap and then drove to visit Laurel Bauman at Lima Memorial Hospital.

Journal entry, May 26, 1983

I learned that Laurel Bauman's condition has worsened, so I dropped everything and went to his bedside at the Lima hospital. I was alone with him for the last twenty minutes of life, talking to him, thinking he might hear, and praying aloud, as he was dying in peace. A son who had been with him all night wanted me to help plan the services. I could only tell how we had done [at Grant's death]. He thought his siblings would approve of having burial first with relatives present, then a memorial service at the church.

Journal entry, May 30, 1983
I did final shaping up of plans and words and prayers for the private burial service at 2:00 p.m. and the public memorial service at the church at 4:00 p.m. for Laurel Bauman. This was my first experience of being in charge of funeral services.

Journal entry, June 2, 1983
Today I had tests at the doctor's office, as ordered by my doctor. Tomorrow I go to get results of these tests, then call my doctor and decide where to go from here. Who knows? I may soon be going to my permanent home in heaven. It is evident that I am losing blood internally. I am as lacking in pep as I was before the blood transfusions in Harrisonburg.

Journal entry, June 31, 1983
Today I got the results of the tests. They show I am continuing to lose blood internally. I called the results to my doctor, as requested. He thinks I should make this Sunday, June 5, my last at Grace Church.

Journal entry, June 5, 1983
I decided to wait until after my message to announce that this would be my last Sunday. I sensed that many people were aware of the news and of my health problem. It's uncanny, since I feel good, especially when I am speaking.

For this last sermon, given three weeks early, I took the advice of church secretary Shirley Sommer, who said, "You should give that one you've been saying is needed, "I Can't Do That!" In the message I cited some of God's people in Old and New Testaments who knew they must obey God rather than man and take the consequences. It was a call to first loyalty to God and lesser loyalties to nation or any person or thing.

After my message I announced that this would be my last Sunday at Grace Mennonite. After telling them about my health problem, I said, "The Lord be with you to call you, guide you, discipline you, comfort you, enable you, bless you, and use you in his service. And may you be with him in your first love and first loyalty."

For the benediction I invited everyone to say after me, phrase by phrase, "The Lord bless you and keep you; the Lord make his face shine upon you and be gracious to you; the Lord turn his face toward you and give you peace. Amen" (Numbers 6:24-26). To my delight, the choir's choral benediction was the same passage.

Out in the foyer many waited in line to tell me good-bye. There were tears in the eyes of a number, including a few men. There were hugs and kisses aplenty.

PART EIGHT

IN THE LORD'S WORK
1983–1988

Chapter 38

"He Will Watch Over Your Life"

Harrisonburg, Virginia
June 1983–July 1985

After I underwent gruesome tests and x-rays at the Harrisonburg hospital, I received the report from my doctor: "The x-rays and tests show no significant reason to suspect cancer. Go about normal activities for six more weeks, then have blood and stool tests."

"Is that so the trouble can be more easily detected?" I asked.

The answer was "Yes."

My children and I and sister Katie said "No!"

At everyone's suggestion, I called Joe Gascho, the husband of my niece Barbara and a M.D. at the University of Virginia Hospital at Charlottesville. He immediately got me an appointment with a specialist. It was not a minute too soon in a battle for life.

I saw a doctor July 20 in Charlottesville and a colonoscopy was scheduled for July 22. Surgery for colon cancer was scheduled for August 2 at the University of Virginia Hospital.

Two malignant tumors were removed from my upper colon, along with twenty inches of my large intestine and three inches of my small intestine. One of the two tumors had broken through my intestinal wall and affected my lymph nodes. My gall bladder was not affected by the tumors but had stones, so it was removed. When the doctors sent me home, they told me that only twenty to twenty-five percent of patients with my condition were cured.

Conversations with George

Ten days after my surgery, my brother George and his wife Margaret came to visit. The subject soon turned to women in ministry.

George said, "At Bethlehem 83 [Mennonite Church General Assembly] I publicly objected to the statement in the news sheet that mentioned Daniel Kauffman and George R. Brunk I as being down on women. I told them that sixty years ago Papa invited a woman into his pulpit to preach. I said, 'My sister Ruth Stoltzfus had been a pastor and she says he trained her for it.'" George then said to me, "So we may not be as far apart as we thought."

Two days later George and Margaret came again. This time I had some things to say. "That time Papa invited a woman (Sarah Lapp) into the pulpit, it was not to preach."

"He asked her to speak," said George.

"Yes," I answered, "but it was not to develop 'three points' in a sermon. It was an invitation to tell about her mission work in India. She stood a little to the side to speak and when we got home Papa was pleased that she had. Papa did not believe that a woman should be a pastor. We must not use him for our purposes. We must be accurate in our words about him."

Times of blessing

Six weeks after my surgery, on September 15, I flew to Columbus, Ohio, to see my five-day-old grandson, Jacob Grant Stoltzfus Jost, on my way to give three talks at the Central District General Conference Mennonite women's retreat.

Timothy met my plane and took me the ten miles to their home, where I saw Ruthie with a tiny beautiful baby boy. Ruthie had no problem diapering and nursing the baby with her one and only hand. Timothy helped, and so did Kathie, who had come to provide home-made bread and experienced mother advice to her younger sister.

I borrowed Ruthie's Dodge station wagon and drove to Pandora to join a van load of women going to Camp Friedenswald in Michigan. I was identifying so much with Ohio people that at the opening of the retreat, when the moderator said, "All those from Ohio please stand," I found myself standing as though I did not live in Virginia.

The retreat went well, and after it ended I drove back to Ruthie's for another time of blessing with family and an appointment at the Ohio State University cancer clinic. The oncologist confirmed what I had heard in Virginia: "Twenty to twenty-five percent of those with your kind of tumor were cured. The other seventy to seventy-five percent are not. They are doing research and hope to find an effective drug but have none at present."

Back in Virginia I went for my three-month checkup. The test results were good from our human viewpoint, which tends to misunderstand God's plan and expect that we stay on this earth forever. I told family and friends, "God knows my day and my hour. He is watching over my pilgrimage. He does not intend that we have roots too deep here. Like the apostle Paul, I want to stay and I want to go."

New toys

Meanwhile, I was enjoying my new toy, a Commodore 64 computer. Allen and son-in-law John Fairfield ordered components, called the companies for removing bugs, and helped me wade through instructions. When I left Pandora, the church people gave me a gift that paid about one third of the computer cost.

I tried to take a brisk thirty-minute walk every evening, sometimes listening to music on my other new toy, a Sony Walkman, sometimes praying. I bought a cassette recorder and took it as a gift to my sister Katie and her husband, John, with a note that said, "To Katie and John, a token of appreciation for umpteen ten-dollar meals, for taking me shopping and helping me pick out clothing."

Raising questions

On Sunday, May 13, Calvin Shenk of the Eastern Mennonite College (EMC) faculty came to me and said, "Last Saturday night I attended the Women in Ministry conference [held at Harrisonburg Mennonite Church] for the first and only time. I could not believe the clapping that followed Virginia Mollenkott's presentation [approving of homosexuality]. I want to express appreciation to you for your courage in asking those two questions."

After Virginia Mollenkott's presentation I had said, "This is the voice of age, trying to be stronger. I have two questions: About the Virgin Mary—do we gather [from what the speaker had said] that she was irregular morally because she was an unwed mother? Secondly, is the church to give its blessing to any and every covenant?"

On the first question, Virginia Mollenkott essentially had said "no." On the second, "yes."

Calvin said, "A male in the audience could not have asked the questions."

Kathie said to me later, "It needed to be said by a woman who is for the Women in Ministry effort."

A few days later I had lunch with Pam Beverage, chair of the planning committee for the conference. A Virginia Conference leader had told her and the other planners that the Women in Ministry conferences should come under some church authority, and he would suggest this to the Virginia Conference bishops. The bishops had called Pam to appear before them and give an account. She had persuaded Margaret Foth (speaker on Your Time, successor to Heart to Heart) to go with her, and she was sorry they went. One bishop had said God was male and only male.

Those same Virginia Conference bishops issued a statement on the ordination and licensing of women:

> It is our desire to affirm the gift of the Spirit as exercised by the women in the church. . . . With our present understandings we will consider requests for the licensing or ordination of women for diaconate ministries. In light of the continuing theological discussions, we feel that we cannot at this time consider requests for the licensing or ordination of women to the office of pastor.

When I was visiting Kathie a few days later, she said she had heard that I told someone the male critics of the Women in Ministry conference "can just be glad we didn't ordain each other."

I told her I didn't remember, but it sounded like me. I recalled that years earlier I had told Willard Swartley, when he was on the faculty at EMC, that we women leaders, like the early Anabaptists who baptized each other, should ordain each other. Willard had said, "But please let us men be present."

Tribute to George

I thoroughly enjoyed giving my "Family Tribute" to my brother George at the July 22, 1984, celebration of his fifty years of ministry. I told family stories about George and then gave this appreciation:

> Years ago you stayed in our home when you had revivals at Weavers Church in our Harrisonburg area. Helen, our youngest of five, was

captivated by your attention to her. She said later, "Mama, I wish I could be a 'Gawge.' "

While in high school, our son Eugene sustained a head injury on the gym floor. At the hospital the specialist said, "We will know at about midnight which way this is going to turn." Far down the hall I saw a big tender man coming to be with us in our anxiety.

When Grant and I suffered mental anguish over a grown child having serious struggles in matters of the Christian faith, you came to our home and entered into our pain with us.

When Ruthie was seventeen and x-rays of her most useful arm showed bone cancer, you came to talk and pray with her before we flew to Mayo Clinic where her arm was amputated. You called ahead to friends in Minnesota whom you had come to know in your revivals and arranged for them to seek us out and stand with us during those nightmarish days and nights.

At Assembly 73, during open discussion on the role of women in the church, you spoke out in all fairness and said, "Mennonite men have sinned against Mennonite women." In 1982 when you did not approve of my being an interim pastor in Ohio, you were still a gracious brother. Near the time of my departure you phoned and said, "I came by to help you load your car, but you were not at home."

You were about six when Papa was away from home for months

Margaret and my brother George Brunk II. [Gerald Brunk family album].

because of heart trouble and thought he might not live long. At that time he wrote to us children individually. He wrote to you, "Be a good boy. Help work. Don't quarrel. And grow fast so you will be a good, big, farm, church man."

You did become a good, big, farm, church man and I thank God for your life and work.

After the meeting, George gave me a kiss and appreciative words. The next day he said on the phone, "Thank you for all the nice things you said yesterday. You had the audience captivated." He called again a few days later and said he had listened to the tapes and been moved by what I said. "It was more than I deserved," he said.

In connection with the celebration, Virginia Conference set up a ministerial training trust fund "to help worthy young people in their preparation for Christian service." I sent in a donation with these words, "I trust the Virginia Mennonite Conference will respect, recognize, encourage, and assist in the development of the gift of leadership God gives to some women."

"My times are in your hands"

At the end of September I went to the University of Virginia for end-of-one-year x-rays and blood tests. Everything looked fine, my surgeon said. These Bible verses meant more than ever: "My times are in your hands" (Psalm 31:15) and "He will watch over your life" (Psalm 121:7).

I told friends, "When I came home from the hospital, I did not expect to live long, so I subscribed to the newspaper for only three months and hired Jane Burkholder to work for me full time until I died. I kept on not dying, so I told Jane to resume working for other people."

On December 15, I wrote in my journal, "I'll be seventy in three months if I live that long! Beginning six weeks after my August 2, 1983, surgery, I've had thirty-one speaking appointments in six states and Ontario. It is only by God's enabling in every way."

Office hours by appointment

When I told a friend I was working hard on messages for Ontario conference, she said, "Why don't you just use messages you have already given?"

"No," I said, "each one must be born again."

When I listed the speaking engagements that crowded my already full schedule, Eugene asked, "Are you complaining or bragging?"

I tried to keep to a schedule. Mornings I had Bible meditations plus study of several pages in each of a little stack of books and pamphlets. Evenings I was too tired for study and scanned the daily newspaper, *Newsweek*, and Christian publications. Morning and evening and much of the time in between I had background classical music going on cassette tapes.

I listened over and over to tapes of Elizabeth Achtemeier's lectures on preaching, given that fall at Associated Mennonite Biblical Seminaries. Her lectures were not only a good course in preaching, but they deepened my convictions and gave me insight into the acts of God, "the Mighty One," in the long sweep of sacred history. My brother Truman, then 82, retired bishop, former moderator of the denomination, told me, "I never heard anything like it and wish I had heard it long ago."

I wanted to work on a book of stories from my years, but I had interruptions every day and a steady trickle of new requests that I hated to turn down, like speaking to Weavers Church Sunday school classes of fifth, sixth and seventh graders about sex and growing up; writing an article on intimacy for *Voice*, the Mennonite Church women's magazine, and co-writing the annual *Voice* devotional guide on the book of Ruth.

My one-bedroom apartment was buzzing with activity and people needing an hour to five days of my time, depending on whether they had a bad case of the flu and needed a place and care, or just needed someone to listen to their concerns.

I had commitments to give messages and attend churchwide meetings and lead spiritual renewal meetings and workshops at Wayland, Iowa, in the fall, "God willing," as I wrote them. I had promised articles to editors. Where was I to draw the line between other people's needs and my own?

I put a sign on my front door: "Office hours by appointment."

Advice from Helen

That year Helen sent me a birthday letter and a homemade book. The letter said, "Glad you're not slowing down or giving in to the stereotypes of 'old women.' Goodness, Mither [pet name], you're not old at all! I still brag about you to my friends, telling them how I have a mother who preaches and marches and writes and all the rest of it. HAPPY BIRTHDAY!"

She advised me to leave my upstairs apartment unrented. "If you could send the people up there (who need a place to stay) to fend for themselves, you could have the time, privacy, you so desperately need. You really need time and space to keep yourself from going nutty. And what will we do with a nutty mother on our hands?"

Her homemade book was illustrated with big cutout pictures and these captions:

> Places You Will NOT Find My Mother:
> With her nose in the latest FASHION section of *The Times* . . . in the kitchen whipping up some apple strudel . . . poring over the perfume/cosmetic counter at Bloomingdale's.
> WHERE CAN SHE BE FOUND???
> Well, she was here a minute ago—maybe she's at her computer . . . no? Well, call Kathie. Maybe she's taking care of . . . no? Or maybe she went to Ohio for a weekend; didn't she have six speaking engagements . . . no? Or she's probably in the library, getting away from it all . . . no? Or she had that lunch appointment with Eve . . . no? I know. She's taking her walk—see, her Walkman's gone . . . no? She probably went to EMC to do some Xeroxing . . . no? Well, call Mildred—maybe she. . . .

Called to preach

On March 17 I gave the Sunday sermon at Doylestown Mennonite Church, "Discipleship means . . ." The next day I gave a talk to the Clayton Kratz Fellowship in the evening and to a luncheon for business and professional people.

The Fellowship had planned a series of quarterly talks on the theme of being called: "Called to Teach" given by a teacher, "Called to Guide" by a guidance counselor, and "Called to Heal" by a physician. When I was invited and the series was described, I suggested my topic be "Called to Preach" but was told that would not go over well, coming from a woman.

I settled on the title "Called to Faith," and I had a good time. When Vernon Bishop introduced me, he recalled that many years earlier I had done bookkeeping by mail for his brother. He said, "When you sent him a report showing he owed a lot of taxes, you sent along two aspirins."

I closed my message with Romans 15:13: "May the God of hope fill you . . . with hope by the power of the Holy Spirit." I had us say it together several times, substituting our own names where the word "you" appeared. It was a benediction without being pronounced as such by a woman.

When I returned home, I received two calls in one evening from congregations, asking me to preach. Immediately I made notes of ideas that began to flow. I wrote in my journal, "I guess because this is my calling it is almost impossible to say no, and makes my heart sing in spite of the work involved."

History in the making

On March 28, Joe Longacher Jr., congregational chairman of First Mennonite Church in Richmond, Virginia, phoned to ask if I would consider being co-pastor for an interim of one year. The other co-pastor would be Wayne Speigle, a student at Union Theological Seminary, who needed to work a year at a church as part of his education.

Lloyd Weaver Jr. called to say he hoped I would consent. Since there were problems with ordaining or licensing a woman in Virginia Conference, I would be a "commissioned minister with a certificate," he explained. The Richmond congregation was looking for someone with experience, wisdom, and maturity, he said. They had been in a conflict situation since their pastor Bruce Yoder had married a divorced woman. It looked like five couples and maybe more would leave to form another church when Bruce left at the end of May.

When Lloyd said I should not decline because of my health, I joked, "I guess they'd excuse me if I died during my term."

"Wayne needs someone to lean on," Lloyd said, "someone broad-minded, with a variety of experience to be his mentor. You touch base with people. You are not pushed about, but you can listen." He said that Joe Longacher had talked with members most likely to object to a woman minister, and they had said, "We don't object if it's Ruth."

P. T. Yoder called to continue the conversation. Like Lloyd Weaver, he did not just give his consent, but strongly urged me to go. It would help the conference and the congregation, he said. As a medical doctor, he thought my health would be fine for another year at least. "It may be you have come to the kingdom for such a time as this," he said, "and it may be that your health is holding up so you can serve at Richmond."

"I never dreamed I would live to hear such affirming words from Virginia Conference leaders," I wrote in my journal. "He spoke as though he would be glad to be involved in a commissioning service. He expects the ordination of women will come in two to five years."

When I consulted my nephew George, he said, "When I first learned about it, it felt right."

I told him, "Whenever a church official calls to engage me for speaking appointments, my heart rejoices as soon as I hang up, and I start making notes."

"God put those juices in," George said.

Sam Weaver told me that my going to Richmond would help other women. Harold Eshleman said the Richmond congregation had no "attitudes against women."

"History is in the making!" I told friends.

Even my brother George seemed to be changing. When I asked him if it was true that he had made the statement that he did not object to the ordination of a woman but objected to her being a sole pastor, he said, "Yes."

Joe Longacher called to report definite interest for my coming, and I agreed to meet with the pastoral council and the congregation. "Is it faith or foolishness that I am considering this when I already have schedule problems?" I wrote to friends.

While driving to Richmond on April 14, I prayed, "Lord, open or close the door according to your will. But please make it plain." At the meeting, at their request, I told about the flag issue at Grace. Then I gave a message, "The Story of a Man Who Changed," about Isaiah's vision (Isaiah 6:1-8), and stated my vision for the wider church.

Members of the church were asked to respond to a proposal that Wayne and I be commissioned for one year of service within the congregation, beginning July 1, 1985. I would be Wayne's mentor/supervisor, attend First Mennonite at least two weekends a month, preaching one Sunday and observing Wayne preach one Sunday.

On May 10, 1985, Joe Longacher called to say the vote was ninety to ninety-five percent favorable to Wayne Speigle's and my being co-pastors. The commissioning service was set for Sunday morning, July 7, with overseer Lloyd Weaver Jr., officiating.

A great feeling

I flew to Columbus to help Ruthie, whose second son, Micah, was born on June 4. While playing with two-year-old Jacob, I got the sanctified notion to drive to Pandora for church. It was a great feeling to see the wide acres of cropland, but greater still to see the people as I slipped in the side door and sat at the end of one corner. I arrived in time for most of the worship service. Pastor Don Longbottom asked me to speak a bit and have the benediction. His family and another joined me at the home of Phyllis and Dwight Suter for Sunday dinner. I felt gratitude for the faithfulness of the people, despite the controversy over the flag and civil religion.

Chapter 39

Co-Pastor, First Mennonite Church

Harrisonburg and Richmond, Virginia
July 1985–May 1986

Journal entry, June 21, 1985

I am dictating my journal into my Panasonic tape recorder as I drive to Richmond for the first time since First Mennonite Church voted for Wayne Speigle and me to be their pastors. Phyllis Tyson has consented to type my dictation. Not only at my desk at home, but as I travel to and from Richmond, I will be dictating and will not need to type out everything, as I have been doing for years.

Now I am crossing the mountain. It reminds me of what my niece Audrey wrote: "God bless you, Poofie. Be all you can be. You're not old yet. Remember Caleb, who said, 'Give me this mountain.'"

Audrey came by just minutes before I left, on vacation from her work in Choice Books Caribbean. She says she thanks God for my open door in Richmond. She is grateful to her father for giving her a pulpit—writing the Sunday school commentary in the *Sword and Trumpet*. She gives messages in churches and is nothing in the world but a woman preacher. But her mother (my sister Stella) and her father (Ward Shank), along with many other well-meaning Virginia Conference people, object to a woman being a pastor.

It is now 10:30 p.m. and I am headed toward Harrisonburg after a three-and-a-half-hour meeting of the pastoral council. It was decided that Wayne and I would each have the title of co-pastor.

Ron Kraybill is coming this week to work with the congregation. Even those who are breaking away from the church want mediation in order to have the best possible relationship between the two groups.

The council meeting was long, but it was good to see how the members work together. One from the group that is leaving said they want to have a more informal type of worship. I asked if that was a reaction to the past worship or a perception of the future. "That's a hard question," she said, "but informal worship is easier in a small group."

I pray God to help me to be forthright and yet easy to work with.

The car is running fine, Beethoven's music is playing, and I am feeling fine, considering that my day began about 6:00 a.m. I thank God that things are as well with us as they are, as my father prayed so often.

Letter to Doris Gascho, June 24, 1985

I pray to be more conformed to God's will, and feel that his Spirit bears witness with my spirit that I am his.

I am thanking God for an efficient secretary to whom I take tapes of my dictation.

I am struggling with displeasure that the June 13 Virginia Conference newsletter mentions me as mentor but avoids the title "co-pastor." Then feeling disgust at myself for not knowing that discrimination is still with us and not knowing better how to serve without proper recognition.

Journal entry, June 27, 1985

Yesterday I received something I had never received before: the Virginia Mennonite Conference reports to be read by assembly delegates before the next annual conference. By being co-pastor with Wayne Speigle, my name appears as a delegate from First Mennonite in Richmond.

Letter to Doris Gascho, July 1, 1985

This was the beginning of my service at First Mennonite as mentor/supervisor for Wayne Speigle, to observe his sermon once a month and discuss it with him. Union Theological Seminary requires such a person.

Journal entry, July 7, 1985

Wayne Speigle and I were commissioned as co-pastors at First Mennonite Church, Richmond. Ken Stevanus was commissioned to listen to Wayne's sermons and critique them when I am absent. We three were introduced by Joe Longacher Jr., chair of the congregation, and asked for a response. I spoke a few minutes about my vision for the church, saying that I would like to see it be a hospital for healing, a garden for growing, and a base for going.

Paul Wenger Jr., a former pastor, had the morning message. Overseer Lloyd Weaver Jr. conducted the commissioning, including a litany in which the congregation and the pastoral team voiced commitments to each other, followed by a commissioning prayer.

We newly commissioned ones participated in serving the communion. My part was to read from 1 Corinthians 11:23b-26, give thanks for the bread, and assist in serving the cup. Near the close we had a foot washing service in which the men stayed in the auditorium while the women retired to the library to wash each other's feet.

Journal entry, July 15, 1985

Made three trips to the Virginia Conference sessions. I told the editor of conference newsletter that Wayne and I are co-pastors, that "mentor" was a term from Union Seminary. At the conference commissioning Wayne and I were in the "lay pastor" category.

There was a commissioning prayer for me at Park View Church on July 14. Someone said later, "Why don't they just ordain you?" Enough affirmations.

Journal entry, July 21, 1985

I am remembering the Sunday morning, July 21, 1974, when Grant died unexpectedly after a pain in his chest Saturday night, the first such pain in his life. I can see him in the early morning, sitting in his favorite chair with his favorite Book with his head bowed in prayer. He was not a perfect man but he was a man of God and he was the man for me.

Years ago Kathie told me that John had said of Grant, "He is without guile." I understood that he meant [Grant] was without pretense. He always encouraged me in my church work and never said one negative word about it. He shared the parenting of the children and in some of the housework at times. I am finding that [some other] women with leadership abilities are not blessed with helpful husbands who aren't threatened like the one I had.

The title of my first sermon is "As It Is Written." The Scripture is Luke 24:13-35, and the points that emerge from this charming story are that the written word stands, the risen Lord comes, and his redeemed ones witness.

I pray God not only to enable me to give the message, but that it may burn in my own heart and in the hearts of listeners. I ask him to help me to practice what I preach, and to live a life in harmony with the messages I give. I thank him for his grace in using me for his service in spite of my flaws.

Journal entry, July 23, 1985

I am traveling toward home on Interstate 64 West. The music in my car is "Nearer My God to Thee." Since leaving Richmond at 5:30 a.m., and for the last half hour, it has been a worship experience to recount the experiences of the past few days in Richmond, and to be ministered to by my favorite hymns while traveling on this beautiful, tree-lined highway, uncluttered by traffic this time of the morning.

I have needed restoration in my own soul after seeing and feeling more deeply the hurts of the people because of the split in the church. At the annual church picnic Sunday afternoon, I had conversation with many who let down their hair. When I asked Marie for counsel in meeting the needs of the congregation, she said, "Margaret (former co-chair of the pastoral council) and I were talking and we agreed that, judging by your sermon this morning, you had a good understanding of the needs of the congregation."

At the swimming pool I sat at the edge and dangled my feet in the water. A young mother swam over to talk. With tears she spoke of the hurt she feels during church worship because of those who have left. There are people still attending First Mennonite Church who have not made the final decision to leave and there is evidence that some of them will decide to go.

I had good conversation with Bruce Yoder at breakfast Monday morning. He resigned as pastor after he saw that not enough members went along with his marriage. He's relating low-key to the break-off group, who first met without his knowledge.

Journal entry, August 4, 1985

I am heading toward First Mennonite Church, where I will be worship leader. I'm more comfortable giving the message, though it takes more work. Today I will have my first experience of critiquing Wayne's sermon.

Journal entry, August 19, 1985

I attended Mennonite Church General Assembly in Ames, Iowa, August 9-14. I spoke to the Women's Missionary and Service Commission (WMSC) and at a meeting on the women in leadership ministries report. After consulting nephew George, I went to a mike and said, "In all of my seventy years I have not asked for any office but only the freedom to speak the message I felt God gave me. But I found time and again that maleness was considered a qualification and femaleness a disqualification. I believe—though this may be harsh—that those who held and do hold that position are under the judgment of God."

Letter to Doris Gascho, September 2, 1985

Date of tests and x-rays changed to September 16 so I can attend, with Wayne, a morning session at Union Seminary for pastor/supervisors and students in ministry. Thanks if you prayed a week early. Thanks if you'll pray again! I've not had any medicine or treatment these two years (statistics show it doesn't help in my kind of case), yet I feel good and am energetic.

Good experience leading worship yesterday. During sharing a young woman said, "I've often shared about happy times. Today I confess anger with God. Please pray for me." This sparked my comment, "There was a time in my life when I said, 'God, it isn't fair!' The Psalms often begin with complaints and end with words of faith like 'Hope thou in God.'" Many hands went up when I asked how many of us have had times of such anger. I mentioned her in the prayer that followed, spoke to her later, and want to make it easy for her to talk with me further. There are times when our most important ministry is not preaching.

On the way home I stopped at Bridgewater [Virginia], where Kathie's have moved beside a narrow river. Kathie is expecting any day now, worried that at 37 she may not have a normal baby. I had a normal one at 41! At that time we didn't know the risk.

Journal entry, September 3, 1985
Born today: Andrew Robert Wenger Fairfield.

Journal entry, September 9, 1985

It is 6:40 a.m. and I am on my way to First Mennonite Church, where I will meet Wayne Speigle and go to Union Theological Seminary for a session for pastor/supervisors and students in ministry.

Yesterday morning at Park View Church we had the largest college-age Sunday school class, eighteen in all. Peggy Landis, Sunday school superintendent, said that a college-age class has been tried many times, but this is the first it has held together for a whole year. I can only thank God for this continued communication with the young people.

Now I am on the way home from the seminar session at Union Seminary. I felt more comfortable than expected with the other supervisors and the students-in-ministry. Kurtis Hess, director of the seminary office of field education and placement, led a moving opening prayer. He explained the expectations for supervisors and described the Doctor of Ministry program. In the list of students-in-ministry, under Wayne Speigle's name I am listed as supervisor—a supervisor who cannot be licensed or ordained, but the one she supervises will have no problem being so recognized.

Letter to Helen, September 11, 1985

Took supper to Kathie's last Sunday evening. Held the delicious baby Andrew while they ate, and could not believe how much it looked and felt like holding baby Eugene in 1946. Little dark fuzz of hair and something about his face like Eugene, but not the eyes, so he's a mixture. Kathie's strength is about up to par. Does enough law stuff from home to pay rent to keep her office in town for later. She brings baby in the morning for me to keep about an hour. Pure pleasure.

Ruthie told Micah (while in my arms), "Enjoy the limelight while you can. You'll soon have competition," or words to that effect.

Thanks again for coming here and taking care of me when I came home from the hospital in August 1983. I'm blessed with such dear children. And I have such interesting and exciting work to do. I wish all people were so blessed.

Letter to Doris Gascho, September 17, 1985

I had tests at the University of Virginia hospital. My chances to live are better now that I have lived two years since colon surgery, and no trouble was found during yesterday's tests and x-rays. Two years ago a twenty percent chance, now forty percent, surgeon Jones figures.

I have thoughts about not getting things done if my time is short. Mennonite Publishing House is interested in a book of stories from my years, and was also interested in a book of daily thoughts for parents until I put it on a back burner. The fact that I am not getting those things done tells me that the speaking appointments are my priority.

I have felt strongly a call to a speaking ministry. In spite of the hard work and obstacles, it has been and is a joy beyond words. I don't recall ever turning down a speaking request except when there was a conflict or, one time, an illness. Now, when church leaders finally do recognize my gifts, I hesitate to respond negatively. There is more at stake. Again and again, young women have thanked me for helping to pave the way for them.

I have more appointments than usual right now, but there is a tremendous breakthrough that I see as being in God's providence. Instead of typing or photocopying pages here and paragraphs there from pre-Apple computer sermons (on which I had spent hundreds of hours) for use in new sermons, I have Phyllis type previous sermons on the computer and save them on disks. I have the fun of selecting, combining, adding new material on the screen, and printing it for delivery. I love it. Phyllis rattles the keys the fastest I have ever seen and fills disks so quickly that I had to have Allen format more!

I have lots of laughs, loaf some, read in bed, watch a little TV, enjoy being a music nut, seeing children, grandchildren, friends, and enjoy tremendously the work I do. Morning Bible meditations are often rich: "You have made known to me the path of life; you will fill me with joy in your presence, with eternal pleasures at your right hand" (Psalm 16:11).

Ten more Eastern Mennonite College students came to our college-age Sunday school class, making a total of twenty-eight, counting me. We had a good time!

In the next three days I have no appointments, a nice part of work/rest rhythm. Will make a pastoral call to elderly couple from Richmond, now here at Virginia Mennonite Home. Have better grasp on the six messages for Iowa. Immersed myself in clippings from church papers, so I can "sit where those farmers sit," as nearly as possible.

Received a "Certificate of Ministry." Never expected to see it.

Journal entry, September 27, 1985
Kathie just called to say that eleven-year-old Joshua has brought up the question of getting TV. In his argument he said, "Grandma is a righteous woman, and she's got TV."

Journal entry, October 6, 1985
I am driving to Richmond to critique Wayne Speigle's sermon. First I will begin a series during the Sunday school hour on "Singleness, Marriage, and the Family." It will be a heavy morning, since I am to be worship leader and will have a five-minute children's sermon. I have a question for the children: "What have you been putting in your mind lately?" I will tell the story of a boy in my fifth grade class years ago, who said when it was time to read a story after recess, "Read something about somebody getting killed." I will hold before them Philippians 4:8, which I have written on a long piece of white wrapping paper. I will have the children say with me, "Whatever is true, whatever is noble, whatever is right, whatever is pure, whatever is lovely, whatever is admirable—if anything is excellent or praiseworthy—think about such things."

Journal entry, October 13, 1985
My new friend Cathie Scott and I each drove about eighty miles—she drove south and I drove north—to meet for fellowship. We ate a meal together, then drove over the countryside and stopped at an old church. We went to the cemetery, read information on some tombstones, then sat under a tree to talk.

Appropriately enough, Cathie asked, "What are your thoughts about death?" Our conversation ended with prayer.

Last week I received this note from her:

> Let me tell you again how much your long, wonderful prayer meant to my aching soul in that cemetery we wandered into!
> Ruth! It finally got through my hard head! Jesus is the Son of God! I am reading *Mere Christianity* at the suggestion of Chuck Colson on

your tape. Unbelievable the long, winding route the Lord is patient to take with us doubters. I can't believe it took me forty-four years!! What a waste—all that pain and grief.

C. S. Lewis has been a hero since *Narnia*, and now through a circuitous route by a friend's bookshelf, there *it* was. You're probably laughing great cosmic chuckles just like God is at me! He knew he was gonna get me. God bless you for all your help in this.

I didn't know I was helping. We had not discussed the divinity of Christ. Yet God, in his great grace ministered to my friend's need. What a thrill!

Letter to Doris Gascho, October 21, 1985

My sister Katie's husband, John Shank, died unexpectedly in his sleep at 3:30 a.m. three days ago. I canceled everything at Richmond: my sermon and Sunday school series, a meeting with the young mothers' group, and pastoral council.

Katie and John had been active in church work (he as an ordained minister) in this area and in Jamaica, where they were administrators of the Peggy Memorial Home for twelve years. Only several weeks ago they did Choice Books Caribbean work in London. Upon returning, John resumed his work as a retired cattleman on their farm ten miles from here. They had no children. We had been including Katie and John in our family celebrations like Christmas and will still include her. My children loved them.

[My daughter] Kathie's John paid no attention to staying at Katie's bedroom door while talking to her, as we suggested to visitors to avoid spread of the flu. He rushed to her bed, kissed her, knelt and put his head in the covers beside her, then talked to her at length on his knees. Ruthie's Timothy sat on the bed near John and held Katie's hand.

Today Katie caught herself thinking that someone said John was coming. I understand that reaction. I would catch myself thinking the person driving up was Grant or thinking I must tell or ask him something.

Sunday morning, after my first night back home from Katie's, I had the strong impression that I'd be asked to speak in the Goshen area and said audibly, "I'll go." Half an hour later a Mrs. Rempel phoned. "I've been trying to call you. Could you speak at the women ministers' session January 27, 1986, during Ministers Week at Elkhart?"

Letter to Doris Gascho, December 2, 1985

Kathie said she overheard her son Joshua telling a friend, "One of my grandmothers is old-fashioned, the other modern. The old-fashioned one [Grandma Fairfield wears earrings and has anything but the traditional look] lives on a farm and they have bees and things. The modern one has a computer."

Journal entry, December 3, 1985

Yesterday I called the children to come up front for Bob Eshleman's story, "I Remember Christmas." There were only two boys who could be called children. The rest must have been away at Grandma's house for vacation. What to do? I asked, "How many of us feel like children and are willing to come up to these front benches?" Young adults quickly scrambled up front and I came down from the pulpit.

Got the notion to look at cars on the way home from Richmond. Prices were high, so I've decided to have the rusted floors welded and keep the old Peugeot until I have time to decide on another car. Water had splashed up from rainy highway. Kept floor carpet wet. Icy cold air flowed in.

Letter to Doris Gascho, December 9, 1985

After I took the old Peugeot to have welding done, the welders called back and said they find the rust problem is more extensive than they had thought and they advise me not to put any more money in the car and to discontinue driving it except locally. Last Thursday in freezing cold I looked at used cars in three places and test-drove some. Not one seemed right, and all were more than I wanted to pay.

I phoned about cars advertised in the paper, including a 1981 Plymouth Reliant. I went to see it, consulted Allen and Eugene, took it the next day for my trusted mechanic to check, called my bank for book value, and bought it Saturday night for $150 less than the owner first asked because it needed front tires and fan belt replaced and had 73,000 miles on it.

The car drives like a dream. I like its maroon color, medium size, clean-cut look, and AM/FM tape player. Got oil changed yesterday and it was low. Got new front tires this p.m. Will have mechanic do rest of servicing, then annual inspection on Friday.

Grant used to say I was happy when I had wheels under me.

Journal entry, December 15, 1985

I am driving to Richmond to do another in a series on "Singleness, Marriage and the Family," then the sermon, "My Spirit Rejoices," based on the experience of the blessed Mary in Luke 1. This is the first time I am making the trip in my 1981 Plymouth Reliant. It is performing beautifully and is a pleasure to drive. In spite of the bitter cold, the heater is functioning well, and as I drive along, I have hymns and classical music playing on the AM/FM cassette player.

I'll be seventy-one in three months, if I live that long. I thank God for his hand of providence in getting me around all kinds of obstacles and over the rough places so that at last in my old age I can exercise my Spirit-given gift of preaching with some freedom.

Letter to Doris Gascho, December 31, 1985

I had told the leaders before, but for the first time I told the congregation at Richmond of my uncertain prognosis at the close of my message, "How Can We Face the Future?" (Based on Habakkuk's cry of "why?" turning into a cry of trust.) I used an article I wrote by request of editor Dan Hertzler for *Gospel Herald*. He had advised me to make the personal reference. "Otherwise you're talking into thin air," he had said. We preachers must pray for wisdom to say enough yet not too much about ourselves.

I had prayer with a longtime member before she went for delicate surgery for artery trouble in her neck. She came through better than she feared and wrote me, "The prayer on Sunday was a turning point for me." There are some keen joys in ministry.

Letter to Doris Gascho, January 7, 1986

Had noon meal with Joe Longacher, church chairman, and his family. Talked with him about papers from Union Theological Seminary in regard to Wayne, also things Joe wanted to discuss about getting a permanent pastor. There are reasons it may be delayed. Would I consider an extension of this present system beyond my year? I said I'd have to think about it—maybe I could be on call.

It's a struggle, but I refuse almost militantly to give up starting my day with two devotional books, Bible, and reading a few pages from three other books. I've learned that I have to keep fed spiritually as a separate thing from studying for messages, but ideas do flow for messages.

Journal entry, February 2, 1986

I am heading home from Richmond on Sunday evening. Wayne Speigle's sermon was good, and after the service I affirmed his definite progression, the summarization of his points, and applications he made.

Rosalie Eshleman has been wanting a group of older mothers to meet with me, so after the service we planned that on the third Monday of the month, when I stay over for pastoral council meeting in the evening, I will meet with women of any age. The young mothers group will meet with me at 10:00 a.m. the same day.

Journal entry, February 13, 1986

Yesterday I received a call from James Lapp, moderator of our denomination, asking if I would represent the Mennonite Church as one of twelve people from Mennonite and Brethren in Christ churches in North America on a study tour to Central America, June 2–20, visiting churches, then be available to speak in churches back home.

It was hard for my brain to process the information and tell him whether I was leaning toward a positive or negative answer. We agreed that he would mail me the information and call me next Tuesday evening. Meantime, I will think and pray about it and consult some people, including the following by phone today: Doris in Kitchener, Ruthie in Columbus, and Kathie, John, Eve, Allen, and Mildred here at home. I will pick Phyllis's brain when she comes to type on Friday evening.

Journal entry, February 16, 1986

James Lapp says the idea of the trip is for us to visit and listen to our brothers and sisters in the faith—to see their painful situations and to counsel together as to faithful Christian responses for us North Americans.

The congregational chair and pastoral council chair here will consult about rearranging my schedule and give me my answer tonight. One of them said, "I have my answer now, because you would come back and report to this church."

Church leaders are asking the congregation about the possibility of extending the present interim pastoral service beyond June 30. I'm not sure how I feel about this. It does seem that I continue to have some work to do in the wider church.

Journal entry, February 18, 1986

I'm back from Richmond, where it's all "go" as far as consent and even encouragement from church leaders for me to go to Central America in June.

At 10:00 a.m. Monday I met with young mothers, who kept their children with them during the discussion instead of having a baby-sitter in the nursery, as usual for our monthly meeting. During the discussion I said that most of the children in First Mennonite Church are away from their grandparents, uncles, and aunts. What to do? The children are deprived and the grandparents are deprived when they are separated too much. One mother suggested that the church have adoptive uncles, aunts, and grandparents for the children. I made a mental note to present the idea at our pastoral council meeting. Then I went back to my room at the Discipleship Center, where the young voluntary service workers live, and had a nap to prepare for the rest of my day.

In the afternoon I went to the church library, where the women's support group had gathered to meet with me for the first of a series of monthly get-togethers. I began with a devotional and read John 1:6-18. In order to make the passage personal, I went back to the verses and suggested that when I raised my hand each woman would give her own name. Verse 12 became "Yet to Ruth, Joan, Dory, Rosalie, Gloria, Sarah, Dorcas, Caroline, Constance, Ida Mae, Carolyn, Sharon. . . ."

As a group (better than any one person) we planned the format of our monthly meetings: brief time for informal visiting, devotions (by different ones, at my suggestion), input by me on some theme, sharing time on theme or anything on our hearts, eating together at a place nearby.

The final meeting of this busy day was the pastoral council, who gave solid support for my going on the study tour to Central America.

Journal entry, February 20, 1986

Two evenings ago James Lapp called and I consented to represent our denomination as a member of a study group in Central America.

Yesterday I called my surgeon, R. Scott Jones, at University of Virginia Hospital to ask if he would say "Go ahead," as he did for requests in the States. Going to Central America will involve typhoid, tetanus, hepatitis shots, anti-malaria tablets, etc.

"You should go ahead the same as the others in the group," he said, "but be careful because that is an area of violence."

Letter to my family, March 1, 1986

Joe Longacher, chair of Richmond Church, has asked if I could continue at Richmond for all of 1986 and maybe a few months more, until they get a permanent pastor.

P. T. Yoder, formerly my doctor, now in church work full time, said, "How's that for confidence that you are going to be all right?" He had called to ask if I would serve a three-year term on the Virginia Conference Discernment Committee, which suggests personnel for boards. I told him someone else may be able to do it better.

On the front page of my devotional book, *Light to Live By*, I have listed the names of all twenty in our family. I often pray for each one. At the bottom I have written my prayer: "Until the end of time, from generation to generation, bring each one of us to Jesus Christ, the way, the truth, and the life, the way for wanderers like us, the truth for doubters like us, the life for dying people like us, and as my father used to often pray, 'without the loss of one.'"

Journal entry, March 16, 1986

I gave my sermon, "Seven Last Words of Jesus." Toward the close I felt moved to give this invitation: "Is there someone in the audience today who feels a call to seriously take Jesus as personal Savior and Lord? If so, you can raise your hand or stand, remain silent, or speak a few words, just as you feel moved." There was no response.

I continued, "Is there someone in this audience who feels the call to love Christ more dearly and follow him more nearly? I know of one person." At this point I raised my hand to indicate I was that one, and then I asked, "Are there others?"

Several dozen people raised their hands. I then led a prayer for us all.

Letter to Doris Gascho, April 18, 1986

This weekend, nephew George R. Brunk III and I will serve together at Durham (N.C.) Mennonite on "Women's Role in the Church." He begins on Friday with "Why Do We Disagree?"

Letter to Doris Gascho, April 20, 1986

It was a miracle day at Durham Mennonite on Saturday. The night before, I got three hours of sleep. Ruthie, Timothy, and two babes, Jacob and Micah, arrived at 12:20 a.m. instead of 11:00 p.m., as expected. The babes bawled, off and on, until 2:20 a.m. Then I slept until 5:20 a.m.! I'm glad they came, nevertheless!

I took off for Durham at 7:30 a.m., equipped with Pepsi to keep me awake. Had an emotional/spiritual experience listening to a tape of Galatians, then hymns by the Mormon Tabernacle Choir. Arriving at 11:50 a.m. and finding the church locked, I decided to take a nap on the front seat of my car. Before long, a member of the church came and unlocked the doors. At his suggestion I went to the nursery, spread out a thin mattress on the floor, and dozed off into shallow sleep several times—enough to feel rested. Never mind such problems when I get to preach! I never think about how I feel while speaking!

The two sessions—1:30 p.m. and 3:30 p.m.—were keen joy. The audience was small but intensely interested in the overall theme, "Women's Role in the Church." It was more like a seminar than a regular church service.

Serving with nephew George R. Brunk III was an enjoyable experience. During a recent sabbatical he made a special study of "headship," at the request of some church agency. I didn't know where he came out on the question until this day.

Toward the close of the last session, he and I stood together in the pulpit in discussion with each other and with the audience. I said, "Could I ask you if your emphasis is more on the fact of 'decency and order' than it is on which sex leads the order?"

He answered, "Exactly. Precisely. I'm glad you asked that question," and enlarged on the point. If I understood him correctly, he said if the Apostle Paul were teaching in our time, his teaching on headship would be different than it was in his time.

He and I believe we must be very, very cautious on this point!

Journal entry, May 19, 1986

As requested, I spoke a bit before my sermon yesterday about going to Central America. Sermon title was, "How Can We *Really* Work for Peace?" I called for action, warning them that some of my ideas are controversial—protesting war taxes, for example.

One woman said it was the first message on peace for a long time at First Mennonite [Richmond]. She has a son who spent time in jail for protesting at missile sites. A few others thanked me warmly. Most were silent on the question. I only hope I have God's smile of approval.

Letter to Helen, May 21, 1986

On June 3 you will be thirty!

Memories flood my mind of your childhood years: the time you stood patiently beside me even though you were too little to see over the counter where I was studying what to buy at the department store, the good baby you were in church and elsewhere as long as I was holding you, your stage on the front porch and family audience on the front lawn, your perceptive questions, like the one after I read you a Bible story, "How do we know there is a God?"

Your growing-up years hold only pleasant memories, with thanksgiving that you did not cause Daddy and me mental anguish in that difficult time of coming to self-identity.

Now you are a woman of thirty: tall, beautiful, gifted, creative, so dear, well-meaning, honest, and forthright. I think Daddy and I did a good job with you and you responded well to our care and training!

Now you say you and Albert are going to be married.

I can see that he is a fine man. You know my concern that there should be mutuality of religious belief in a marriage, for the sake of both spouses and their children. This, without shifting from the centrality of Christ and the Bible in your life. This, without any substitute for his church—his true church.

I love you much, dear daughter.

Chapter 40

God's People in Central America

El Salvador, Nicaragua, Honduras
June 2–20, 1986

At the top of a steep mountain our group of twelve visited Mesa Grande refugee camp, inhabited by 11,373 refugees who were bombed out of their homes in El Salvador by the government. I have a drawing by a child from that camp. The picture shows the Lepan River and the air force bombing civilians and a soldier with an automatic rifle. We went into a room where twenty-three people from three families lived.

The refugee camp had three open-air kitchens where the 700 people who lived there eat beans and cornmeal. The refugees told us how they had been forced to flee from their homes because the government is trying to clear guerrillas out of the mountain areas. One man said, "We want to go back to our homes. President Duarte says that these areas are being cleared out to get rid of the guerrillas, but it's the civilians who are being killed."

One father said he went without food for twelve days. Another said, "We tried to escape by way of a river, but the water was so high children and old people drowned." Some got across only to face soldiers with rifles.

We went to a political prison that held people because they were sympathetic to the wrong side of the conflict.

On our way to the refugee camp we had passed the cathedral where Archbishop Romero was murdered in 1980 while conducting mass. Several Mothers of the Disappeared, wearing black shirts and white scarves, were marching in front of the cathedral. Later we visited the Mothers of the Disappeared and heard their stories of children taken out of their homes at night.

"We went to the security office and the dumps, and no one would tell us where our children were," they told us. One woman said, "My son was taken four years ago and I haven't heard from him since." Others said, "We are marching. We are holding banners. We are saying, 'You took our children. They left us alive. We want them back alive.' "

After listening to the stories of eight mothers, I told a member of our group that I felt like I had been to 5,000 funerals. He said, "That's how many the Mothers Committee say have disappeared."

We visited Pastor Gomez, a Lutheran pastor, who told us how their organization is serving the people through mobile health units, teaching about agriculture, education, and pastoral services. "The government calls us subversives," he said. Sure enough, he was denounced in newspapers and on radio and TV for working against the government.

Along with five or six others of our group I went to his Sunday morning service. We heard Pastor Gomez say to his people, "You perhaps know that I have been accused of being against our government. I want you to know the accusations are false. I want you to know, too, that I don't expect to leave the country. I'm not going to leave you. I'm going to stay with you. I want you to pray that I will be faithful to my duty as a pastor—that I will be a shepherd willing to give his life for his sheep."

One small group after another surrounded him with tender touches. I went up front and knelt at the rail for communion. I felt the reality of Christ's body broken and his blood poured out for us.

In Nicaragua and Honduras we had unhindered fellowship in churches. We were told in orientation, "You'll go into Mennonite churches where they do a lot of clapping, and when somebody is up front praying, so is everybody else in the audience." Far outside of Tegucigalpa, the capital of Honduras, we attended such a church. It was filled with 750 people on a Saturday night. Two men on the platform and people all over the audience were praying audibly.

At the small Danli Mennonite Church, members of our group spoke a few words that were then translated into Spanish. A chorus of "Amens!" came from the people after each presentation. When the pastor spoke he said, "I could hardly contain tears because of the Spirit." They could not thank us enough for coming to listen to them, worship with them, and hear with them the call of Christ on our lives. They said, "Remember that you have a family here." In his closing words to us, a Mennonite leader said, "Take a holy kiss from the Honduran Mennonite Church."

In each of the three countries we were told, "Please tell your government to stop sending military aid. As long as aid continues, our suffering continues."

When I returned from Central America, I could not forget the words of those who lived in fear of their own government—the so-called democracy of El Salvador that from 1979 to 1986 killed more than 50,000 of its own people with an army trained and financed by the United States.

Chapter 41

Associate Pastor, First Mennonite Church

Harrisonburg and Richmond, Virginia
July 1986–June 1987

Letter to Doris Gascho, July 15, 1986

I just heard about the wedding of Helen and Albert Greenberg: They drew the few attending in a circle around them and they had singing and Jewish and Christian prayers, including a prayer by Ruthie. Then Ruthie, Helen, Helen's friend Janine, and Timothy sang "Praise God from Whom All Blessings Flow" from the *Mennonite Hymnal*. The ceremony was on video and we'll be seeing it here when it arrives.

Back at the apartment they would occupy, Helen and Albert introduced to a housewarming group the video as "a production (drama) we've been working on." Only when the people saw the words CLERK OF COURT, did it begin to dawn that there had been a wedding earlier that day!

Letter to Doris Gascho, October 7, 1986

Paul R. Yoder, chairman of Park View Mennonite, asked me at church if I plan to go with the group forming a congregation at the Eastern Mennonite College Campus Center. I said yes, I think I will sign up to relate there, one year at a time. He expressed concern that my college-age class continue at Park View, and for the young people coming on later (his daughters included, I assume). I told him, "I hope the new congregation will be a part of Park View, and we'll come back here for the second hour." Some of us think there should be a swarming rather than the big building program planned at Park View.

I can only thank God for the privilege of relating to young people. Surely his Spirit is at work. The class is like a little church, with prayer and occasional singing and a benediction.

Letter to Eve MacMaster, November 14, 1986

Park View Mennonite is going to own the new congregation, Campus Center Mennonite Church (CCMC). On October 26, while I was away, those beginning the congregation stood up and were commissioned at Park View. November 2 was the first service of CCMC. I was there with the group of about eighty-six, which included some students and a few from other churches in the community. CCMC bulletin is an insert in PVM bulletin, and both churches give out both bulletins in that form.

The testimony of a Peace Corps commercial I saw this morning was pretty cute: "It's the hardest work I ever loved." That just about describes my fourteen months in Ohio as interim pastor at those two churches.

I just had a call from Overseer P. T. Yoder, asking me to serve on a Virginia Conference committee to work on a statement on "headship." If it were not for him and nephew George also serving, I would not want to consent.

Letter to Doris Gascho, November 24, 1986

It's a Monday morning at Ruthie's in Columbus, and I'm writing at the kitchen table while Timothy is getting ready to take me to the airport.

I enjoyed speaking at Neil Avenue Mennonite Sunday morning about "God's People in Central America." This is a "sanctuary" church—giving haven to refugees—and the sanctuary committee asked me to come.

In the afternoon Ruthie and I attended a lecture about women in the sanctuary movement. I am encouraged that there is a group in Columbus who are interested in giving sanctuary to illegal aliens. I am convinced that our government is responsible for the atrocities committed in El Salvador by the army they train and finance. This explains the mindset that makes it illegal to give sanctuary to people escaping the terror in El Salvador.

Letter to Doris Gascho, December 9, 1986

I survived the meeting of the Virginia Conference committee on "headship" today. Chairman P. T. Yoder, said, "How shall we start?" I suggested that we first discuss what headship is not, to try to clear away the myths and misinterpretations of Scripture before forming a statement—just as rubbish must be removed from a property before a building can be constructed.

He wrote on the board WHAT HEADSHIP IS NOT and under it "domination, oppression, superiority, gender specific (?)" in line with our discussion. It was peaceful, considering that pastor Roy Kiser and I are poles apart, as shown by his last words that a woman should certainly not be in pastoral leadership.

Pray that I can know what to say and when to keep quiet. Nephew George is a prince of a guy in the committee—a gentle Brunk with a good grasp of the Scriptures and a knack for presenting his views while commanding Roy's respect. I told George I'd hate to serve on the committee without him.

Letter to Doris Gascho, February 12, 1987

Two days ago at our Virginia Conference study committee on headship, Roy Kiser said, "The men don't try to do a woman's role—child bearing. Why do women try to do a man's role—leadership?"

I answered that the Bible gives instructions to fathers about their duty to children. Both parents have home duties. But those Bible verses are interpreted in such a way as to exclude fathers from home duties. Then 1 Corinthians 12 and Romans 12 are interpreted to exclude women from using their gifts in the church.

Then he asked me, "Who says what the gift is?"

"The Holy Spirit decides," I said, "but there are men who think they know better than the Holy Spirit!" What is so disgusting is the idea that a biological function is considered a substitute for other work. What about the years after the children are grown and flown when usefulness is still important? If a mother's highest calling is to be a mother, why isn't it a father's highest calling to be a father?

But it was a good meeting. While studying "the head of Christ is God," chairman P. T. Yoder and my nephew George developed the thought that God gave authority to Christ!

Where was it taking us? P. T. Yoder said, "God turning over

authority to Christ means that men should give authority to women in leadership."

Roy Kiser said, "I'm the only one on this committee who takes the traditional view."

Surprised at my congenial feeling, I told him it's good for us to hear each other.

Journal entry, February 13, 1987

Helen welcomed me at the airport with hugs, kisses, and a beautiful bouquet of big daisies and sprigs of greenery. We went sightseeing and rode over the famous Golden Gate Bridge. I was amazed at the hills in and around San Francisco. I thought that like the Atlantic, I would see just a great body of water. If you just step off the highway, it seems you'd roll down a half-mile or so. The land was just turned up sideways by earthquakes.

Friday evening we drove to a retirement village and had a delightful evening there in the apartment of their Quaker friend Morgan, a man in his eighties. Albert said, "He is my mentor." At the meal everyone joined hands for prayer and instead of it being silent as Helen and Albert usually do, Morgan called on me for a "Mennonite prayer." Morgan has friends across the boundaries of race, class, and religious belief. He and Albert got acquainted when Morgan went to a performance of A Traveling Jewish Theater which Albert and two others founded eight years ago.

Albert is a wonderful man and Helen spoke of these friends as being "family," but my heart is heavy concerning the matter of mutuality of belief in a marriage.

Journal entry, February 14, 1987

At noon I took Helen and Albert out to eat and then we were off to the airport for my flight to Los Angeles and the meeting of the Council on Faith, Life and Strategy (CFLS).

Journal entry, February 15, 1987

This morning our council members scattered to seven different churches. Wayne North and I went to Faith Mennonite Church in the morning. James Lapp, Phyllis Pellman Good, and I attended Pasadena Mennonite Church in the evening, when the church has its regular Sunday worship service.

Three hours before the evening service began, I discussed with young pastor Jim Brenneman what my theme would be for the evening message. I made a number of suggestions, but when he said that my message would be preceded by a drama sketch on Jesus and the Samaritan woman, we agreed that I would take that as a springboard for my thoughts.

It was a new kind of excitement to speak only from my small brown Bible with a few words written in the margins, with nothing else except some points and stories from memory. There was plenty of time for eye contact!

At the close of the meeting two young men from Fuller Seminary came to talk to me. One said he had never heard a woman give a sermon before. He asked if I believed women are equal to men. How did I interpret the Scriptures on the question of man's headship and silence of women in church? What books would I recommend for him to read? I promised to send him a list in the mail.

Journal entry, February 16, 1987

CFLS is like a board of elders breathing over the whole denomination and seeing what we can do for the welfare of the church. First on our agenda was the concerns of the Los Angeles area church leaders. We also discussed the training of ministers, the relationship of General Board to General Assembly and program boards, relationship of conferences and churchwide boards, minorities and race relations in the church, how to make mission for Christ our priority all over the church, and more.

For some time I have been concerned that nothing was done about the dilemma of those who cannot conscientiously pay the portion of their federal taxes that goes for the military, a tax withheld by a church agency. After consulting my nephew George about the wording, I drew up a memo to CFLS, pointing out "the new questions of church subordination to the state when a church agency is forced to side with the state against the conscience of its own members, especially when the church is on record supporting the conscientious action of its members in nonpayment."

I questioned the tactic of calling for a churchwide study and suggested that "CFLS review and evaluate the way the concern was processed and call for a plan whereby the request of employees be respected and taxes for military purposes not be withheld by church agencies."

In the discussion that followed, I held to my point that it is a contradiction for the church to be on record as supporting individuals of conscience on this question, yet not respecting their position.

Journal entry, March 6, 1987

Sunday morning I enjoyed giving the Sunday morning message at Frazer Mennonite Church [in Pennsylvania]. The bulletin said I would have the sermon, but a woman said afterwards, "I appreciated your, uh, talk."

On Sunday night nineteen attended the first Keystone Bible Institute class on "Singleness, Marriage, and the Family," and eight attended the one on Colossians. For the morning class on "Women in the Bible," which began Monday morning, eight people came. A man told me he photocopied my *Gospel Herald* article, "Jesus and the Role of Women," for his conservative mother and it helped her.

Journal entry, March 17, 1987

My first presentation at Hesston (Kan.) College was to 500 students at chapel on "What Is Real Love?" My opening words were "Greetings to all of you people who are keeping a growing edge by being in college. Keep studying and reading and experiencing, all the rest of your life."

Chapel was followed by informal dialogue at the faculty/staff coffee break. A woman commented, "You said to the students what we cannot say."

Journal entry, March 19, 1987

My first appointment was a prayer breakfast for faculty, staff, and students. I spoke on, "How Can We Know God's Will?" My beginning story was of grandson Andrew, one and a half, who crawls up on a chair and gets into things on the kitchen table. While he is messing into the sugar, the salt and pepper, he says, "No, No." I said some older people are doing things they know are not God's will, so the first requirement for knowing God's will is to WANT God's will.

A young man from the group came to me later saying, "I hope to be married in several years, but expect to go into a voluntary service program. My problem is money. How am I going to have enough for a marriage?" I said, "Take the next step that is clear to you, and God will make a way as needed later on. I am glad to see that you are giving service the priority at this time."

My chapel talk was "Singleness and Marriage." I wanted to speak to both since not all the students will marry, but the limited time did not allow for a full discussion of either subject. Next, as prearranged, I met with a class on roles of men and women. Dwight Roth, the professor, thought they were surprised that a woman my age would discuss sensitive aspects of the sexuality study now recommended in our churches.

Letter to Doris Gascho, March 27, 1987
To meet the Virginia Conference printing deadline, I needed to study Isaiah at least enough to formulate themes of three morning Bible studies during Conference, July 16–18. It's the first a woman is to have the studies.

Letter to Doris Gascho, April 8, 1987
I don't know if others besides me suggested Shalom Mennonite Church, but that may become the name of the new Campus Center Church.

Letter to Doris Gascho, April 27, 1987
I let down my hair to the college-age Sunday school class and told them I can hardly stop my early morning studies in the *NIV Study Bible* (which I now prefer to *Thompson's Chain Reference*). I told them I wish I had had something like it fifty years ago. I showed the features of the book and said, "To give this book may be the best contribution I could make to anyone's life. I want to give it to those interested in using it for serious Bible study. Is that too harsh?" I asked.

They said, "No."

"How can I do it?" I went on. "I won't treat you like children and give stars for passages studied. I need your ideas rather than to make the decision alone."

One person said, "I think a good way would be for anyone to come to you personally and express interest."

"Yes," I said, "that's good. Thanks for that. The person would be accepting my offer and need not hesitate."

Another said, "I think it would be good for the persons accepting the gift to let you know, say in six months or so, about their use of the book."

"That sounds good," I said, "but I wouldn't want anyone to feel obligated."

This all showed me once again that you can get by with stumbling ways and uncertainty about procedure, not only if others share the decisions, but if you genuinely care for the persons involved.

Journal entry, May 9, 1987

I am in a comfortable room at Spruce Lake Retreat in the Pocono Mountains north of Philadelphia. I arrived last evening in time for the first of four talks with the Allentown congregation, who are having their annual retreat.

Journal entry, May 10, 1987

A bonus at the retreat was to talk with Lois Gunden Clemens, who came with her husband, Ernest, to join the bird watchers group in session at Spruce Lake the same weekend as our retreat. Besides talking with her during a meal, I also asked her to come by my room to discuss the head covering, which seems almost gone in the Mennonite Church. We discussed the problem of not wanting to offend people who still hold to the practice and yet not wanting to be two-faced. We discussed whether Paul meant to be teaching in his time about a prayer covering to be worn by women in our time.

My practice this weekend was to wear my beaded hairnet all of the time except for the Sunday morning service, when I wore my black head covering.

Letter to Doris Gascho, May 14, 1987

Our May 13 Virginia Conference headship committee meeting was a delight, despite disagreements. Amazingly, our meetings were peaceful. Tremendous freeing insights came from nephew George on passages having to do with headship, submission, silence, also serving as leaders.

Journal entry, June 7, 1987

I left home this morning at 7:55 for First Mennonite Church,

Richmond, and am now on the return trip after my last sermon of the two years I have been relating to the congregation. It was a special children's day program with the children doing skits and music.

After the service there were kind comments about my work and regrets that my time with them is at a close. Joe Longacher, former chairman of the congregation, said he regretted that there was no sharing time for people to express appreciation.

Ida Mae Leatherman, my first and one-half cousin, represented the cordial, well-meaning people in the church who are not fully happy about women as leaders. She gave me an affectionate good-bye and said, "But I still don't believe in women preachers."

Wayne is now the permanent pastor of the congregation and will be ordained soon.

Journal entry, June 21, 1987
This is the day Wayne Speigle was ordained to the ministry. The woman whose job description was to be his mentor/supervisor and critique his sermons will never be ordained. No one has ordained me except the Lord.

Chapter 42

Free to Prophesy

Harrisonburg, Virginia
June 1987–December 1988

On June 22 I had a confrontation with my brother George on the woman question when he came to borrow folders from Grant's files. Before he went out the door, I called, "Shouldn't you be a little more courageous in letting [some conservative leaders] know that you do not object to a woman being ordained, but you do object to her being sole pastor?"

He answered, "I think they know where I stand."

"I don't think so," I said. "Write it to them and send me a copy. Did you select those excerpts in the May Fellowship of Concerned Mennonites' *Informer* from [Sanford] Shetler's writings on women in ministry?"

"Yes."

"There is no sign there that you allow for any kind of ordination of a woman. The excerpt citing the Baptist Church as a model in its refusal to ordain women is disgraceful." I said more.

The next day when George brought back Grant's folders, I saw that he wanted to talk, and talk we did. He said he and Shetler agreed that a woman should not be a pastor. I had no idea how he reconciled that with his former acknowledged statement that he did not object to a woman being ordained but did object to her being sole pastor. I wanted to talk more about that, but was too busy giving him "both barrels" about the fragile Mennonite male ego perpetuating the patriarchal system, not calling for the slavery system but still calling for oppression of women.

He interrupted a couple of times, but when he said, "Are you through?" I said, "No!" He laughed and said, "Can I talk now?"

I said, "Yes." As he was leaving, I said, "I want to kiss you. It's not a Judas kiss. I love you, dear brother."

He kissed me and said, "I love you. Do you hear me honk when I drive by?"

I said, "Yes, and I appreciate it."

Affirming brothers

At the Mennonite Church General Assembly at Purdue University in July 1987 I spoke briefly to the assembly about the woman question. Afterward Pastor Menno Heinrichs, executive secretary of New York State Fellowship, asked if I would consider being interim pastor at Clarence Center–Akron Mennonite Church in New York, and if he could present my name. I said I would be willing to enter into dialogue but could not promise at this point.

After I led three Bible studies on Isaiah at Virginia Conference Assembly in July, Sam Weaver sent me a handwritten note saying "Thanks for helping to make our Assembly a success. Too bad you are not about forty years old. We could use you for another thirty years. Maybe Virginia Mennonite Conference woke up too late."

A pastorate that didn't happen

On July 21, 1987, the thirteenth anniversary of Grant's death, I wrote in my journal, " 'Love truth and peace' (Zechariah 8:19) on his tombstone represents so much about Grant as a teacher and writer of truth, of peace, of efforts on churchwide and interfaith committees, and the way he always took the side of the underdog."

That same day Menno Heinrichs phoned to talk further about the possibility of my becoming interim pastor at Clarence Center–Akron Mennonite. We agreed that I would fly to Buffalo on August 29 to meet with the pastoral search committee, preach at the Sunday morning service, attend a noon potluck meal, and dialogue with the congregation.

Menno said they wanted someone to bridge the time until the coming of a permanent pastor, and perhaps be a mentor for the young man they were considering as permanent pastor. The position could be part or full time, four months to a year.

When Menno wondered if my title could be "pastoring elder," I said, "If I do the work of a pastor, I would not warm up to that idea. I did serve as an elder in the Park View Mennonite Church. I would not see my work at Clarence Center–Akron as being the work of an elder."

At Clarence Center I first met with the search committee and answered questions about my life, work, and call and asked some questions of my own, following the five pages of handwritten suggestions Doris Gascho, a Mennonite Church leader in Ontario, had sent me.

Someone said, "It would be good for us to discuss whether this committee is ready for a woman to serve in a pastoral role." All proceeded to express themselves favorably except one, who said, "No comment. I stated my position earlier." I gathered from our conversation that another member of the search committee who was absent was also negative to a woman pastor.

Menno brought to the meeting a poll to be distributed at the close of my dialogue with the congregation. My nephew George had suggested to me that such a poll be taken, to ascertain whether it was acceptable to them for a woman to be a pastor on an interim basis.

After the worship service came a potluck meal and a meeting with about forty members of the congregation. Most of the questions were asked by a man who said it was the first he had seen a woman give a sermon from a pulpit. "Have our women in the church been influenced by the ERA and thus feel that they have been discriminated against?" he asked.

I answered that the Bible teaches freedom and equality for women.

Someone else asked, "What is it that you think you could do in this church that a man could not do?"

"I am not interested in coming to this congregation in a pastoral role if the people are not ready, or if my gifts cannot be fully used," I answered. "I am praying that God will open or close the door according to his will. It does not matter to me which it is."

During the meeting an elder and a member of the pastoral search committee said, "This has been a mountaintop experience."

Afterward the man who asked most of the questions was friendly and we shook hands. I thanked him, saying, "That helped me to focus on questions that must have been in the minds of others also."

I was overwhelmed by the people, many of them women, who thanked me for helping them to "learn so much in the meeting."

As he drove me to the Buffalo airport, Ray Yoder told me that the results were seventy-nine percent positive, and he and his wife began asking what kind of housing I'd prefer. Living in a big house with a widow? Living alone in a trailer? In a furnished apartment?

"The final vote of the church will be the test," I said.

Menno Heinrichs called the next day. "The meeting was a good experience," he said. "I had been praying for a miracle and Sunday afternoon it happened. It was a historical, significant step. You talked about your call being a speaking ministry. Your teaching is biblical and touches us where we live. You could meet with groups and lead in Bible study."

On September 11 he called to say that the pastoral search committee had decided to recommend to the congregation that the young man and I serve together on a pastoral team for up to one year. A ballot would be distributed September 12 and the vote taken on September 27. The ballot listed three options: calling both the young man and me as a pastoral team for up to one year, calling the young man as interim pastor for up to one year, calling me as interim pastor for up to one year.

The day after the vote, Menno called to report that the results were not high enough for me to serve in a pastoral role. While the poll of the 35 or 40 (of a congregation of 130) attending the August 30 meeting had been 79 percent favorable, the final vote was 39-yes, 32-no, and 31 absentee ballots yet to be counted. In the unlikely event that all absentee ballots were in favor, there would still not be the necessary 75 percent. To further complicate things, the young man the pastoral search committee had recommended to serve with me had withdrawn.

Later Menno Heinrichs reported that the final count of votes was 53-yes, 43-no. The congregation had chosen "a young man who has been with the congregation for six months." Menno wrote, "He had some training in Bible school and does quite well as a teacher. He is a son-in-law of one of the elders. I believe he has potential."

Freeing God's daughters to prophesy

John Lederach from Philhaven Hospital in Mount Gretna, Pennsylvania, invited me to speak at one of their teleconference luncheons for clergy and church workers. Seated with Eastern Mennonite Seminary people in Harrisonburg on November 12, I spoke by phone connection to eight groups at mission boards and seminaries in Pennsylvania, Virginia, and Indiana. My topic was "Freeing God's Daughters to Prophesy."

My broadcasting experience helped me visualize the unseen audience beyond the seminary gathering. I began by saying:

> I appreciate so much the men and women in the church who have worked to bring about greater freedom for women to use their Spirit-given gifts in the church, but we still have more work to do and to do together. I feel like I've waited fifty years to give this message, so—thanks to God's providence—John Lederach and some significant others came on the scene before I move off of the scene.
>
> Fifty years is about how long I have felt (and it has been reflected to me by persons over the church) that the Holy Spirit gave me gifts for a prophesying ministry. I have three big notebooks bulging with stories from my years. I will not speak *of* those experiences but *out of* those experiences.

I spoke about prophetesses and other women leaders in Bible times, longstanding myths about women, and Jesus' treatment of women. Then I gave my suggestions for freeing women to prophesy. Delivery was pure delight, even though I had to read fast to stay within the thirty-minute limit, making my words a bit snappy. The responses of those who came up front afterward were gratifying: hugs, comments, and requests for tapes and printouts.

Chided

The next day I sent copies of my talk to four of my siblings as one more effort to help them understand "where I'm coming from." In a covering memo I wrote, "You know, happily or unhappily, that you have a sister who is some kind of preacher. I have felt God's call for decades and am as sure of my calling as any of you have been about yours."

My brother George called a few days later and chided me for calling my messages sermons and for saying that I preached. "Papa didn't believe in a woman being a preacher," he said.

I answered, "He didn't believe in having a piano in the home either" (meaning, "as you do").

Later I told my daughter Kathie that after the confrontation my face was flushed and it was hard to get back to my work. "When something like that happens, you must talk it out promptly with someone," she said.

I still regarded George as a great preacher and a loving brother in his own way, but I considered his chiding to be irreverence for the work of the Spirit in my life. Our main disagreement was whether a woman should be sole pastor of a church. To me, this had all kinds of implications as to whether the male/female, superior/inferior system should continue.

In the Lord's work

I drove in a different car than planned when I headed north on January 9 to teach at Keystone Bible Institute in Lansdale, Pennsylvania, and give a Sunday morning message and a chapel message at Christopher Dock Mennonite High School. As I was leaving home at noon, the gears to my car would not function properly. I turned back not knowing what to do next. At a motor sales place I impulsively turned in and talked to Wade Arbogast, the owner, whom I scarcely knew. "Could you rent me a car?" I asked. "I'll pay you whatever car rental companies charge."

He brought around an '81 Oldsmobile Cutlass, fixed up the papers, and gave me a copy. I transferred my suitcase, books and papers to the Olds. As he was seeing me off, I said to him, "I love you!" I trusted my gray hair to help me get by with such a statement without being misunderstood.

At Lansdale, Mary Jane Lederach Hershey said to me, "Years ago, when you and I were in a group of women at Washington, D.C., visiting government offices, you told us you were ordaining us, and you said, 'Now go and do the work of the Lord.' I always took this seriously."

Pastor John E. Sharp said, "One family did not attend this morning because a woman was giving the message." He added, "There was never a more powerful sermon preached at this church." In the same breath and with tearful eyes he said, "I thank God and you for the message."

An Eastern Mennonite College (EMC) student's wife said, "No honest person listening in their right mind could say women don't belong in the pulpit."

About twenty-two women and two men attended the daily Bible classes. One evening, as the teachers ate together, I mentioned the comment of one of the other teachers, Paul Lederach (a bishop), after my Philhaven teleconference message. He had said, "The main theme we tend to miss is that the subservience of women is related to the Fall, which Christ came to redeem, and by continuing to assign a secondary status to women we are perpetuating the Fall. This theological background needs to be understood."

Paul said, "I would like to make a list of instructions to slaves as given in the New Testament and then ask some of our brethren who object to women serving in public which of these verses we should be keeping today."

When I arrived home from Pennsylvania, I checked in with Wade Arbogast to pay for six days' use of his car, expecting the bill to be several hundred dollars (for which I would be reimbursed by Keystone Bible Institute). "How about fifty dollars, which would be half-price?" he asked. As I started to write the check he said, "I won't charge you anything. You were in the Lord's work."

Like the early Anabaptists

After the worship service at Shalom Mennonite (formerly Campus Center Mennonite) on April 3, Chris Gill, commissioned pastor, told me that an EMC student who had been meeting with us was requesting baptism. Chris said, "Since you are licensed, would you do the baptizing?" I told him I was not licensed but had been commissioned a number of times as interim pastor or co-pastor.

The previous September I had been asked to baptize Chris and I had answered, "I'd like to do it if it wouldn't break up the church." At that time I had talked with Sam Weaver, and he had said, "Get permission from Overseer P. T. Yoder and go ahead." I declined out of consideration for a member at Shalom who was opposed to a woman pastor, but who later left Shalom.

Chris Gill and I agreed to baptize the student together, though neither of us was ordained. Like the early Anabaptists, who baptized each other, we served as representatives of the congregation. I suggested we use the words "*We* baptize you" instead of "*I*." I also suggested that P. T. Yoder stand with us, to show approval.

P. T. graciously went along with our ideas until he talked with some Virginia Conference men who were ordained pastors. They said the baptism should be done by someone ordained. Later he called to say he had a change of heart and would stick by the original plans. He thought that included my doing the baptism, but when he came back and the three of us met again, I said, "I feel that

Chris should do it, because he is the commissioned pastor and has been instructing Michelle."

We each spoke five minutes, and Michelle gave a testimony. I poured the water into Chris' hands from a pitcher.

Good news and bad news

My granddaughter Katie was baptized at Community Mennonite July 3, 1988. In the bulletin, along with statements by pastor Duane Sider and Katie herself, was a statement by Katie's parents, Allen and Anne:

> As Katie's parents, we want to commit ourselves to support Katie in her decision to accept Christ as her salvation and reconciliation with God. At this time we are especially aware that we have responsibilities for others, for each other, and in this case for Katie and her eternal life. We pray that you as part of Christ's church and Community Mennonite will be the Lord's strength, support, and wisdom for Katie as you are for us.

It was an answer to prayer. I thought of Monica, mother of Augustine, who had gone to the priest with concern for her wayward son and how the priest said, "The son of so many prayers cannot be lost."

But then came bad news. On October 21, after traveling from Pittsburgh to Washington, D.C., to Harrisonburg, my son Eugene paid me a surprise visit, saying, "I have bad news. Pat and I are separating. I don't know if we'll get together again or not."

Anne came by on November 4 with her contribution to the monthly Stoltzfus family letter. In her letter she asked Pat and Eugene, "*Are you out of your minds?*" She stressed the need to work at the marriage. In her closing she wrote in large capital letters:

THIS IS THE STOLTZFUS FAMILY AND WE TALK ABOUT
THINGS UNTIL WE DRIVE EACH OTHER CRAZY BECAUSE WE
KNOW THAT THIS IS THE ONLY WAY TO LOVE AND LEARN
AND LOVE AND LIVE AND LOVE AND SURVIVE AND LOVE
AND GROW AND LOVE AND LOVE FOREVER.

When I sent the November family letter, I added a handwritten note to the pack I sent to Pat: "I'd like you not only to stay with

Eugene, but to stay in our family. Tell me, as much as you can, what's back of this separation idea. I care for and about you. Mother Stoltzfus."

Eugene and Pat did not reconcile, then or later.

PART NINE

ORDAINED MENNONITE
MINISTER
1989–2000

Chapter 43

Controversy

Harrisonburg, Virginia
January–September 1989

Journal entry, January 12, 1989

This morning Christopher Gill, pastor of Shalom, called for an appointment to come this evening to talk. I thought Chris might be coming to say more about renewal meetings that Shalom servants' council may ask me to lead sometime in March. But what he said was, "Since December there has been talk around about your being ordained to the ministry. I thought it was time you knew."

Paul (P. T.) Yoder has talked with Chris, suggesting that any request for my ordination should come from a congregation. Owen Burkholder, pastor of Park View, where I still have my primary membership, said he does not object, but one of their elders does not approve. Owen suggests that any request come from Shalom.

Chris thinks the stated reason for ordination would be for some advisory role at Shalom and for my speaking ministry in the wider church. The Shalom servants' council gives full approval, but the matter would need to be processed with the congregation. Then, if approved, it would be taken to the Council on Faith and Life of Virginia Conference.

I told Chris I have felt ordained by God for years and affirmed by enough people in the church; I would never ask the church for ordination, even though I've known for decades that if any man were involved in the work I've been involved in, he would have been ordained long ago. Even though I would never ask to be ordained, if Shalom Mennonite wishes to request it, I would lean toward consenting.

I go along with Chris' idea to wait a month and discuss things further when Shalom servants' council meets in February. "At age seventy-three, I have waited a long time already, and I can wait longer," I told him.

Journal entry, January 13, 1989
Chris Gill called to say that P. T. Yoder suggests that Shalom servants' council discuss my ordination further and the matter be brought before the congregation with me present and if the congregation approves, the request be made to the April meeting of the Council on Faith and Life.

I asked Chris, "What started this whole thing?"

"P. T. Yoder came to me, saying your ordination is long overdue," Chris said.

"I wonder if someone in the wider church nudged him," I said.

Journal entry, January 31, 1989
On nephew George's advice, I interviewed Virginia Conference leaders John R. Martin, Owen Burkholder, and Sam Weaver. John Martin, conference moderator, said that two districts are opposed to the ordination of a woman, but there would be enough support if I consented. He advised waiting until the decision of the Council on Faith and Life before contacting my siblings.

Owen, chair of the Council on Faith and Life, said that conference leaders are cautious. A woman who was licensed recently came out as a homosexual and announced that she and her husband are separating. There are women waiting for ordination, Owen said: a hospital chaplain in Richmond and a married couple in North Carolina. "Because of your credibility," he said, "I think the majority of the leaders in Virginia Conference would want you to be ordained before other women are ordained."

"Do you know what I believe?" I said. "The Lord has put them in a corner so they *need to* ordain me. Could some politics be in this?"

"Yes," he answered.

In response to my question, Owen said, "No, there has not been 100 percent consensus for decisions made by Council on Faith and Life. Of the eleven members of the council, I would expect two to vote against your ordination."

When I spoke with Sam Weaver, executive secretary of Virginia Conference, he told me that in October 1988, shortly before I spoke at the annual meeting of Southeast Conference, Martin W. Lehman, general secretary of that conference, said to him, "Why doesn't Virginia Conference ordain Ruth Brunk Stoltzfus?" At that time, Sam said, he had talked to P. T. Yoder, but he had heard nothing more until now.

Sam thinks Chris Gill, who is commissioned, should be licensed and I should be ordained in the same service. He mentioned my age as the reason some would object. I told him that in 1988 I had twenty-seven appointments in six states, with nine of the appointments being a series. I said of medical tests showing normal for more than five years since surgery and of surgeon Jones' words, "You are home free," of the miracle of strength I experience, and my daughters' statement that I have more energy than they do.

Sam said, "The time you really broke through in the church was when you spoke at Bowling Green on women in leadership."

Journal entry, February 2, 1989

Chris Gill and P. T. Yoder came at 10:30 a.m. to talk with me. P. T. suggested that Shalom hold a special congregational meeting for discussion and decision. Chris told P. T. the grounds for ordination that Chris and I had discussed: an advisory role at Shalom and my speaking ministry in the wider church.

After Chris said, "Ruth preaches at Shalom about as much as anyone," P. T. said an advisory role could be performed without an ordination. He suggested instead that the grounds for my ordination be to assist in the preaching at Shalom Mennonite and my speaking ministry in the wider church. Ordination would not be for my ministry in the past, he said, but my past work would be given recognition at the ordination.

He would like to see it happen in May, after approval at Shalom council, Shalom congregation, Harrisonburg District, and the Council on Faith and Life of Virginia Conference. This would be well before the annual Virginia Conference Assembly (July 12–16), where new ordinations are announced.

I told them that Owen Burkholder had spoken as if some conference leaders would like to see me ordained in advance of other women. "Could some politics be in this?" I asked Paul.

"Just enough for flavor," he answered.

When we talked about how I can face my pain and that of my siblings in our disagreement on women in ministry, I told them that the last time I called Kathie she said, "Mother, you'll have to go through the pain for the sake of other women."

As they left, P. T. said, "We'll walk with you in your pain."

Journal entry, February 9, 1989

Yesterday morning I talked briefly by phone with nephew Truman about this ordination question, and we arranged to talk longer this morning. Truman said yesterday, "I pledge to be in prayer for the next twenty-four hours." This morning he said, "Someone is needed with experience, seasoning, and careful words to plow the way for other women. There is no one else to do it."

I also called my brother Truman this morning. He said, "If I were not old and feeble, I'd want to be there for your ordination." Regarding others who would question my ordination, he said, "Simply say, 'There is talk in the conference about ordaining me and it's in the hands of the church leaders. It's the responsibility of church leaders, and I'm an obedient servant of the church.'"

This evening after eating supper with my sister Katie, as I was putting on my coat to leave I said, "There is something I want to tell you before you hear it from someone else. There is talk in the conference about ordaining me. It's in the hands of the church leaders. I have not asked for it. I have plenty of work to do."

"It's against the Bible," she said, "but we'll still be friends."

Journal entry, February 28, 1989

This morning at 2:00 a.m. my sister Edna, age eighty-two, had a massive stroke. The doctor said there is no hope of recovery. When Katie and I visited Edna, she seemed to understand when I kissed her forehead and said, "I came to tell you I love you . . . God is watching over you."

Journal entry, March 18, 1989

My sister Edna Frances Brunk Hertzler died on March 11, 1989. I miss her but am thankful that she did not need to suffer during those eleven days in the hospital after her massive stroke.

Around Edna's death bed—near 1:20 a.m.—we had a wonderful time, along with the pain of parting. Because she still had meaning in her eyes, we believe she likely heard our words even though she could not speak. Present were her husband Arthur and their sons Bob and Ray, also my brother George, sister Katie and I, and niece Reba Brunk—a wonderful nurse who stayed with Edna many hours.

There were prayers at her bedside before, but when Edna's breathing became slow and halting and the end seemed near, I asked Arthur if we could have prayer and called on George to lead. While Edna was dying, George was praying. While Arthur was crying, George called on me to lead a prayer for him. We sang, "In the sweet by and by, we shall meet on that beautiful shore" (except when some of the rest of us broke down from crying). Then we just stayed around her bed and told stories about Edna—even her humor—for an hour. It was good therapy, and it helps me now to tell about it.

Journal entry, March 19, 1989

After the Sunday morning service at Shalom Mennonite, I saw on the bulletin board a copy of the February 9, 1989, minutes of the servants' council. I read with special interest the references to the question of my ordination.

According to the minutes, P. T. Yoder listed as reasons for ordination to "affirm Ruth's ministry over the years; recognize Ruth's ministry in the wider church and give it more authenticity; enhance her function at Shalom; help to open the door for increasing credentialing of women in the Mennonite Church."

When Owen Burkholder was asked, "Since Ruth has membership at Park View Mennonite Church and associate membership at Shalom, why not do a joint request for ordination?" he answered, "The elders at Park View have already done some processing and have raised concerns about 'irregularities' of age, sex, and membership."

After discussing the possibility of negative repercussions, time, and procedure, the council decided to recommend to the congregation that they ordain me for teaching and preaching in the wider Mennonite Church and to assist at Shalom in the ministry and in the administration of ordinances.

Journal entry, March 29, 1989

At last evening's congregational meeting it was decided that Eastern Mennonite College (EMC) student Paul Groff will serve as coordinator since Chris and Linda Gill are moving to Michigan and Carroll and Nancy Yoder are going overseas for a year. The last item on the agenda was my ordination. Chris Gill read a recommendation for the congregation to make to the Harrisonburg District. I was invited to leave so they could have freer discussion.

After the meeting Chris called to say, "There was unanimous consent to ask for your ordination. This will go to the Harrisonburg District meeting April 12 and, if approved, it will go to the Council on Faith and Life at the end of April. P. T. Yoder will be contacting you. There is a questionnaire to complete and there is feeling that your membership should be at Shalom."

Journal entry, April 18, 1989

Today I filled out the Virginia Conference "Examination for Ministry" and returned it to P. T. Yoder.

Journal entry, April 19, 1989

Today Shalom pastor Chris Gill presented a request to the Harrisonburg District from Shalom congregation that I be ordained to "assist our congregation," to formally recognize and affirm my ministry, and "to encourage Virginia Mennonite Conference in the future ordination of other ably-gifted women who are called to leadership positions in the conference."

P. T. Yoder called to say the Harrisonburg District has approved my ordination, but some were not sure about ordaining someone beyond retirement age.

Speaking of the pain of going against the beliefs of all my siblings except Truman, I asked him, "Why must we always have a struggle?"

P. T., a physician, answered, "It's the only way to have a birth."

Journal entry, April 24, 1989

I received a call from P. T. Yoder, saying, "Your 'Examination for Ministry' showed wisdom and experience." He asked my okay to talk to my brother George. Expressing no doubt that the Council on Faith and Life would approve, he asked which Sunday would suit for the ordination service.

Journal entry, April 30, 1989

P. T. Yoder called to say the Council on Faith and Life—the last step in the process—has approved the request of P. T. Yoder and the Shalom congregation for me to be ordained to assist at Shalom, to acknowledge my work in the wider church, and to help pave the way for other women.

Journal entry, May 1, 1989

I felt more settled and secure about being ordained after I took out of my files "Headship and the Leadership Roles of Women," the paper drawn up by our Virginia Conference ad hoc committee on headship. The statement was approved April 28, 1988, by the Council on Faith and Life (bishops and overseers).

The part that gave me relief appears in the concluding section of the document:

"It may be helpful if at least some parts of the church test the use of women in new levels of leadership. This kind of issue in the church is one that finds resolution only as we try new directions and then test the results in the light of the total spirit of Scripture."

Thank God!

Journal entry, May 4, 1989

Earlier I consented when P. T. Yoder mentioned asking Owen Burkholder about using Park View Church, since Strite Hall in the Campus Center, where Shalom Church meets, might be too small. But I'd rather not do that, because Owen, though he does not personally object to my ordination, does not favor the request for my ordination to come from Park View Church, where my membership is. One elder objects, and no doubt so would a number of members.

Journal entry, May 9, 1989

P. T. Yoder came to talk. He quoted my brother George (in an interview he had with him), "You didn't come for my blessing and you don't have it. I blame the conference more than I blame my sister." He added that he would not block my ordination. George wrote Paul several days later, "The more I think about it, the more irregular it seems."

"I told him we are not ordaining Ruth to be pastor," P. T. told me. (Meaning, I suppose, that I would be assisting in the leadership at Shalom Mennonite.) Then he said to me, "I see your ordination as mainly recognizing and affirming your ongoing churchwide ministry and paving the way for other women."

This time P. T. seemed more willing to have the ordination after, rather than before, the annual Virginia Conference Assembly in mid-July.

Letter to my children, May 12, 1989

I called nephew George to ask, "Do you think it would be a good idea for the man who had the message when a woman was commissioned to have the message when she is ordained?"

"I would have no objection on the basis of principle," he answered. He wants the weekend to weigh everything, then will call me.

Journal entry, May 15, 1989

Nephew George called to say he will give the message at my ordination. Praise the Lord!

Journal entry, May 18, 1989

I called P. T. Yoder to tell him that my nephew George has consented to have the message at my ordination, and that his first choice of date is July 23. P. T. will officially ask him and talk to Chris Gill about leading the service. P. T. will give the charge. I will write to Owen Burkholder, asking that my membership be transferred to Shalom.

Journal entry, June 5, 1989

My brother George brought me a copy of his letter to P. T. Yoder and Sam Weaver, which made reference to the question of my ordination:

> This letter will relate to the recent conversations that we have had with reference to women's ordination—the ordination of my sister Ruth, in particular.
>
> These conversations have revealed that there is wide divergence of understanding and opinion on this matter. We certainly cannot both be right. Somebody is seriously wrong, for certain. The various new interpretations of the Scriptures relating to this matter are somewhat amazing.

As both of you know, I have taken serious exception to the way in which the work of the Conference has been managed. In our conversation on Friday, I made reference to three examples—the handling of [a case involving an EMC professor], the incorrect and false assumption that this is a personal difference between [that professor] and Brunk, and the handling of the matter of ordaining a woman to the ministry.

As I pointed out to you, Sam, your statement in our Friday meeting that there was only one negative vote on this matter of ordaining Ruth, I consider to be misleading and unfair. As you certainly know, it is not correct that all the others on the Council on Faith and Life are in favor of that action. If my understanding is correct, when the issue was before the Council a year or more ago, there were a number of votes against it. The constant pressure to push this matter has, in my opinion, caused some of the brethren to conclude that there is no use to make any further objection. They see that you intend to go through with this at all cost.

Also, Brother Sam, as I pointed out to you on the telephone since our Friday conversation, it seemed unfair for you to give the impression that my brother Truman is in favor of Ruth's ordination. You did not respond well to my comment that I believe we should come down on the side of obedience to the Scriptures. That does not appear to be a matter of major concern to you. I was at that time (and still am) amazed at your answer on that occasion which was this—that you are guided by a comment from your mother on one occasion when she said that you should not be the first by whom the new is tried nor yet the last to lay the old aside!

I would like to take this occasion to remind both of you that the utter lack of consensus, both in the leadership of the Conference and in the membership thereof, make it somewhat presumptuous (to say the least) for you to proceed with your plans for the ordination of my sister Ruth. Would it not be a safe assumption that the majority of the membership in the Virginia Conference is opposed to the ordination of women to the pastoral role? However, having said that, I do not believe that consensus of the membership is a deciding factor. I believe that there are some issues now being decided by default on the basis of the fact that the majority of the membership no longer support a certain practice taught by the Scripture. I want to say again what I said before, that I believe that you are unaware of the seriousness of the action which you are about to take. It appears to me that neither one of you is really certain in your own mind that this is what you ought to do. One of you made that acknowledgment in our Friday meeting.

My conviction is that if you proceed with this action the day will come, sooner or later, when you will see the wrongness of your move and suffer regret for the action which you will have taken. When that will occur, I am not prepared to say.

Both of you know that I hold my sister Ruth in high respect and appreciate the unusual gifts which the Lord has given to her. But your comment, Sam, to the effect that according to Ruth, I am a "secret believer" in the ordination of women to the ministry—well, this is a total misrepresentation of where I have stood and continue to stand.

I continue to believe that your action in this regard will be displeasing to God and in disobedience to the Holy Scriptures.

On the very day that the first woman is ordained to the ministry in the Virginia Conference, I shall automatically thereby consider myself no longer to be a member of the Virginia Conference. You will not be surprised if I publish my reasons for that decision.

Journal entry, June 7, 1989
Early this morning I drafted this response to George's letter:

Dear George—and I mean dear,
On August 9, 1980, at the Lancaster, Pennsylvania, celebration of your ministry, and again on July 22, 1984, at a similar celebration at Trissels Mennonite Church here in Virginia, I spoke on the program as requested by the planning committees. Both times I had positive things to say about you and your ministry and I still have positive things to say.

Since you gave me and others a copy of your June 5, 1989, letter to P. T. Yoder and Sam Weaver, I think I should write down a response.

For years I have kept careful letter/journal notes, and on April 11, 1985, I made this entry:

I asked my brother George this morning if it is true that he made the statement that he does not object to a woman being ordained, but objects to her being sole pastor. He said, "yes."

That "yes" is the basis of my comment some time ago (heard by Sam Weaver) that I think you are a "secret believer." Now that you are backing off from your April 11, 1985, statement and showing a changed position by telling me it's that you do not object to a woman being ordained a *deaconess*, and since you are holding Virginia Conference leaders and me and others to your changed position, I think you should acknowledge that you have changed.

I have felt ordained of God since 1950 when, by his leading and Grant's encouragement and help, I began the Heart to Heart broadcast which brought calls to speak in many pulpits across the church—many times along with Grant—and led to my serving twice during 1982–1983 as an interim pastor in Ohio, then in 1985–1987 as co-pastor at First Mennonite Church in Richmond, Virginia. I see the providential hand of God in thus getting me around all kinds of obstacles.

I would never ask to be ordained, but when I learned in January of this year that Virginia Conference leaders were talking of ordaining me—it was not as sole pastor—I decided to leave it up to them. That is still my position.

Love to you, Ruth

I called nephew George, who had not gotten a copy of his father's January 5 letter to P. T. Yoder and Sam Weaver. He came down and I gave him a photocopy of it, also a copy of my January 7 response. I told him that since his father says he will no longer be a member of Virginia Conference on the day the first woman is ordained, I would not ask him to have the message as planned if we go ahead with my ordination. He said he'll support me in going ahead but isn't sure what his role should be.

Journal entry, June 8, 1989
Today at the close of an evening meal with my sister Katie, she handed me the following letter, which George had asked her to give me:

My Dear Sister Ruth:
I am responding to your letter of June 7 in which you remind me of the way in which you stood by me on past occasions, which I have not forgotten. That fact has made it doubly difficult for me to take the position which I have felt necessary to take.

I see no point in prolonging the debate on whether I have changed my mind or not. You say I have. I say that I have not. I could live with a long-term situation in which a woman was ordained to serve in a subordinate role if it was understood without any question that it would not go beyond that. You know, however, that is not the case. You are in favor of women in charge as pastors and I am not. This move toward your ordination is only a step in the direction of full-time pastoral responsibility for women in the Virginia Conference. You know that this is true.

If you have felt ordained of God, as you say, since 1950, then why can you not continue to serve in those situations where doors are open for you to do so? I am puzzled to understand why you seem to be pushing for ordination. I am also puzzled that it seems you have been feeding upon literature written by persons who, in my judgement, are radicals.

Again, let me say that I love you dearly and I thank God for the gifts that you have, rejoicing in your exercise of those gifts within the limitations of the Holy Scriptures. Admittedly, we are far, far apart on this question and I could not be more convinced that your position is contrary to the Scripture.

Loving you, never-the-less, George R. Brunk II, Editor

Journal entry, June 9, 1989

I appreciate the softer tone of George's June 8 letter. I would like to reply that the most radical literature I read is the Bible. Also that my children would never let me get by with his kind of logic—that he made no change when switching from approving the ordination of a woman as *pastor* to approving only the ordination of a woman as *deaconess*, the rationale being that it's not a change since he's concerned that she serve always in a subordinate role. But I will let the matter rest.

At 4:00 p.m. P. T. Yoder came to talk. He mentioned that we have processed the question of my ordination in congregation, district, and conference, and it has been approved. "How do you feel?" he asked.

I told him I asked the Lord for a miracle to help me sleep when I first read George's June 5 letter to him and Sam Weaver. "Emma Richards called from Lombard, Illinois," I said, "and she encouraged me to go ahead. Her words were like oil of healing to me."

P. T. and Sam Weaver see three options: drop the whole thing for fear of a split in the Conference, license me, or go ahead with my ordination.

I said any of the three was all right with me. As for ordination, my public ministry over the years has already been a kind of ouchy thing to most of my brothers and sisters, but they have respected and loved me. I still feel that my biological brothers and sisters cannot determine my calling, but how much should a person concede when opposition is this strong and your brother threatens to leave the conference and publish his reasons?

Journal entry, June 11, 1989

Today, with Shalom coordinator Paul Groff as leader, I was received as a member of the congregation, as advised by P. T. Yoder. I had kept my membership at Park View Church while an associate member at Shalom almost since its beginning on November 2, 1986.

Journal entry, June 14, 1989

Yesterday and today daughter Ruthie called from England to talk about flying home one week early in order to be here July 23 if I'm ordained. I told her, "There's a civil war here about it, but it seems likely that I'll be licensed or ordained."

In the evening, in response to my phone call, my nephew George came to see his father's and P. T. Yoder's latest letters about my possible ordination and to counsel with me, as I asked. My brother George has been on a collision course with Virginia Conference. He may have been near to leaving for a long time before this issue came up. If I'm not ordained, other women will soon be.

Journal entry, June 15, 1989

Today conference leaders met for a final decision about my ordination. Toward evening P. T. Yoder called. He said that at the Harrisonburg District meeting yesterday, the feeling was to proceed with my ordination. At the meeting today, conference leaders decided that they would be happy for us to proceed with licensing, "in light of the family dynamics."

When P. T. asked my brother George if he could live with my being licensed, he had said yes. "We see this as a step forward," P. T. told me.

I called my nephew George to report the conversation. He had heard Sam Weaver say today that the licensing route might help my brother. I asked, "Is licensing a Band-Aid solution, since it's likely that women will be ordained soon in the conference?"

"Yes."

"But I would not get the blame for precipitating the ordination of a woman, right?"

"It might lessen the objection," he said.

"Really," I said, "is there much difference between being licensed or being ordained?"

"Some perceive a difference," he answered.

"Which route would you favor," I asked, "licensing or ordination—if you were in my shoes, and knowing all that you know about the situation? Also, would you be more comfortable giving the message if I were licensed than if I were ordained?"

He answered, "I'll think over this and call you tonight." When he called back, he encouraged me to take the same position as before and go with the decision of conference leaders, but to check out the following with P. T. Yoder:

> 1. What assurance do you have that George II will back off on his threats to leave the conference and publish his reasons if I am licensed instead of ordained?
> 2. How much weight are you giving to fear of damage or loss to the conference beyond one or two persons who threaten to leave?
> 3. Will licensing be a temporary Band-Aid solution that will only postpone the problems for a short while and mean facing them when women are soon ordained in the conference?
> 4. What difference in sequence do you see for women to be ordained if I am licensed instead of ordained?
> 5. What "family dynamics" do you mean would be better served by licensing? My brothers and sisters? Nephew George? George II's grandchildren and mine? Other?

Journal entry, June 16, 1989

P. T. Yoder came at 10 a.m. to report further on the meeting of conference leaders yesterday and to discuss where to go from here. He went over the five questions nephew George and I drew up last evening. He doesn't think any whole congregation would leave the conference if a woman is ordained, but individuals might.

The paper "Headship and the Leadership Roles of Women" was approved by the Council on Faith and Life [last year], but it was not brought to a vote at Virginia Conference Assembly. When P. T. read it to the assembly, only one question was asked: "Does this mean that the conference will ordain women?" He answered, "Steps will be taken for a woman the same as for a man."

P. T. suggested postponing my licensing or ordination, because there might be an eruption of some kind if it comes soon after Virginia Conference Assembly. In the middle of this discussion I was surprised to hear him say that the conference leaders have decided to leave it up to me whether I am to be licensed or ordained.

I said I had expected to abide by their decision. He had wanted me to be the first woman in Virginia Conference to be ordained, and I began to like that idea, but it may be best for me to be one of the women licensed in the conference in an effort to ward off, if not prevent, a blowup with my siblings and a breakup in the conference.

We agreed that after taking some time to think and pray about the matter and calling my brother Truman for consultation, I would call P. T.

When I called Truman, he said, "There is no difference between being licensed and ordained. The woman is in the pulpit, in any case." Then he said, "Forget everything I have said and stay by your position of leaving the decision up to the conference leaders."

Next I called nephew George, and as we talked two decisions jelled: I will tell P. T. Yoder that I stay by my position of leaving the decision of licensing or ordination up to conference leaders; and I favor postponing the date.

George said because of schedule problems, postponing the date makes it more likely that he could have the message. I take it that a licensing instead of an ordination service would also make it more likely. What a bind for him.

I phoned P. T. Yoder and told him of my decisions. I said the burden is beginning to lift.

Letter to Doris Gascho, June 17, 1989

I called Virginia Conference moderator John Martin, as you suggested, and asked him to suggest wording for my announcement of the latest plans so that what I say to friends ties in with conference perceptions. He suggested, "Because of family and conference considerations, my credentialing is postponed until fall."

Because of family dynamics I can see why the conference leaders would want to let me have some say-so as to whether to go ahead with ordination as they had approved.

John Martin did say, "We leaned toward the idea of licensing," and added "not because you are a woman."

My brother George said yes when P. T. Yoder asked if he could live with my being licensed. That's a step forward from several years ago when he gathered up a corps of men, met Virginia Conference leaders, and protested the licensing of women.

Yesterday morning Eve MacMaster, in the area for the weekend, encouraged me to be open to licensing "as the humble way to go." I ask, how can we do the Anabaptist way of *no hierarchy*, yet free women to use their leadership gifts?

Rejoice with me in the peace I have in the path I have chosen through this tangled maze, which is willingness to be licensed instead of ordained as a compromise for the sake of peace. Ruthie said when I called her yesterday, "It's like meeting violence with nonviolence."

At the same time, I feel strongly that it is a part of the slower but surer process toward ordination, maybe even mine, for women in Virginia Conference. God has been in the process, and it has been good for me to learn yet more about the wisdom of consulting others. "In the multitude of counselors there is safety" (Proverbs 11:14).

Journal entry, June 23, 1989
P. T. Yoder called to ask the bottom line question: "If you look at family considerations (siblings' objections) and not conference considerations (some persons possibly leaving) which do you say—to license or ordain you?"

I said, "While I hate to go against my siblings and am concerned about conference implications, I leave it to conference leaders. We love and respect each other, but I don't know that biological brothers and sisters should determine my calling. Even if I'm licensed, I think they will still feel touchy about my public ministry. So if conference leaders say ordain, I'm willing to be ordained."

"That answers my question," P. T. said.

Journal entry, June 24, 1989
In the evening I talked with Allen and Anne about the question of my "credentialing." Allen said my time of going through a wringer is not over. According to Anne, there may be more people in the conference who protest if I'm *not* ordained than if I am.

Journal entry, June 25, 1989
Emma Brubaker reported to me the rumor that if I'm ordained four congregations in Virginia Conference will leave, and if I'm not ordained four congregations will leave!

Journal entry, June 29, 1989
Doris said John Martin commented to her when she called him about my being licensed or ordained, "Virginia Conference *is* going to ordain women."

Journal entry, July 7, 1989
Today's mail brought the August 1989 *Sword and Trumpet,* in

which my brother George announces the plan of Virginia Conference to ordain a woman as one of three reasons he has decided to sever his membership in the conference.

Letter to my children, July 12, 1989
I am willing to be licensed—that's done for trial periods usually—instead of ordained, for the sake of peace, but P. T. Yoder has written the Council on Faith and Life that Harrisonburg District, after another meeting, does not consider licensing an appropriate option and still requests my ordination, as approved earlier.

Journal entry, July 13, 1989
As a delegate from our fledgling Shalom Congregation, I was at Virginia Conference Assembly from 8:30 a.m. until 3:30 p.m. Owen Burkholder gave the report of Mennonite Church General Board on the question of withholding the military portion of the federal tax and I felt moved to go to the microphone to speak to the issue.

During the bishop/overseer district reports, Harrisonburg overseer P. T. Yoder reported: "July 23, 1989, was announced for the ordination of Ruth Brunk Stoltzfus. Because of family and other considerations it has been postponed."

Wayne Speigle was chosen as moderator-elect of the conference. In commenting about it from the platform with Wayne beside him, Warwick District overseer Lloyd Weaver said, "While Wayne was interim pastor for two years at First Mennonite in Richmond, Ruth Brunk Stoltzfus was his mentor."

NEWS FLASH! At 9:25 p.m. P. T. Yoder called to say, "I'm planning to go ahead with your ordination on September 10, but let's sit tight for two more days" (until Virginia Conference Assembly is over).

Journal entry, July 15, 1989
It was an ordinary-looking letter that I opened today from the EMC Alumni Association. But the words were not ordinary: "Congratulations! On behalf of the Awards and Nominations Committee and the Alumni Association of Eastern Mennonite College, it is my pleasure to report that you have been selected to receive the 1989 DISTINGUISHED SERVICE AWARD."

The award is to be given Saturday evening, October 14, at the annual alumni banquet as part of Homecoming '89 activities. I'm invited to suggest the person to present the award to me and to submit a guest list of close relatives to be invited.

First was a time of numbness and then I began to think of the people in my life whom God put in my path—those who loved, nurtured, taught, guided, disciplined, shaped, understood, forgave, inspired, and trusted me. Most of all I thought of God's grace and providence.

Journal entry, July 19, 1989
Nephew George and I talked by phone. He will be at my ordination, now scheduled for Sunday, September 10, 1989, but declines having the message because of his father's opposition. He offered to have the Scripture and prayer instead.

"It is good to make some concessions," I said, "but the time comes when we must respect who we are and what our position is." I had in mind, also, the time I felt I needed to consent to being licensed instead of ordained. George concurred.

After consulting P. T. Yoder and nephew George, I called John R. Martin to ask him to have the message at the ordination service.

Next I called nephew Truman. In answer to my question, he said that his father seems at peace about my ordination. I told Truman that I'd like his father or him to have comments and a prayer at the close of the service. He suggested putting just the name Truman Brunk on the program so it could be either Sr. or Jr. I said if Sr. had the closing prayer, I would want Jr. to have the prayer after the Scripture reading by nephew George. "I'd love to have you two nephews up there together," I said.

Journal entry, July 26, 1989
I called P. T. Yoder about ordination plans. He said my brother George called him this morning to ask if they will license or ordain me so that he can make decisions.

"What decisions?" I asked.

"About leaving the conference," P. T. replied.

"I would like to request prayer for George," I said. "He must be in pain, too."

Receiving the 1989 Eastern Mennonite College Distinguished Service Award presented in part by nephews Gerald Brunk (in background) and George Brunk III.

Journal entry, July 29, 1989

Today the *Daily News-Record* religious services page announces "Paul E. Groff will be commissioned as lay leader at Shalom Mennonite Congregation Sunday. Kenton Brubaker will bring the message and Ruth B. Stoltzfus will commission Groff. . . ."

How can an inferior female, seventy-four, commission a sacred male, twenty-one? There goes the female subordination bit down the drain in one tiny Virginia church.

Journal entry, August 18, 1989

I went to eat the noon meal with sister Katie. These days I usually eat one meal with her on Wednesday and one on Friday instead of daily, Monday through Saturday, as I used to do. We have not discussed my ordination since I first told her of the possibility months ago. It's too painful, but we love each other in spite of our disagreement.

Journal entry, August 23, 1989

Today P. T. Yoder left with me a copy of his memo to the *Gospel Herald* and *Mennonite Weekly Review:*

> Ruth Brunk Stoltzfus will be ordained by the Virginia Mennonite Conference to the Christian Ministry on Sunday, September 10 at 7:00 p.m. at the Shalom Mennonite Congregation, Eastern Mennonite College.
>
> The ordination is in recognition of Sister Ruth's many years of ministry and leadership in the Mennonite Church. It also affirms and authenticates her current ministry in the Shalom Mennonite Congregation in Harrisonburg and the wider Mennonite fellowship.

Journal entry, August 25, 1989

At 2:45 a.m. daughter Ruthie called to say that contractions are eleven minutes apart and she expects to go to the hospital soon to give birth to their third baby boy. Later Kathie called with the news that the beautiful baby, David Eugene Stoltzfus Jost, weighing in at about seven pounds, was born. Kathie will fly there to help out.

Chapter 44

Ordination

Harrisonburg, Virginia
September 10, 1989

Several hundred people gathered in the Lehman Auditorium on the evening of Sunday, September 10, for my ordination. All five children and their families were here, even Ruthie, who flew from Columbus, Ohio, with her son David Eugene, age two weeks.

The service began with a greeting by Paul E. Groff of Shalom congregation. After Faye Yoder led the congregation in singing "The Lord Is King," my nephew George read passages from Philippians. In his prayer of blessing George related the servanthood of Jesus to the ordination: "O God, of all creation . . . we, too, bend our knee before your Son and confess him to be our Lord. We adore your Son, Jesus Christ, for all that he is to us. We acknowledge his supreme example of servanthood."

We sang "Come Gracious Spirit" and then John R. Martin spoke on "The Servant's Servant." After John's message, P. T. Yoder gave the ordination charge and then invited me to join him, saying, "Sister Ruth, in the wisdom and foreknowledge of God, you have been called to the Christian ministry. The community of faith, enriched by your ministry, has recognized your gifts and calling. You are now being called and affirmed to assist in the pastoral ministry of the Shalom Congregation and for service in the wider Mennonite fellowship. Will you accept this call and responsibility in all earnestness and sincerity, promising to give yourself to this work by the grace and power of God?"

"I will."

"Do you promise to study the Word of God diligently with all faithfulness? Will you seek to understand its message, making it a guide for your life? Will you preach the Word of God with all its

345

Paul T. Yoder gives the ordination charge.

purity and power? Will you diligently teach all who come under your care—witnessing, as you have opportunity? Will you serve the community of faith as an ambassador for Christ?"

"I will."

"In this ministry, will you teach and preach the Word of God as revealed to you by the Holy Spirit, and in the context of the interpretation and practice of the Mennonite Church? Will you seek to evangelize the lost, comforting the sorrowing, rebuking those in error, dealing with each person in love and gentleness? Will you work in harmony with the congregation and with the Virginia Mennonite Conference?"

"I will."

"In response to your promises before God and his people here, I charge and ordain you in the name of Jesus, head of the Church, to preach the Good News, to call sinners to repentance, to nurture believers, to share your gifts in leadership and decision making, to counsel with prudence, to discipline believers with gentle love and to equip the saints for ministry. Be strong and of good courage. Live your life in harmony with the teachings of Jesus. May your ministry be fruitful, a glory to God, and a rewarding personal experience. Amen."

At that point he invited friends to join us on the platform in a prayer of dedication. Then he presented me with a Certificate of Ordination from Virginia Conference.

We sang "Lord, Speak to Me," and then I gave my testimony.

Doris Gascho and Jim Burkholder responded, and then Kathie read a statement from Phil Ebersole, pastor at Bancroft Mennonite Church in Toledo:

> Your short note and the memo announcing your ordination was moving to me. I cried as I read it to myself, our secretary, and the congregation: "This is a notice about my life; I'm living through God's miracle."
>
> I, along with the congregation here at Bancroft rejoice with you on this joyous and solemn occasion. You have served the larger church in ministry for many years, but Bancroft will hold a dear spot in your heart, for it is there that you were first called to pastoral ministry in January of 1982. I shall not forget who preceded me in pastoral ministry here. Yes, Ruth, you were appreciated here as a pastor, your teaching, preaching, concern for families, ministry in crisis, visitation. We affirm those gifts and share with you in the authentication of those gifts today. Ruth, may the joy of the Lord be yours today and in the days ahead.

Then came the congregational response and closing comments by nephew Truman. After the service, everyone was invited to participate in a reception held in the Campus Center.

Chapter 45

Pastoral Advisor

Harrisonburg, Virginia
September 1989–January 1991

At my ordination I was charged "to assist in the pastoral ministry of the Shalom Congregation." So I was startled when, less than three months later, Paul Groff, with whom I served on the eldership team at Shalom, informed me, "It's not necessary [according to a vote at Shalom servants' council] for you to attend council meetings."

Later, in a combined worship committee and servants' council meeting, I mentioned that I never knew of a person ordained for any type of service in a church who was not expected to attend regularly, to say nothing about being at liberty to attend council meetings at any time.

I began to think that my ordination may have been in part to confirm my years of service in "the wider Mennonite fellowship," but mainly to pave the way for other women to be ordained in Virginia Conference, rather than for me to serve in any significant way at Shalom Mennonite.

In the wider fellowship

I had more than enough speaking assignments to keep me busy. In October 1989 Eastern Mennonite High School (EMHS) faculty member Galen Horst said encouraging things about a talk I had given at an EMHS chapel. "We were very blessed," he said. He then reported this conversation in his Bible class preceding chapel:

Student: "Who's speaking in chapel?"
Galen: "Ruth Brunk Stoltzfus."
Student: "Who's she?"
Galen: "A prophet." [The class had been studying the prophets Amos and Micah.]

"Then, when you spoke in chapel," Galen told me, "your first words were, 'Greetings to all you rich people.' At our next class the students asked, 'How did you know?' "

Other assignments took me farther from home. In January 1990, I was at Community Mennonite Church, Lancaster, Pennsylvania, where I gave the message, "Jesus and the Roles of Men and Women." I enjoyed the service, including questions in the sharing time about my message. The congregation gave serious attention and more than the average number came up front afterwards for dialogue.

Several women asked why I wore a devotional head covering. I said that one reason I liked to wear it for divine services was so that I did not offend the women who still wore the covering.

One of the women said, "But what about offending the people who do not wear it? To them the head covering is a sign of oppression."

I told them that my father, George R. Brunk I, a bishop, never said anything about the covering being a symbol for a woman's submission to her husband. "Even though I question whether the apostle Paul meant to say what women should wear in our century, I lament all the stuff women wear since the covering is gone—all the junk they put on their bodies," I said.

Milestones

On March 15, 1990, P. T. Yoder and Clarence Bauman came to talk about the idea of a Virginia Conference scholarship fund for young adults, male and female—with priority to females—to assist them in training for church work. They first suggested that the fund be named the Ruth Brunk Stoltzfus Scholarship Fund, but gave me the choice of calling it the Grant and Ruth Brunk Stoltzfus Scholarship Fund. I chose the latter, saying that Grant would be much in favor, that he gave me support and never said a negative word about my work in the church.

I suggested that instead of "priority" to females, it would still be progress to say "equal opportunity" to females. Kathie told me "priority" was only fair.

Pastoral advisor

By invitation I attended Shalom servants' council on March 1, 1990, to work on a job description for a lead pastor. On May 17,

Al Fuentes, a seminary graduate and Mennonite Central Committee trainee from the Philippines, was recommended to be on the pastoral team, as well as Paul Groff, who was the administrative coordinator under the title of "enabler." I was asked to be the mentor for the pastoral team. My title was "pastoral advisor."

I had the message, "What Is Your Gift?" on September 2, when Al Fuertes joined Paul Groff and me as a member of the leadership team. With students present for the first Sunday in the school year, attendance was forty-nine. Despite the real bond of fellowship between me and the other members of Shalom, I was feeling the effects of ageism.

Chapter 46

Radical Evangelical Anabaptist

Harrisonburg, Virginia
May 1992–November 1993

I attended a reception at Eastern Mennonite College (EMC) in late spring of 1992 at which President Joseph Lapp presented model trucks commemorating the Brunk Revivals of 1951–1982 to George and Margaret and their family. It was a cooperative fundraising effort to benefit the new building for Eastern Mennonite Seminary. I paid 100 dollars for a truck and seventy-five went to the seminary.

I showed the children the truck I had bought, with the original design, "The Whole Gospel for the Whole World." Then I said, "I want to write another check to the seminary for the new building and thought of ordering a truck for each grandchild, but most of them are too old to play with them. I need my children's advice."

Kathie said, "I'd say get the trucks. Minutes ago I showed and explained the truck to Andrew." Showing him the brochure, she had said, "See, that's Uncle George, Grandma's brother."

I told the family that in my travels for appointments in hundreds of churches, I met many people or heard of those in the neighborhoods who came to Christ in the Brunk Revivals and were deeply changed. "The trucks will symbolize the whole story as part of our Brunk family history," I said.

I experienced more family history on May 31, 1992, at a meeting held at Warwick River Mennonite Church to celebrate the 1912 vision of my father and three other men for a Mennonite school. This led to the establishment of Eastern Mennonite High School and College and Seminary at Harrisonburg.

I could not keep back tears when, as part of the drama, nephew

George walked in from a door up front wearing Papa's hat and long, plain coat and pushing and dumping a wheelbarrow load of sand, symbolizing the bigger load of sand Papa had dumped on the chosen site of donated land across from our home.

Radical evangelical Anabaptist

I wrote this letter for the editorial page of our *Daily News-Record*:

> Edward M. Glick's May 18, 1990, column calls Barbara Bush "a startling success even though she dropped out of college to marry George Bush and bear his children." Now that we are near the end of the twentieth century, wouldn't it be wonderful if those children could also be her children?
>
> I'm sending a copy of this revolutionary idea to Barbara Bush at the White House, also to Edward M. Glick, c/o *Daily News-Record*.

In response to a letter of request from Marian C. Franz of the National Campaign for a Peace Tax Fund, Washington, D.C., on April 22, 1992, I wrote to the House Ways and Means Committee:

> I am a conscientious objector to participation in war-making and war preparation. Because of deep religious conviction I have been a resister of the telephone tax and the military portion of the federal income tax for many years.
>
> As an ordained minister in the Mennonite Church, a historic peace church, I can tell you that we have thousands upon thousands of members who will take no part in human destruction, but practice the call of Jesus Christ to give their lives in sacrificial service to build up and help masses of people in material or spiritual need in the United States and over the world.
>
> We appreciate the provisions of our United States government for conscientious objectors who cannot give their lives for the purpose of taking human life.
>
> We ask that same religious liberty so that we do not give our money— the military portion of our taxes—for the purpose of taking human life.

When I filled out Renee Sauder's "Women in Ministry Survey," skipping the pages that referred to seminary experience, which I never had, I needed help in answering a question about my theological position. I called Hubert Pellman, and he saw me as "evangelical Anabaptist." Then I called nephew George Brunk, who said, "radical evangelical Anabaptist."

"There's nothing like a little help with my self identity," I wrote in my journal.

Questions for the grandchildren

While Anne was finishing pharmacy school in Richmond, I frequently had Allen and the children for vegetable soup suppers. My place was a hotel with restaurant, laundry, taxi, and banking services for all the local grandchildren and their friends. I loved it when family members came and when they needed me for this or that. I also enjoyed taking them out to eat.

One time while at a table in a Taco Bell restaurant, I told the grandchildren, "I want to tell you a story and at the end ask you a question." The story:

> There was once a woman seventy-seven years old who had a car eight years old and when she would back out from her place and drive on the street the front wheels would sometimes go wobble-wobble and then straighten out okay. But she thought, "I might need to have this car repaired."
>
> One day she saw in the newspaper pictures of new cars and the offer that she could buy a new car and just make payments each month. The payments would be about the same amount that she was paying each month for her children and grandchildren to eat with her.
>
> Now the question: "Which would be the best for her to do—sit in a new car or sit at a table with her children and grandchildren?"

Peter, then twelve, who was sitting next to me, said, "Well, the grandchildren would know how to answer that!"

I tried in other ways to teach the grandchildren responsibility in managing funds that God had put in our care in a world of much physical and spiritual need.

On Andrew's seventh birthday I wrote him a birthday note:

> HAPPY BIRTHDAY!
> Here is $7 because you are seven.
> What will you do with the money?
> Maybe you will *give* some.
> Maybe you will *save* some.
> Maybe you will *spend* some.
>
> Those are three good things to do with money; don't you think?
> Grandma thinks you are such a fine boy. I love you very much.

Family milestones

There were four funerals for relatives in 1993. My sister Stella's husband, J. Ward Shank, died on March 6. Grant's sister Verna Yost died on May 13, and his brother Ivan on August 6. Then, my sister Stella Shank followed her husband home on September 16. Each one was missed and remembered fondly.

Reconciliation between brothers

I couldn't stop praising God after my brother George called November 17, 1993, to report that Lawrence had phoned him from Florida to say, "I have been searching my heart and want to come to see you."

"He sounded weak," George told me. He invited Lawrence and his wife Dorothy to come for Sunday dinner. George said to me, "That, after these twenty years [of no communication—forty years since their quarrel and split]. I tried to work for reconciliation twenty times."

As I thought of Lawrence and Dorothy traveling toward Harrisonburg, I prayed, "O God, give Lawrence surges of strength to continue on the journey."

On their way to visit George, Lawrence, and Dorothy stopped in Newport News to visit brother Truman and Ruth. Sister Katie called me and reported Truman's comment by phone: "I couldn't believe how different Lawrence is. They came at 4 p.m. Lawrence went for food and we ate together. They left at 9 p.m. We hugged both hello and good-bye. He wanted me to come to the Valley, too, so all four brothers could be together." Truman, ninety years old, was not able to make the trip.

Lawrence and Dorothy arrived Saturday at the home of our brother Menno and his wife Sebe in Dayton.

At quarter till eight on Sunday morning I called pastor Earl Zimmerman to say I hated to miss either the Shalom or Park View church service but since Park View Mennonite was having a fortieth anniversary celebration, I expected to attend there. "We were members there for decades," I told Earl. "For years I was on the coordinating committee, which did planning with pastor Harold Eshleman, and later served as an elder."

As Earl and I decided, I met him at Shalom Mennonite at 8:15 a.m. instead of the usual 8:30 a.m. to discuss church matters and pray together before I'd need to leave for the 9:00 a.m. Park View service.

I told Earl, "I can't resist telling you of a miracle happening in this area today. Have you heard of the estrangement between my brothers George and Lawrence?" Maybe he hadn't heard while serving for years in the Philippines, I thought.

"Oh yes," Earl said, "everybody in the world has heard." Then I told him of Lawrence's call to George and the visit to Truman and Menno on the way to visit George. During prayer time Earl led a moving prayer for Lawrence and George.

During Sunday school at Park View Mennonite I taught the older women's class because they were without a teacher. The lesson, "Being Forgiven," was based on the story of the brothers Jacob and Esau (Genesis 33). I could not resist telling the women, "A miracle of forgiveness is taking place today between two brothers about two blocks away," and told them about George and Lawrence.

There were tears—mine, and those of some others. The more I thought of Earl's words, "Everybody in the world has heard," the more I thought it was in order to let the story of this forgiveness and reconciliation be known far and wide.

Lawrence (leading singing) and George (at the pulpit) about a year before their estrangement. [Menno Simons Historical Library & Archives, Eastern Mennonite University, Harrisonburg, Virginia]

Sunday evening Katie invited me to eat supper with her. Lawrence, Dorothy, and Dorothy's sister Mabel Shenk, who lived nearby, were there too. When I arrived, I went to Lawrence and said, "Any charge for a kiss?" It was the first friendly meeting in twenty years or more. He was a changed man yet still full of stories—a Brunk trait.

Katie called on him to lead the prayer at the table, also as we stood and held hands before parting. We were in touch with God and all said "Amen." Before they left Lawrence said something to the effect that he no longer judges people.

On Monday I called Katie to find out more details of the reconciliation between George and Lawrence. As near as I could tell, this is what happened:

Near the time for the Calvary Sunday morning service to begin at the Eastern Mennonite Seminary chapel, George waited outside for Lawrence and Dorothy. When they arrived, Margaret and Katie joined George, Lawrence, and Dorothy in a conference room where George and Lawrence talked things over, asked forgiveness, embraced, and kissed each other.

On the long walk from the conference room to the chapel, George and Lawrence planned their part in the church service, which would follow the scheduled sermon by Harold Lehman.

At the service George, Margaret, Lawrence, Dorothy, and Katie sat together in the second row up front. Following the sermon, George took Lawrence and Dorothy up front with him and soon asked Margaret to come up, too. George spoke first to pave the way for what followed. He mentioned the years he and Lawrence worked together in the Brunk Revivals, the years of estrangement that developed between them, and now the efforts toward reconciliation. Then Lawrence spoke. Dorothy and Margaret spoke. George and Lawrence embraced and kissed. It was a sermon in action.

But the service was not finished. George gave an invitation for anyone who had a need in the area of reconciliation to come up front while Lawrence led, "Just as I am," the invitation song he had led hundreds of times in their tent revivals. Five people responded.

Katie kept saying, "It's a miracle."

On Monday morning George and Margaret and Lawrence and Dorothy went to Katie's, and George and Lawrence signed Brunk Revival model trucks.

I told Katie, "When I think how both George and Lawrence preached so much about the Holy Spirit, I'm really puzzled about those years of estrangement."

George came on Tuesday morning for me to dub a tape of one of his sermons. I had been wondering what prompted Lawrence to make the move toward reconciliation. Before I asked, George said, "I asked Lawrence how the change of attitude came about and he said, 'I almost died in recent weeks with the burden of this alienation.'"

I liked to think that if "there is rejoicing in the presence of the angels of God over one sinner who repents" (Luke 15:10), then our parents in heaven knew their sons were reconciled at last.

Chapter 47

The Next Generation

Harrisonburg, Virginia
August 1992–February 2000

A specialty of our small Shalom congregation was to unearth gifts of Eastern Mennonite College, now Eastern Mennonite University (EMU), students and other young people. We asked them to teach Sunday school, give their faith story, or give a message if there was ability and interest. One young woman requested baptism and asked that I baptize her.

November 22, 1992, I had the message, "What Is Your Gift?" at Shalom, then conducted a commissioning service for believers in their day-by-day vocations. Paul Groff had us gather up front and read responsively our Shalom Covenant and sign a paper as members or associate members, as we did annually.

Afterward, two Japanese Eastern Mennonite High School students came up front, and one asked what it meant to sign the paper. I explained and she signed. "I am a Christian," she said, "and my father is the pastor."

What about the other? It was hard to discern her belief and degree of interest. "Would you like to talk with me some evening about this?" I asked her.

"Yes," she answered.

"When?" I asked.

"Monday," she answered. We arranged to meet at 6:00 p.m. at the EMU cafeteria and then come to my place.

That evening I called EMU faculty member Calvin Shenk, who was experienced in dealing with people of different cultures. Then I called my friend Mildred Pellman for suggestions on telling the story of Christ to the Japanese student.

When she came, the student brought along a Japanese dictionary but we had good communication without it. I asked if she was of the Shinto or Buddist religion, and she seemed to say neither one, but she and her family went to the Temple about once a year.

She paid close attention as I opened my Bible to the Gospel of Matthew and spoke and read passages about Jesus. I hoped and prayed for her to become a seeker of Jesus.

Out to pasture gradually

Beginning Sunday, September 5, 1993, the Shalom church bulletin listed Earl Zimmerman as pastor and me as associate pastor. On Sunday, October 3, 1993, as planned, P. T. Yoder installed Earl Zimmerman, a returned missionary from the Philippines, as our new pastor and commissioned Paul Groff for service in Kenya for three years under Menonite Central Committee.

At a meeting of ministers in the Harrisonburg District, they cracked up when I said, "Now that I'm seventy-eight I'm thinking of retiring."

When I told P. T. Yoder in casual conversation that I felt some ageism at Shalom, he said I should resign. So I gave Earl Zimmerman a notice to this effect for the December 12 church bulletin:

> On December 31, 1993, Ruth Brunk Stoltzfus will resign as associate pastor of Shalom Mennonite. She will continue with appointments in the wider church and still relate to this congregation.

Earl encouraged me to change my resignation to a later date, and he thought the notice should say that I would be available for service in the congregation. We agreed to change the date of my resignation to June 1994, and to change "still relate to this congregation" to "still be available for service in this congregation."

Earl and I met June 26 as usual to discuss church matters and have prayer together before worship began. Before closing our time of discussion and prayer, he asked if we would meet together before worship the next Sunday.

"Next Sunday is July 3, and my resignation is at the end of June," I said.

"I have talked to several people about being on the leadership team with me," Earl said, "but until that is settled, I'd like you to continue on the team. I can't carry this alone."

I consented to continue for awhile. P. T. Yoder advised that I retire in spite of my reports of good relationships with the students and requests for appointments in the wider church. He himself planned to resign in about a year as Harrisonburg District overseer. He would be sixty-seven in 1995. I would be eighty.

Two EMU students, Marc Hershberger and Debbie Stoltzfus, were commissioned on January 15, 1995, to replace me on the Shalom leadership team. I considered both of them friends and gave each a copy of my twenty-eight-page collection of congregational prayers and benedictions. They encouraged me to have a message once in a while at Shalom, so that put me out to pasture gradually.

Disciplined but unrepentant

Daughters Kathie, Ruthie, and I drove together to Newport News for Truman and Ruth's seventieth wedding anniversary celebration on January 16, 1994. I had phoned Truman Saturday evening, "Don't let Truman Jr. preach until we get there." We arrived at Warwick Mennonite Church in time for nephew Truman's good message, "As for Me and My House" (Joshua 4:1-7; 24:14-18).

In the middle of his sermon Truman said, "I see my Aunt Ruth is here and I'm asking her to come up later and respond to the sermon and lead a special prayer for my parents." I loved it.

I spoke briefly but to the point, saying, "I appreciated the sermon. I called Truman Sr. last evening to say I was coming and to not let Truman Jr. preach until I got here. The sermon was a wonderful combination of memories and Scriptures—the Word of God with the power to change us, nurture us, and equip us—the Word that is living and active and sharper than any two-edged sword."

By being brief about the sermon I figured I could tell a few short stories about Truman and Ruth, but, as I had often noticed, men can speak on and on but soon think a woman needs curbing. The worship leader came and stood beside me and explained that there would be time later for stories after the meal. Since it was not yet near noon, I said, "I want to tell one more brief story." It was in support of his point that I was speaking too long: "When Grant and I traveled to speak in churches, he said one time, 'You know, Ruth, when we get up to speak we should distinguish between time and eternity.' "

A woman came to me afterward and said, "He did that to me one time."

I told her, "I feel disciplined but unrepentant."

The next generation

I traveled to eastern Pennsylvania to give the Sunday morning message at Salford Mennonite Church in October of 1994. While I was in the area, I also spoke at two women's meetings planned by the Mennonite Women's Council on Leadership of the Franconia Mennonite Conference. I had a wonderful time with a receptive and engaged audience. We focused on the question of women using their gifts of leadership given by God's Spirit.

The first topic they requested was about my journey. I gave the gist of my childhood, youth, marriage, motherhood, grandmotherhood, and my call to public ministry. I told the audience that if I were to give a title to my talk I would call it, "How God Made a Way When There Wasn't Any Way." Attention for my second message, "The Bible and the Women Question," was perfect as it seemed everyone present was in public ministry or had the gifts for such ministry.

Between sessions I displayed eight documents on a table for the women to review and to select those they would like me to mail them. The documents included lists and articles I had written on the role of women. When I met young women in ministry, I often gave them copies.

More milestones

"Mama, I'm holding a beautiful baby girl—Lydia," Helen said when she phoned from a hospital in Berkeley, California. This twelfth grandbaby joined our family tribe on June 17, 1994.

January 7, 1995, I wrote to my brother Truman, who was seriously ill:

To T. H. Brunk

The world's most wonderful big brother
and loving uncle to our five children—
A big and big-hearted bishop always caring
for others whether children or adults—
A big man with a big vision
for calling others to ministry in the Church—

Love to you from your little sister Ruth,
and to Ruth, that wonderful woman
you married January 16, 1923!

When I phoned him, he said, "I've lived ninety-two years and now I wish the angels would come and take me." At his age and with his health condition, it was time for Truman to go, and on January 12, 1995, he departed this life.

Venture capitalist

In August 1991, Allen had talked with me about ways I might be able to furnish funds for his and John Fairfield's language software, an innovative way for grade school, college, university students, and others to learn foreign languages.

We had a family meeting about it in October and discussions continued at Christmas. Should Mother risk capital so badly needed? I gave a modest check to each of the five children for Christmas and let each one decide whether to invest or lend the amount in the project or neither. They agreed that the project, if successful for teaching languages, should also be a channel for money to flow from the more wealthy to the poor.

Allen wrote in his February 1, 1992, family letter: "The product is dynamite. Here I am distracting much of my family into some fantastical scheme. And spending the hard-earned and frugally saved dollars of my almost seventy-seven-year-old widowed mother. Am I crazy?"

In February Allen called with the news that Eugene was moving to the Valley to work for the company. February 24, 1992, Fairfield & Sons, Ltd. opened up an office in Harrisonburg.

Allen wrote in his family letter dated March 29, 1993:

> I don't forget that it was generations of thrift, and thrifty parents and a mother I discover in my advancing middle age (I have always been so unobservant about so much) is not just a speaker and a writer and a church leader and a preacher but also a venture capitalist, the most nervy kind of capitalist. A venture capitalist in a new industry soon to be born.

Our company got orders from all over the world for the language program, named Rosetta Stone, available on CD-ROMs of ninety-two lessons each for English and a growing number of foreign languages.

While I was getting my supper together on December 19, 1995, Allen came and quietly started writing a check. When he handed it to me and I saw how much it was for, I said, "I feel like fainting or crying."

When Allen left, I knelt at my bed and asked God to guide. "Lord," I prayed, "as to the thrill of depositing this check at the bank, help me to spend the rest of my life teaching and writing about the thrill of depositing Your Word in our hearts."

With the profits from our family company, I opened a fund to help international students pay tuition at Eastern Mennonite University in 1996.

So it will stand

Before he or another family member left on a trip, Grant often read Psalm 121, including the words, "He will watch over your life; the Lord will watch over your coming and going, both now and forevermore."

And so he has. Throughout my life, the Lord has been faithful. And now, at age eighty-seven, I look back and say, with Isaiah 14:24, "Surely, as I have planned, so it will be, and as I have purposed, so it will stand."

At my desk in 1993.

Epilogue

What a shock that son Allen Grant died September 30, 2002, at the age of fifty-nine. I never dreamed or imagined that a child would go before I would. It was a heart attack that took him. It is a great comfort that he faithfully attended church at Community Mennonite. I believe he is safe at home in heaven seeing the Lord, Grant his father, and other relatives. I'll soon be age eighty-eight and am telling the Lord I'd like to go home.

Index

The Editor

Eve Bowers MacMaster has been a friend of Ruth Brunk Stoltzfus since the early 1970s. Her ministry has included writing, editing, teaching, and working for peace and justice. Currently she serves as pastor of Emmanuel Mennonite Church in Gainesville, Florida.